ACCOUNTS FOR SOLICITORS

ACCOUNTS FOR SOLICITORS

Lesley King LLB, Dip Crim (Cantab), Solicitor

JORDANS

1999

Published by
Jordan Publishing Limited
21 St Thomas Street
Bristol BS1 6JS

British Library Cataloguing-in-Publication Data
A catalogue record for this book is available from the British Library.

ISSN 1353–3584
ISBN 0 85308 583 8

Photoset by Mendip Communications Ltd, Frome, Somerset
Printed in Great Britain by Hobbs The Printers Ltd of Southampton

PREFACE

This book is written primarily for The College of Law's Legal Practice Course but it is hoped that it will be useful for others.

It is divided into two parts. The first part deals with principles of double entry bookkeeping. The second part deals with the accounts of solicitors and in particular the need to account for client's money.

For the sake of brevity, the masculine pronoun has been used to include the feminine.

I would like to thank Nancy Duffield, Frances George, Amanda Heaslip, Tony Morgan, Jane Vanderuliess, Catherine Stuart, Amanda Seager, Rebecca Atkins and Carol Wadsworth-Jones for their help in the preparation of this book, and the staff at Jordans for their support during the production process.

The law is stated as at 1 June 1999.

LESLEY KING
London

CONTENTS

TABLES

References in the right-hand column are to paragraph numbers.

Table of Cases

Table of Statutes

Table of Statutory Instruments and Regulations

ABBREVIATIONS

The following abbreviations are used throughout this book.

ACT	advance corporation tax
ASB	Accounting Standards Board
FRC	Financial Reporting Council
FREDs	Financial Reporting Exposure Drafts
FRRP	Financial Reporting Review Panel
FRSs	Financial Reporting Standards
SSAPs	Statements of Standard Accounting Practice
UITF	Urgent Issues Task Force
VATA 1994	Value Added Tax Act 1994

INTRODUCTION TO COURSE

1 WHY DO I NEED TO KNOW ABOUT ACCOUNTS?

The short answer is because The Law Society says you must. However, that does give rise to a further question – 'Why does The Law Society say that?' The answer to this question is that knowledge and understanding of accounting principles will help you enormously in your professional and personal life, in the following ways.

1.1 To deal with the affairs of clients

A great deal of the work done by solicitors requires an understanding of accounts.

- In commercial work you may be involved in shares or asset takeovers and will need to be able to 'read' the accounts of the company involved to understand the problems of the transaction.
- In private client work you may be involved in the valuation of shares for taxation purposes.
- In divorce work you may have to look critically at the accounts of a business run by a spouse when you are trying to agree the amount of a cash settlement.

1.2 To liaise with accountants

Particularly in commercial work you may have to work closely with accountants on certain aspects of transactions.

You will find it helpful to understand some of the concepts and jargon accountants use. Accountants have studied law and have some understanding of the solicitor's job. As a profession we are at a disadvantage, if we have no understanding of theirs.

1.3 To deal with your own financial affairs

It is likely that you will have money to invest, already or in the not too distant future. An understanding of the principles of investment is vital to your financial well-being.

1.4 To run your own business

If you become a partner you will have to manage the financial affairs of your firm. To do so adequately you must understand profitability and solvency, and the crucial importance of cash flow.

1.5 To comply with The Law Society's requirements as to professional conduct

The Law Society requires a solicitor who handles money belonging to clients to keep particular accounts and to record dealings with such money in a particular way. While you are unlikely to have to make the entries yourself, you will be responsible if errors are made by others.

You will frequently have to decide whether a payment which is to be made by your firm for a particular client can be made from the client bank account or must be made from the office bank account. Similarly, when money is received from a client, you will have to decide whether it should be paid into the client or office bank account.

2   HOW TO USE THIS BOOK

This book is not designed for passive reading. It is a work book. You will find that throughout the text there are exercises for you to do. These exercises are an integral part of the course. They are designed to develop your understanding and confidence, not merely to test you on the material you have just read. Solutions to the exercises appear at the end of the relevant chapter. It is essential that you study these solutions as you go through the text.

PART I

ACCOUNTING PRINCIPLES

Chapter 1

BASIC BOOKKEEPING – AN INTRODUCTION

1.1 ACCOUNTS, BOOKKEEPING AND FINANCE

Anyone who has any money needs to keep some sort of record of what happens to that money. You probably keep pay slips, bank and building society statements, and (if you have any) share certificates and dividend warrants. These documents provide a useful personal record, allowing you to calculate your financial position, and assist you in your dealings with the Inland Revenue by providing the information necessary to calculate your tax liability.

Anyone who runs a business needs similar information to keep track of the financial position of the business. However, because so many different events occur in the life of a business, it is not enough to rely on individual documents to provide the full picture. It is preferable to take the relevant information relating to a particular type of transaction from the individual documents and enter it in a separate record book. These records are then summaries of the individual documents and are normally referred to as 'accounts'.

While a business is small the proprietor will probably do everything single-handed, including keeping the accounts. However, once a business expands the proprietor will employ people to assist in particular areas. It is common to employ a bookkeeper to keep the accounts. This is because accurate day-to-day bookkeeping is vital to the success of a business, allowing the proprietor to judge whether the business is making a profit and whether or not there is sufficient cash to pay bills, but it is a fairly tedious and time-comsuming process which can be handled by a relatively unskilled person. The proprietor is then free to plan the strategy for the business, improve the quality of the product and the level of customer satisfaction.

In order to plan a business strategy, it is vital that the proprietor should receive accurate, up-to-date information from the bookkeeper and be able to interpret it correctly, drawing conclusions about past performance which will enable him to make decisions as to future development. An area where correct interpretation of information provided by the bookkeeper is particulary important is the financing of a business. Should cash be contributed by the proprietors, borrowed from outsiders or, in the case of a company, raised by the issue of shares?

People whose job involves the provision of finance, for example bankers, analysts, lawyers and accountants will probably make no bookkeeping entries themselves but will have to be able to understand the accounts presented to them so that they can correctly interpret the information the accounts contain.

1.2 WHAT ARE ACCOUNTS?

As suggested in **1.1**, accounts are simply summaries of information contained elsewhere. There will be separate accounts for every type of business transaction and all aspects of each transaction will be recorded. For example, if in the course of your practice as a solicitor you want to make a payment on behalf of a client, you will requisition a cheque; the bookkeeper, having received your requisition, will issue the cheque (which will be signed by an authorised person) and will then record the payment in the accounts. The bookkeeper will record two separate consequences of the payment:

(a) the firm has less cash in its bank account;
(b) the firm is now owed money by the client.

1.3   WHAT DO ACCOUNTANTS DO?

Accountants can be involved in one or more of a number of different aspects of managing the finances of a business.

1.3.1   Recording information

We have already seen that it is very important to have records so that the proprietor can make informed decisions. The accountant will follow rules that govern the way in which information is recorded. It is important that there are rules since it means that anyone who has learnt the rules can understand accounts kept by another person on the basis of those rules.

1.3.2   Reporting

The accountant can analyse the information contained in the day-to-day accounts, summarise it and present it to management. Management can then use that information as the basis for decisions on strategy. However, it is not just management who need financial reports. There is also a demand for information from outside the business. The Inland Revenue demands tax returns and, in the case of companies, the government, potential investors and shareholders demand published accounts. Employees may also demand information about the financial health of the business, usually as a prelude to wage negotiations.

1.3.3   Auditing

Not all accountants are qualified to audit accounts. Only those who are registered auditors are authorised to sign a statutory audit report.

Companies (other than 'small' companies – see below) are *required* to have their accounts examined by a qualified auditor who must provide an opinion as to whether the accounts give a 'true and fair' view of the affairs of the company and its profit (or loss) for the relevant period. The auditors will have access to all the books and documents of the company. They are under an obligation to the members of the company and are also subject to disciplinary action by their professional body for misconduct. There have been cases recently where shareholders have alleged negligence or misconduct on the part of auditors and so the process must be carried out with great care.

In addition to the statutory audit required by the Companies Acts, auditors may be invited by management to carry out an audit as a means of obtaining an independent appraisal on the efficiency of the organisation.

A 'small' company, as defined in s 249A of the Companies Act 1985, is entirely exempt from the audit requirement if its turnover is not in excess of £350,000 and its Balance Sheet total is not more than £1.4m. Public companies must satisfy other criteria set out in s 249B.

There is an overriding provision that holders of 10 per cent or more of a company's issued share capital may require an audit.

As from 1 September 1998, firms of solicitors are required to employ a registered auditor to give an accountant's report on the quality of the solicitor's bookkeeping insofar as it relates to money held for clients. The requirements are now set out in Part F of the Solicitors' Accounts Rules 1998. Prior to that date, solicitors were required to employ an independent accountant. The change stems from The Law Society's attempts to reduce the costs of default. It became apparent from the reports of the Monitoring Unit and from inspections carried out by the Solicitors' Complaints Bureau's Investigation Accountants that some reporting accountants were not carrying out their duties effectively and that serious breaches of the SAR, and, in some cases, frauds, had not been identified.

1.3.4 Preparing Profit and Loss Accounts and Balance Sheets

All businesses need an annual statement of profits (or losses) and of assets and liabilities. These are required for the proprietor's own purposes and for the purpose of the Inland Revenue. Accountants are frequently asked to prepare these 'Final Accounts' from the day-to-day accounts kept by the bookkeeper for the business.

1.3.5 Dealing with the Inland Revenue

Accountants frequently prepare tax returns for submission to the Inland Revenue on behalf of individuals and businesses. They can advise on the availability of deductions, exemptions and reliefs and on the correct treatment of income and capital gains.

1.4 WHO NEEDS FINANCIAL REPORTS?

1.4.1 The proprietor

As we have already suggested, the proprietor of a business will need to know how much profit the business has made in the most recent accounting period, how much cash is in the bank and what liabilities and other assets the business has at the end of the accounting period.

The proprietor will use this information to decide what action to take in the following period. If the business is basically profitable but currently short of cash because of over-enthusiastic expansion, the proprietor may try to borrow more money to improve cash flow. If machinery is outdated, it may be desirable to scrap the existing machinery and buy something more modern. If business is thriving, the proprietor may want to consider taking on more staff and premises and expanding the scale of operations.

1.4.2 Taxation records

These are extremely important. The government has a variety of different taxes all of which require detailed records. If the business is unincorporated the proprietor (or proprietors, if it is a partnership) will include the profit or profit share of the business on his income tax return. If the business is incorporated, the company itself will be liable for corporation tax.

If the business employs staff, it will have to operate the PAYE (Pay As You Earn) scheme. This requires the employer to deduct income tax from the employee and to account for it to the Inland Revenue. Records will have to be kept of salaries so that the Inland Revenue can check that the correct amount of tax has been deducted and certificates of deduction of income tax can be issued to employees.

The business will also have to deduct national insurance contributions from the employees. Again, detailed records will have to be kept for the Inland Revenue.

Finally, if the business is registered for VAT (value added tax), it will need to keep records of VAT charged to customers and of VAT charged to the business by suppliers. It will have to account to HM Customs & Excise for the correct amount of VAT every quarter.

1.5   REGULATION OF ACCOUNTS

1.5.1   Introduction

There is a great deal of regulation of accounts. Some of it is self-imposed by the accountancy profession and some of it is imposed externally, for example by the government insisting that companies produce final accounts at the end of the accounting year in a particular form.

1.5.2   Self-imposed regulation

Why do accountants want uniformity?

A person could prepare a set of accounts for his own use on any idiosyncratic basis he wished, but such accounts would be useless to an outsider trying to understand the affairs of the business. Clearly, if accounts are prepared on a uniform basis (ie if the same conventions have been followed and the same practices adopted), they will be usable by anyone.

Frequently, people want to compare the accounts of one business with the accounts of another (for example, when investing or considering the purchase of a business). It is impossible to make a valid comparison unless the accounts have been prepared on a uniform basis.

The accounting profession has, therefore, tried to achieve a measure of uniformity.

1.5.3   Accounting standards

There are six major accountancy bodies in the UK and Ireland. They established the Accounting Standards Committee which aimed to lay down definitive standards of financial accounting and reporting. The Accounting Standards Committee issued a number of Statements of Standard Practice (SSAPs). These standards describe methods of accounting for application to all financial accounts. The aim is to give a true and fair view of the financial position of an enterprise and its profit or loss. Although SSAPs had no statutory force, non-compliance by an accountant could lead to disciplinary action by the appropriate governing body in a similar way to disciplinary proceedings against a solicitor. The accountancy bodies could enquire into apparent failure by their members to observe the standards or to disclose departures therefrom.

In 1990, there was a fundamental structural change in line with the recommendations of the Review Committee chaired by Sir Ron Dearing in 1987 which had conducted a general review of the system of developing accounting standards. As a result of the Committee's recommendations, the Accounting Standards Committee was replaced on 1 August 1990 by a new body, the Accounting Standards Board (ASB). The ASB's function is to issue (or withdraw) accounting standards on its own authority.

To guide the ASB in relation to areas of public concern and to see that its operations are properly financed, a Financial Reporting Council (FRC) has been established.

To assist the ASB in areas where there exists or may develop some unsatisfactory or conflicting interpretations of accounting standards or statute law, a body called the Urgent Issues Task Force (UITF) has been established. Its pronouncements are published and made publicly available for the preparers and auditors of financial information.

A Financial Reporting Review Panel (FRRP) has also been established, primarily to enquire into departures by large companies from accounting standards. It may take into account pronouncements of the UITF in deciding whether financial statements call for review.

Diagrammatically, the structure may be shown as follows:

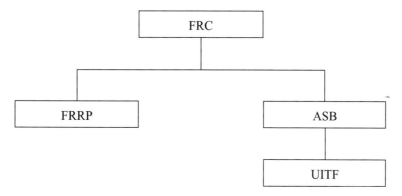

The ASB adopted the 22 SSAPs extant on 1 August 1990, thus giving them the status of accounting standards within the meaning of the Companies Act 1985 (see below).

Accounting standards issued by the ASB are to be known as Financial Reporting Standards (FRSs). Before an FRS is approved, the Accounting Standards Board issues an 'exposure draft' for general comment. These are known as Financial Reporting Exposure Drafts (FREDs).

The Dearing Committee considered recommending full statutory support for accounting standards but decided against it on the basis that it would make standards too legalistic and inhibit quick change where new developments required it. The Companies Act 1989 incorporated into the Companies Act 1985 a lesser form of statutory support. However, this relates only to the accounts of companies.

Companies which are not 'medium sized' or 'small' companies are required by Companies Act 1985, Sch 4, para 36A to state within their accounts whether the accounts have been prepared in accordance with applicable accounting standards and to give details of and the reasons for, any material departures. To that extent, the SSAPs adopted by the ASB, together with FRSs issued by it, have an element of statutory force.

Companies which qualify as small companies may elect to adopt a single reporting standard known as the Financial Reporting Standard for Smaller Entities rather than to follow all the individual SSAPs and FRSs.

For this purpose, a 'small' company is one which satisfies two of the following criteria:

- turnover less than £2.8 million;
- gross assets less than £1.4 million;
- number of employees less than 50.

Chapter 2

BASIC BOOKKEEPING – THE DOUBLE ENTRY SYSTEM

2.1 WHAT DOES A BUSINESS WANT FROM ITS ACCOUNTS?

2.1.1 Information

A business needs to know:

- what income it has generated in a particular period;
- what expenses it has incurred in the same period.

Note: Deducting expenses from income will allow the business to calculate its net profit for the period. This is done on a Profit and Loss Account.

A business also needs to know:

- what assets it has at a given moment;
- what liabilities it has at a given moment.

Note: Assets and liabilities are listed on a Balance Sheet.

On a daily basis, therefore, a business must keep records of income, expenses, assets and liabilities so that periodically it can produce a Profit and Loss Account and a Balance Sheet.

2.1.2 Classification of items

We referred in **2.1.1** above to income, expenses, assets and liabilities. How do we classify items into the appropriate categories?

Income is what the business is trying to produce. It is the result either of the labour of the business's employees or the investment of its capital.

Examples of income are professional charges for services supplied, the price charged for stock sold, interest received, insurance commission received.

Expenses are items paid (or payable), the benefit of which is obtained and exhausted in a relatively short period (often within a single accounting period) and where the expenditure is necessary to maintain the earning capacity of the business.

Examples of expenses are the price of stock bought, gas, electricity, wages, interest paid, hire charges, petrol and repairs.

Assets must be carefully distinguished from expenses. Like expenses, assets are the result of expenditure. The difference is that an asset gives rise to a benefit which can be spread over a larger period and which will increase the earning capacity of the business. Examples of assets are premises, machinery, fixtures and fittings, vehicles, cash and debtors.

Liabilities are amounts owing. They may be short term (eg unpaid expenses) or long term (eg a loan from a bank).

2.1.3 Specimen profit and loss account and balance sheet

We have set out below a specimen set of year end (or 'Final') Accounts. In later chapters you will see how the various items are built up.

Remember the Profit and Loss Account shows income less expenses over the year in question. The difference between the two is the net profit of the business. The Balance Sheet lists assets and liabilities at the end of the year.

Example

AB & Co
Solicitors
Profit and loss account for year ended 31 December [Year X]

	£	£	£
Income	000	000	000
Profit Costs Billed	478		
Less Opening Work in Progress	(30)		
Plus Closing Work in Progress	40		
		488	
Gain on Sale of Car		2	
Insurance Commission Received		10	
Interest Received		20	
			520
Expenses			
Salaries		98	
General: Paid		55	
Prepaid		(4)	
		51	
Administrative: Paid		35	
Accrued		3	
		38	
Bad Debts		17	
Doubtful Debts		8	
Depreciation on Computers @ 20 per cent		10	
Depreciation on Fixtures @ 5 per cent		1	
Depreciation on Cars @ 20 per cent		8	
Rent Paid		21	
Loan Interest Paid		5	
			(257)
Net profit			263

Appropriated	£	£	£
	A	**B**	
Interest on Capital	5	3	8
Salary		10	10
Share of Remaining Profits	147	98	245
	152	111	263

AB & Co
Solicitors
Balance Sheet as at 31 December Year X

EMPLOYMENT OF CAPITAL

Fixed Assets	£	£	£
	000	000	000
Leasehold premises		218	
Fixtures	20		
Less Depreciation	(13)		
		7	
Computers	50		
Less Depreciation	(40)		
		10	
Cars	40		
Less Depreciation	(8)		
		32	
			267
Current Assets			
Work in Progress	40		
Debtors	80		
Less Provision	(8)		
Cash – Office Bank Account	10		
Petty Cash	1		
Prepayments	4		
		127	
Current Liabilities			
Creditors	(39)		
Accrued Expenses	(3)		
		(42)	
Net Current Assets			85
			352
Less Bank Loan			(60)
Client Bank Account	150		
Less Amount due to Clients	(150)		
			292
Capital employed			
Capital: A	50		
B	30		
		80	
Current: A	124		
B	88		
		212	
			292

Movement on current accounts

	A	B
	£	£
Balance from Trial Balance at 31 Dec	2CR	3CR
Profits	152	111
Drawings	(30)	(26)
	124CR	88CR

2.1.4   Day-to-day records

Although we will be working towards preparing a set of Final Accounts, we need to look first of all at the day-to-day records a business keeps. The Final Accounts are prepared from the information contained in the day-to-day records. The system which all well-organised businesses use for their day-to-day record keeping is the double entry bookkeeping system.

2.2   WHY USE THE DOUBLE ENTRY SYSTEM?

There is nothing to stop anyone inventing their own personal accounting system. However, there is a great deal to be said for using the double entry system which has been developed over hundreds of years and is understood by people all over the world.

It is important to realise that while the double entry bookkeeping system has its own internal logic, the whole system could have been set up differently. For example, we will see later that some things are recorded on the right and some on the left; the initial decision could just as easily have been to record them the other way round.

However, once you have accepted that initial decision, everything which follows builds logically.

2.3   PRINCIPLES OF DOUBLE ENTRY

Lawyers should be particularly well placed to understand the fundamental principle of double entry bookkeeping as it is rather similar to the doctrine of consideration. The principle is that any business transaction has two aspects to it.

The double entry system requires you to make one entry in the accounts for each of the two aspects.

You must never record only one aspect of the transaction.

In order to record the two aspects, accounts are divided into two sides. The two aspects of any transaction are recorded on different sides of the accounts. Remember that things could just as easily have been recorded the other way round.

Income and expenses
A source of income is always recorded on the right. The incurring of an expense is always recorded on the left.

Assets and liabilities
The gain of an asset is recorded on the left. The loss of an asset is recorded on the right.

The incurring of a liability is recorded on the right. The reduction of a liability is recorded on the left.

Cash
Cash is an asset which regularly goes up and down.

Increasing cash is equivalent to gaining an asset, so it is recorded on the left.

Reducing cash is equivalent to losing an asset, so it is recorded on the right.

The following grid summarises the above:

Expense Incurred	Income Earned
Asset Gained	Asset Lost
Liability reduced/extinguished	Liability incurred/increased
Cash Gained	Cash Paid

Remember, every transaction has one aspect which is recorded on the left and one aspect which is recorded on the right.

Examples

Your business carries out the following transactions:

(a) Business buys a machine for £20,000.

It gains an asset (recorded on left) and loses cash (recorded on right).

(b) Business sells stock for £3,000.

The sale of stock earns income (recorded on right); there is a gain of cash (recorded on left).

(c) Business buys stock for £1,000 cash.

The purchase of stock incurs an expense (recorded on left); there is a loss of cash (recorded on right).

Transactions (b) and (c) in the above example illustrate an important point about the double entry system. Initially, you do not worry about the concept of 'profit' or 'loss'. You simply record transactions as they occur and, periodically, usually at the end of the accounting period, you put together all the transactions carried out during the period to see whether, overall, the business made a gain or a loss.

You do not worry about whether the goods bought were 'worth' £1,000 or whether the sale price of £3,000 was a high or low price. You simply record what happens.

Another important principle of double entry bookkeeping is that the business is regarded as completely separate from its proprietor. Thus, when a person sets up a business and puts in some cash you must record that transaction from the point of view of the business. The business is gaining cash but is incurring a liability in that it now owes money to the proprietor. This liability to repay its proprietor is normally referred to as the 'capital' of the business.

Exercise 2A

A starts a business buying and selling goods. Identify the two aspects involved in the following transactions and say whether they would be recorded on the right or left of the accounts.

(1) To start the business A puts in £20,000 cash and a car worth £8,000.

(2) Business borrows £100,000 from a bank.

(3) Business buys premises for £90,000 cash.

(4) Business buys trading stock for £1,000 cash.

(5) Business buys trading stock for £2,000 on credit from X.

(6) Business sells trading stock for £3,500 cash.

(7) Business sells trading stock for £1,000 on credit to Y, a customer.

(8) Business pays X, a supplier, £1,000.

(9) Y, a customer, pays business £1,000.

2.4   'DEBITS' AND 'CREDITS'

So far, when talking about the sides of the accounts, we have referred to the left-hand side and the right-hand side.

However, the labels accountants use are 'Debit' and 'Credit'. '**Debit**' is used as a label for the left-hand side and '**Credit**' as a label for the right-hand side. They are shortened to DR and CR respectively.

Example

(a)   Joe sets up a business and pays in £120,000 to start it.

   The business gains cash (record on left with a DR entry) and incurs a liability to its proprietor (record on right with a CR entry).

(b)   Business buys premises for £100,000.

   Business loses cash (record on right with a CR entry) and gains premises (record on left with a DR entry).

2.4.1   Do they seem to be the wrong way round?

People tend to expect 'Debits' to be payments and 'Credits' to be receipts. This is because that is the way in which your bank statement is labelled. On your bank statement, a receipt into your bank account is labelled by the bank as a credit and a payment is labelled as a debit. For an explanation of the apparent discrepancy with your bank statement, read the following paragraph. Remember that every transaction has to be recorded with two entries – a DR and a CR.

2.4.2   What is recorded on my bank statement?

A bank statement is a copy of the account labelled with your name, which the bank keeps to record its dealings with you. When you pay money into your bank account, the bank receives cash and makes a left-hand (DR) entry on its cash account to record the receipt of cash. However, it also incurs a liability since it owes that money to you; it makes a right-hand (CR) entry on the account it keeps in your name to record its liability to you. You are a creditor of the bank.

Hence, when you see your bank statement the payment which you made into the bank is shown as a CR entry on your account. However, there is also a DR entry on the bank's cash record which you do not see.

When you make a payment out from your bank account the bank loses cash and therefore makes a CR entry on its cash account to record that loss. It owes you less and makes a DR entry on your account to record the reduction in its liability to you.

2.3   WHAT DO ACCOUNTS LOOK LIKE?

Accounts can be presented in a variety of different forms. One form is the 'T' account. This has two sides, one side to record gains and the other side to record losses. Each account is headed with an appropriate name.

Example

DR   **Cash**   CR

As well as the amount involved in a particular transaction it is usual to include the date of the transaction and, for cross-referencing purposes, the name of the account recording the other aspect of the transaction. Hence, the accounts appear as follows.

The name of the account recording the *other* aspect of the transaction is included under the heading 'Details'.

DR   **Cash**   CR

Date	Details	Amount	Date	Details	Amount

This form of presentation makes the two sides of each account very apparent. However, there is another form of presentation – the tabular form – which is now used much more commonly.

Date	Details	DR	CR	BAL

The advantage of the tabular form of presentation is that the balance column provides a running total of the entries which have been made on the account.

Example

Business pays four electricity bills: £1,000, £3,000, £2,000 and £1,500. Each payment will be recorded on the cash account and the electricity account. The electricity account will look as follows:

Date	Details	DR	CR	BAL
1	Cash	1,000		1,000DR
2	Cash	3,000		4,000DR
3	Cash	2,000		6,000DR
4	Cash	1,500		7,500DR

Example

This example illustrates how a business will record day-to-day transactions. If necessary, refer back to the grid at para **2.3**.

(1) On 1 May, A starts a trading business and puts in £100,000 cash.

    Note: The business gains cash so you make a left-hand DR entry on the cash account. The business incurs a liability to the proprietor so you make a right-hand CR entry. You need an account to record this liability. It is normal to call the account recording liability to the proprietor 'capital'.

Cash

Date	Details	DR	CR	BAL
May 1	Capital	100,000		100,000DR

Capital

Date	Details	DR	CR	BAL
May 1	Cash		100,000	100,000CR

(2)   On 2 May, the business borrows £200,000 from Barcloyds Bank.

Note: The business gains cash (DR cash). It incurs a liability to the bank. You need an account to record this liability and you will make a CR entry on it.

Cash

Date	Details	DR	CR	BAL
May 1	Capital	100,000		100,000DR
2	Barcloyds	200,000		300,000DR

Barcloyds Bank

Date	Details	DR	CR	BAL
May 2	Cash		200,000	200,000CR

(3)   On 4 May the business buys trading stock for £20,000 cash.

Note: The business will lose cash and so you will CR the cash account.

The business has incurred an expense of £20,000. You need an account to record this category of expense. It is normal to call such an expense account 'Purchases'. You will DR this account.

Cash

Date	Details	DR	CR	BAL
May 1	Capital	100,000		100,000DR
2	Bank Loan	200,000		300,000DR
4	Purchases		20,000	280,000DR

Purchases

Date	Details	DR	CR	BAL
May 4	Cash	20,000		20,000DR

(4)   On 5 May the business buys goods on credit from X, a supplier, for £30,000.

Note: As in the previous example, the business incurs an expense (DR Purchases). This time it does not pay cash immediately. Instead it incurs a liability. You need an account to record this liability and you will make a CR entry in it.

Purchases

Date	Details	DR	CR	BAL
May 4	Cash	20,000		20,000DR
5	X	30,000		50,000DR

Supplier X

Date	Details	DR	CR	BAL
May 5	Purchases		30,000	30,000CR

(5)   On 8 May the business sells trading stock for £120,000 cash.

Note: The business gains cash and you will record this with a DR entry. It has a source of income which you will record with a CR entry. It is normal to call such an income account 'sales'.

Cash

Date	Details	DR	CR	BAL
May 1	Capital	100,000		100,000DR
2	Barcloyds	200,000		300,000DR
4	Purchases		20,000	280,000DR
8	Sales	120,000		400,000DR

Sales

Date	Details	DR	CR	BAL
May 8	Cash		120,000	120,000CR

(6)   On 12 May the business sells goods for £70,000 on credit to Y.

Note: As in the previous example, the business has a source of income (CR Sales). This time it gains a debt rather than cash.

Sales

Date	Details	DR	CR	BAL
May 8	Cash		120,000	120,000CR
12	Y		70,000	190,000CR

Y

Date	Details	DR	CR	BAL
May 12	Sales	70,000		70,000DR

(7)   On 15 May the business pays X £30,000.

Note: The business loses cash (CR cash) and extinguishes a liability (DR X).

Cash

Date	Details	DR	CR	BAL
May				
1	Capital	100,000		100,000DR
2	Barcloyds	200,000		300,000DR
4	Purchases		20,000	280,000DR
8	Sales	120,000		400,000DR
15	X		**30,000**	370,000DR

X

Date	Details	DR	CR	BAL
May				
5	Purchases		30,000	30,000CR
15	Cash	**30,000**		—

(8)   On 20 May Y pays the business £70,000.

Note: The business gains cash (DR cash) and loses an asset, Y's debt (CR Y).

Cash

Date	Details	DR	CR	BAL
May				
1	Capital	100,000		100,000DR
2	Barcloyds	200,000		300,000DR
4	Purchases		20,000	280,000DR
8	Sales	120,000		400,000DR
15	X		30,000	370,000DR
20	Y	**70,000**		440,000DR

Y

Date	Details	DR	CR	BAL
May				
12	Sales	70,000		70,000DR
20	Cash		**70,000**	—

Exercise 2B

Prepare accounts to record the following transactions:

(1) 1 April   Amanda decides to open an antiques shop.

    3 April   She puts in her savings of £700 cash.

    4 April   Business buys antiques at an auction for £300 cash.

    5 April   Business buys antiques from Alice for £100 on credit.

    6 April   Business sells some of the antiques in the shop for £500 cash.

    7 April   Business pays Alice £100 cash.

(2) 1 June   Beryl decides to open a bookshop.

    3 June   She puts in her savings of £1,000 cash.

    4 June   Business buys books on credit from Booksellers & Co for £2,000.

5 June   Business sells some books for £2,500 cash.

6 June   Business sells some books on credit to Brian for £300.

7 June   Business pays Booksellers & Co £2,000.

8 June   Brian pays her £250.

2.6   RECORDING DIFFERENT TYPES OF TRANSACTION

So far we have looked at the entries required to purchase and sell goods, and to record receipts and payments of cash and amounts owing to and by the business.

We will now look at what entries you would make to record other types of transaction.

2.6.1   Assets

Long-lasting items purchased to improve the efficiency of the business, eg premises, machinery, cars, are referred to as 'fixed assets'. Each category of fixed asset will have its own account. If it is purchased for cash the entries will be:

Entries:
    CR Cash account
    DR Asset account

If it is purchased on credit the entries will be:
    CR Supplier's account
    DR Asset account

Example

On 1 May the business purchases a machine for £30,000 on credit from A.

Entries:
    CR A
    DR Machinery

A

Date	Details	DR	CR	BAL
May 1	Machinery		30,000	30,000CR

Machinery

Date	Details	DR	CR	BAL
May 1	A	30,000		30,000DR

On 1 September the business pays A for the machine.

Entries:
    DR A
    CR Cash account

A

Date	Details	DR	CR	BAL
May 1	Machinery		30,000	30,000CR
Sept 1	Cash	30,000		—

Cash

Date	Details	DR	CR	BAL
Sept 1	A		30,000	XXXX

Notice that the balance of £30,000 on the machinery account will remain there, so long as the business retains the asset. (It may be depreciated – see Chapter 5.)

At the end of every accounting period the business will draw up a list of its assets and liabilities on the final day of the accounting period. The list is referred to as a Balance Sheet. Asset accounts are sometimes referred to as 'real' accounts because they record tangible assets.

The purchase and sale of assets has no effect on the profit of a business. Profit is the difference between income and expenses.

2.6.2   Expenses

Any business will have a variety of expenses. We have looked at purchases, but there are many others such as electricity, wages, rent and rates. A business will have an account for each category of expense. The business will receive bills periodically for these expenses. No entries are made until the expense is paid. Then you will CR the cash account and make a DR entry on the expense account.

Entries:

CR Cash account
DR Expense account   } when bill is paid

Example

1 May   Business has a DR balance on cash of £10,000. (This means that the business has received £10,000 more than it has paid out.)
2 May   Business receives an electricity bill of £1,000.
10 May Business pays it.

Cash

Date	Details	DR	CR	BAL
May 1	Balance			10,000DR
10	Electricity		1,000	9,000DR

Electricity

Date	Details	DR	CR	BAL
May 10	Cash	1,000		1,000DR

As and when bills are paid during an accounting period, the DR balance on the expense account will increase. At the end of the accounting period, the total expenses will be taken into account when calculating the net profit of the business.

Expense accounts are sometimes referred to as 'nominal' accounts. This is because they do not reflect tangible assets; they reflect expenses the benefit of which will normally have been exhausted by the end of the accounting period.

You must be very careful to distinguish assets from expenses accurately because at the end of the accounting period when you are calculating the net profit for the period, expenses reduce that profit but the cost of fixed assets purchased does not.

2.6.3   Profit costs

Solicitors and other professionals do not sell trading stock to produce income. They sell their services.

When a bill is delivered the solicitor wants to record the sale (ie the loss) of services and the gain of the debt now owed by the client to the firm. The sale of services is recorded as a CR entry on an income account, often called 'profit costs'. The client's debt is recorded as a DR entry on an account in the name of the client.

Entries:

CR Profit costs account
DR Client's account   } when bill delivered

Example

On 1 June a solicitor delivers a bill to A for profit costs of £1,000.

<table>
<tr><th colspan="5" align="center">Profit Costs</th><th colspan="5" align="center">A</th></tr>
<tr><th>Date</th><th>Details</th><th>DR</th><th>CR</th><th>BAL</th><th>Date</th><th>Details</th><th>DR</th><th>CR</th><th>BAL</th></tr>
<tr><td>June 1</td><td>A</td><td></td><td>1,000</td><td>XXX</td><td>June 1</td><td>Profit Costs</td><td>1,000</td><td></td><td>1,000DR</td></tr>
</table>

When the client eventually pays, the solicitor will record a receipt of cash and the loss of the debt owed by A to the business.

Entries:
    DR Cash account
    CR A's account

On 10 June A pays solicitor amount due.

<table>
<tr><th colspan="5" align="center">Cash</th><th colspan="5" align="center">A</th></tr>
<tr><th>Date</th><th>Details</th><th>DR</th><th>CR</th><th>BAL</th><th>Date</th><th>Details</th><th>DR</th><th>CR</th><th>BAL</th></tr>
<tr><td>June 10</td><td>A</td><td>1,000</td><td></td><td>XXX</td><td>June 1</td><td>Profit Costs</td><td>1,000</td><td></td><td>1,000DR</td></tr>
<tr><td></td><td></td><td></td><td></td><td></td><td>10</td><td>Cash</td><td></td><td>1,000</td><td>—</td></tr>
</table>

Note: No entry is made on the profit costs account when the client pays the cash due. The profit costs account merely records bill delivered. It does not show whether or not clients have paid their bills.

The balance on the profit costs account will increase every time a bill is delivered. The total of profit costs at the end of an accounting period will form the basis of the calculation of net profit for the period.

2.6.4   Other income

A business may earn income from subsidiary sources. For example, a firm of solicitors may receive most of its income from profit costs but may, in addition, receive some cash from interest, insurance commission and rent on premises let to tenants. A business will have an account for each category of income.

No entries are made until the cash is received. Then you will need a DR entry to record the receipt of cash and a CR entry on an income account to record the income. The CR entry is made on an income received account.

Entries:
    DR Cash account
    CR Income Received account

Example

On 1 March, a business, which has a debit balance of £10,000 on its cash account, receives a cheque for £100 interest.

Cash

Date	Details	DR	CR	BAL
March 1	Balance			10,000DR
	Interest Received	100		10,100DR

Interest Received

Date	Details	DR	CR	BAL
March 1	Cash		100	100CR

Exercise 2C

Prepare accounts to record the following transactions:

1 July   Sally starts to practise as a solicitor. She puts in £5,000 cash.

2 July   Business pays £1,000 rent for office premises.

3 July   Business pays £500 hire charges for office machinery.

18 July   Business pays £1,000 cash in wages.

20 July   Business pays £100 cash for electricity bill.

22 July   Business pays £80 cash for stationery bill.

25 July   Business sends out a bill for £300 profit costs to Sidney, a client.

28 July   Business pays £1,000 cash in wages.

29 July   Business pays £500 hire charges for office machinery.

You will see that already we have referred to quite a large number of accounts. Traditionally, the accounts were kept together in a bound book referred to as the 'ledger'. The accounts are often referred to as 'ledger accounts'. The cash account was usually kept in a separate book. This was convenient because on the whole the cash account was the busiest account. The cash account is, therefore, not referred to as a 'ledger account'.

2.7   TRIAL BALANCE

Periodically, a bookkeeper checks the accuracy of the bookkeeping. This would normally be done every month and always at the end of the accounting period before the bookkeeper starts to calculate the net profit for the period.

The double entry system requires that for every DR entry made on an account a CR entry for an identical amount must be made on another account. If every transaction has been properly recorded, the total of DR entries will equal the total of CR entries. If an entry has been made on only one side of the accounts or if an entry has been written incorrectly on one side of the accounts there will be a discrepancy between the two totals.

It would, therefore, be possible to check the accuracy of bookkeeping by comparing the two totals. However, over an entire accounting period (usually one year), a bookkeeper will make a daunting number of entries. Adding them all up would be a tedious task. As a short cut it is possible to add together all the DR balances and then all the CR balances and if no errors have been made the two totals will agree. You will see why this works if you think about what a balance is. It is the difference between the DR and CR entries on each account. If the correct DR and CR entries have been made on each account the differences between the DR and CR sides of each and every account should agree.

The process of adding together all DR and CR balances and comparing the total is referred to as preparing a Trial Balance.

Example

Look at the solution to Exercise 2C. We will use the figures to prepare a Trial Balance.

Trial Balance

	DR	CR
	£	£
Capital		5,000
Cash	820	
Hire Charges	1,000	
Wages	2,000	
Electricity	100	
Stationery	80	
Rent	1,000	
Profit Costs		300
Debtors	300	
	5,300	5,300

You will see that income and liability accounts have credit balances while expense and asset accounts have debit balances.

Note that a cash account may have either a DR or a CR balance depending on whether the business has cash in the bank or has an overdraft.

A DR balance on the cash account indicates that the business has money, a CR balance that it has an overdraft. If a question does not tell you that a business is overdrawn you may assume that it has a DR balance on its cash account.

Exercise 2D

Prepare a Trial Balance from the following list of balances:

Profit Costs £10,000. Rent £750. Rates £800. Electricity £150. Sundry Expenses £25. Postages and Telephones £175. Wages £2,500. Miscellaneous Income £325. Stationery £50. Cash £2,000. Creditors £300. Debtors £250. Fixtures and Fittings £1,405. Capital £1,750. Motor Car £4,770. Bank Loan £500.

A Trial Balance will not reveal all bookkeeping errors. If one half of an entry has been omitted or written as a wrong amount the error is revealed but no other types of error will be.

Exercise 2E

What types of error will not be revealed by a Trial Balance? List five possibilities.

Solutions

Exercise 2A

(1) Business gains assets (cash and car)	Business incurs liability to proprietor
(2) Business gains cash	Business incurs liability to bank
(3) Business gains asset (premises)	Business loses cash
(4) Business incurs expense (cost of stock)	Business loses cash
(5) Business incurs expense (cost of stock)	Business incurs liability to X
(6) Business gains cash	Business has source of income (sale of stock)
(7) Business gains asset (debt from Y)	Business has source of income (sale of stock)
(8) Business extinguishes liability	Business loses cash
(9) Business gains cash	Business loses asset (debt)

Exercise 2B

(1)

Capital

Date	Details	DR	CR	BAL
April 3	Cash		700	700CR

Cash

Date	Details	DR	CR	BAL
April 3	Capital	700		700DR
4	Purchases		300	400DR
6	Sales	500		900DR
7	Alice		100	800DR

Purchases

Date	Details	DR	CR	BAL
April 4	Cash	300		300DR
5	Alice	100		400DR

Alice

Date	Details	DR	CR	BAL
April 5	Purchases		100	100CR
7	Cash	100		—

Sales

Date	Details	DR	CR	BAL
April 6	Cash		500	500CR

(2)

Capital

Date	Details	DR	CR	BAL
June 3	Cash		1,000	1,000CR

Cash

Date	Details	DR	CR	BAL
June 3	Capital	1,000		1,000DR
5	Sales	2,500		3,500DR
7	Booksellers & Co		2,000	1,500DR
8	Brian	250		1,750DR

Purchases

Date	Details	DR	CR	BAL
June 4	Booksellers & Co	2,000		2,000DR

Booksellers & Co

Date	Details	DR	CR	BAL
June 4	Purchases		2,000	2,000CR
7	Cash	2,000		—

Sales

Date	Details	DR	CR	BAL
June 5	Cash		2,500	2,500CR
6	Brian		300	2,800CR

Brian

Date	Details	DR	CR	BAL
June 6	Sales	300		300DR
8	Cash		250	50DR

Exercise 2C

Date	Details	DR	CR	BAL
July 1	Capital	5,000		5,000DR
2	Rent		1,000	4,000DR
3	Hire		500	3,500DR
18	Wages		1,000	2,500DR
20	Electricity		100	2,400DR
22	Stationery		80	2,320DR
28	Wages		1,000	1,320DR
29	Hire		500	820DR

Capital

Date	Details	DR	CR	BAL
July 1	Cash		5,000	5,000CR

Rent

Date	Details	DR	CR	BAL
July 2	Cash	1,000		1,000DR

Wages

Date	Details	DR	CR	BAL
July 18	Cash	1,000		1,000DR
28	Cash	1,000		2,000DR

Hire Charges

Date	Details	DR	CR	BAL
July 3	Cash	500		500DR
29	Cash	500		1,000DR

Stationery

Date	Details	DR	CR	BAL
July 22	Cash	80		80DR

Electricity

Date	Details	DR	CR	BAL
July 20	Cash	100		100DR

Profit Costs

Date	Details	DR	CR	BAL
July 25	Sidney		300	300CR

Sidney

Date	Details	DR	CR	BAL
July 25	Profit Costs	300		300DR

Note: It would be misleading to label the 'Hire of Machinery' account as 'Machinery'. The title 'Machinery' would suggest that the business owned a fixed asset whereas in fact it has simply paid hire charges. A fixed asset will continue to be a benefit to the business so long as the asset remains usable, whereas the benefit of hire charges ceases as soon as the period of hire expires. In accounting terms, hire charges are 'expenses' which reduce net profit whereas assets are something tangible owned by the business which are a continuing benefit.

Exercise 2D

Trial Balance

	DR	CR
	£	£
Profit Costs		10,000
Rent	750	
Rates	800	
Electricity	150	
Sundry Expenses	25	
Postages and Telephones	175	
Wages	2,500	
Miscellaneous Income		325
Stationery	50	
Cash	2,000	
Creditors		300
Debtors	250	
Fixtures and Fittings	1,405	
Capital		1,750
Motor Car	4,770	
Bank Loan		500
	12,875	12,875

Exercise 2E

A Trial Balance will still balance despite the following types of error.

(1) **Both parts of an entry omitted** The Trial Balance still balances but the accounts are clearly inaccurate.

(2) **Compensating errors** If two errors are made which cancel each other out the Trial Balance will balance but the accounts are clearly inaccurate.

(3) **Errors of classification** An entry may be made on the right side but on the wrong *type* of account. For example, an asset may be purchased and instead of debiting the asset account the bookkeeper debits an expense account. The Trial Balance will balance but the accounts are not accurate. When the net profit is calculated at the end of the accounting period, expenses will be overstated and assets understated.

(4) **Wrong account used** The bookkeeper may make an entry on the correct side and on the correct type of account but on the wrong example of the type. For example, a bill is delivered to client X but the DR entry is made on client Y's account. The Trial Balance will balance but the accounts are inaccurate.

(5) **Reversed entries** The bookkeeper may record the correct amounts on the correct accounts but may DR the account which should be credited and vice versa. The Trial Balance will balance but the accounts are not accurate.

Chapter 3

MORE ADVANCED ENTRIES

3.1 CAPITAL AND DRAWINGS

As we have seen already in Chapter 1, whenever people start businesses they will normally contribute some cash. The entries required to deal with this are:

Entries:
    DR Cash account
    CR Capital account

The proprietor of a business hopes that at the end of the accounting period the business will have made a net profit. Any profit made will be 'owed' to the proprietor. Hence, once the net profit has been calculated, it will be credited to the capital account to increase the amount shown as owing to the proprietor.

If you were running a business you would almost certainly need to withdraw some cash from time to time to live on. Such withdrawals would reduce the cash in the business and would also reduce the amount the business owed you. You will make a CR entry on cash and could record the withdrawals on the DR side of the capital account. However, a large number of withdrawals would clutter the capital account, so it is usual to keep a separate account called a 'Drawings' account on which to record withdrawals.

Thus, whenever a proprietor withdraws cash:

Entries:
    CR Cash account
    DR Drawings account

At the end of the year the balance on the drawings account may be transferred from the drawings account to the capital account so that the picture on the capital account is brought up to date.

Example

On 1 May at the start of the accounting year A has a balance on her capital account of £30,000. During the accounting year she withdraws £3,000 on 31 July, 31 October and 31 January.

At the end of the accounting year on 30 April the balance on the drawings account is transferred to the capital account.

Each time cash is withdrawn:

Entries:
    CR Cash account
    DR Drawings account

	Cash					Drawings			
Date	**Details**	**DR**	**CR**	**BAL**	**Date**	**Details**	**DR**	**CR**	**BAL**
July 31	Drawings		**3,000**	3,000CR	July 31	Cash	**3,000**		3,000DR
October 31	Drawings		**3,000**	6,000CR	October 31	Cash	**3,000**		6,000DR
January 31	Drawings		**3,000**	9,000CR	January 31	Cash	**3,000**		9,000DR

To transfer the £9,000 balance on the drawings account to the capital account:

Entries:
   CR Drawings account
   DR Capital account

Capital

Date	Details	DR	CR	BAL
April 30	Balance			30,000CR
30	Drawings	**9,000**		21,000CR

Drawings

Date	Details	DR	CR	BAL
July 31	Cash	3,000		3,000DR
October 31	Cash	3,000		6,000DR
January 31	Cash	3,000		9,000DR
April 30	Capital		9,000	—

Currently, therefore, the business is shown as owing the proprietor £21,000. However, as soon as the net profit is calculated it will be credited to the capital account (DR entry will be on Profit and Loss Account – see Chapter 4), thus increasing the amount shown as owing to the proprietor.

3.2   CASH, BANK AND PETTY CASH

Most businesses operate by banking all receipts and making virtually all payments by cheque. The so-called 'cash' account is in reality a record of receipts into and payments out of the bank account. However, a business will need a small amount of cash in the office to cover small day-to-day expenses. This is referred to as 'petty cash'. A petty cash account is required to record the periodic receipts of cash from the bank and the various payments made from petty cash.

Example

A business has a DR balance on the cash account of £20,100. On 1 May the bookkeeper withdraws £20 cash from the bank for petty cash and on 2 May the firm purchases a roll of sticky tape for £2 from petty cash.

Entries:
To record the withdrawal of cash from the bank:
   CR Cash account
   DR Petty Cash account

To record the purchase of sticky tape:
   CR Petty Cash account
   DR Office Sundries account

Cash

Date	Details	DR	CR	BAL
May 1	Balance			20,100DR
1	Petty Cash		20	20,080DR

Petty Cash

Date	Details	DR	CR	BAL
May 1	Cash	**20**		20DR
2	Office Sundries		2	18DR

Office Sundries

Date	Details	DR	CR	BAL
May 2	Petty Cash	2		2DR

Any petty cash left over at the end of the accounting period will be an asset of the firm and will be shown as such on the Balance Sheet of the firm.

3.3   DISHONOURED CHEQUES

The bookkeeper will record a receipt of cash on the day on which the firm receives the cheque. Occasionally, a few days after the cheque has been paid into the bank, the bank may inform the firm that the cheque has been dishonoured ('bounced'). The bookkeeper will have already recorded a receipt of cash but it will now appear that this was wrong.

The error must be rectified and the entries made when the receipt was recorded must be reversed.

Example

On 1 June Customer A is shown as owing the firm £100. The firm has £1,000 in the bank. On 2 June Customer A gives the firm a cheque for £100 which the firm banks. On 9 June the bank informs the firm that the cheque has bounced.

Entries:
To record receipt of cash:

DR Cash account
CR Customer A's account

		Cash					**Customer A**			
Date	Details	DR	CR	BAL		Date	Details	DR	CR	BAL
June 1	Balance			1,000DR		June 1	Balance			100DR
2	A	100		1,100DR		2	Cash		100	—

To record the fact that the cheque has been dishonoured you must reverse the entries you made when the cheque was received:

CR Cash account
DR Customer A's ledger account

		Cash					**Customer A**			
Date	Details	DR	CR	BAL		Date	Details	DR	CR	BAL
June 1	Balance			1,000DR		June 1	Balance			100DR
2	A	100		1,100DR		2	Cash		100	—
9	A – Dishonoured cheque		100	1,000DR		9	Cash – Dishonoured cheque	100		100DR

Notice that the effect of recording the dishonouring of the cheque is to reduce the balance on the cash account and to restore the customer to the list of debtors of the firm. The customer will continue to be shown as a debtor until either the debt is paid or it is written off as bad (see **3.4**).

The customer may tell the firm to present the cheque again a few days later when there may be sufficient funds to meet the cheque. In such a case the firm will record a receipt of cash on the later date.

3.4   BAD DEBTS

Debts are regarded as an asset of a business. Periodically, any business will review its debtors to ascertain whether any should be declared bad and written off. The effect of writing off a debt as bad is that the debtor is no longer shown as owing the firm money and, therefore, the total of assets will be reduced. Bad debts are regarded as an expense of the business and, therefore, reduce the amount of net profit at the end of the accounting period.

Any business will need a bad debts account to which all bad debts are debited.

Example

Customer B is shown as owing the firm £200. The debt has been outstanding for some time and B cannot be traced. On 1 May the firm decides to write off the debt as bad.

Entries:
To record writing off the debt:
  DR Bad Debts
  CR B's account

<table>
<tr><td colspan="5" align="center">**Bad Debts**</td><td colspan="5" align="center">**Customer B**</td></tr>
<tr><td>**Date**</td><td>**Details**</td><td>**DR**</td><td>**CR**</td><td>**BAL**</td><td>**Date**</td><td>**Details**</td><td>**DR**</td><td>**CR**</td><td>**BAL**</td></tr>
<tr><td>May 1</td><td>B</td><td>200</td><td></td><td>200DR</td><td>May 1</td><td>Balance Bad Debts</td><td></td><td>200</td><td>200DR —</td></tr>
</table>

If the client paid the debt at a later stage, the firm would DR cash and CR either a separate account called Bad Debts Recovered or the Bad Debts Account.

3.5   ERRORS

All sorts of errors may be made in the bookkeeping entries. Once discovered, an error must be rectified as quickly as possible. The precise entries you would need to make will depend on the sort of error made, but basically you will want to reverse any entries made wrongly (as with a dishonoured cheque) and then to make the correct entry.

Example

The balance on the sales account is £200,000 and the balance on furniture is £15,000. On 10 April the bookkeeper wants to record a purchase of furniture for £3,000. The correct CR entry is made on cash but, instead of making the DR entry on furniture he makes the DR entry on the sales account. After the error is made the accounts look like this:

Sales

Date	Details	DR	CR	BAL
April 10	Balance Cash	3,000		200,000CR 197,000CR

Furniture

Date	Details	DR	CR	BAL
April	Balance			15,000DR

Entries:
To correct the error:
CR Sales account
DR Furniture account

Sales

Date	Details	DR	CR	BAL
April 10	Balance Cash Furniture – to correct error	3,000	3,000	200,000CR 197,000CR 200,000CR

Furniture

Date	Details	DR	CR	BAL
April 10	Balance Sales – to correct error	3,000		15,000DR 18,000DR

3.6 SUSPENSE ACCOUNT

A Trial Balance which does not balance indicates that an error has been made in the double entry bookkeeping. Sometimes the bookkeeper cannot immediately locate the error made. In such a case, a suspense account is opened and an appropriate DR or CR entry is made. It is merely a temporary measure and as soon as the error is (or errors are) located the account is closed and the entries necessary to correct the accounts are made.

Example

The DR balances on the Trial Balance are £100 less than the CR balances. On 30 November the bookkeeper opens a suspense account as a temporary measure. On 1 December the bookkeeper discovers that a DR entry of £100 was omitted from the stationery account and corrects the error.

Entries:
When the suspense account is opened:
DR Suspense account

Suspense

Date	Details	DR	CR	BAL
Nov 30	Error	**100DR**		100DR

When the error is discovered:
   CR Suspense account
   DR Stationery account

Suspense

Date	Details	DR	CR	BAL
Nov 30	Error	100		100DR
Dec 1	Stationery		100	—

Stationery

Date	Details	DR	CR	BAL
Dec 1	Suspense	100		XXX

A suspense account may also be used as a temporary measure when a bookkeeper is not certain how to treat a particular item.

Example

The balance on a firm's repairs account is £1,000 and on premises £100,000.

On 1 March the firm pays £31,500 to builders. The bookkeeper is not sure whether the payment represents repairs or an extension to existing premises. Repairs, being an expense item, would be recorded as a DR on the repairs account but an extension, being a capital item, would be recorded as a DR entry on the premises account. As a temporary measure, until additional information can be obtained, he records the payment on the suspense account. On 12 March the bookkeeper discovers that £1,500 is to be regarded as repairs and £30,000 as the cost of the extension.

The accounts will look as follows:

Cash

Date	Details	DR	CR	BAL
March 1	Suspense		31,500	XXX

Suspense

Date	Details	DR	CR	BAL
March 1	Cash	31,500		31,500DR
12	Repairs		1,500	30,000DR
	Premises		30,000	—

Repairs

Date	Details	DR	CR	BAL
March 12	Balance			1,000DR
	Suspense	1,500		2,500DR

Premises

Date	Details	DR	CR	BAL
March 12	Balance			100,000DR
	Suspense	30,000		130,000DR

Exercise 3A

An extract from the Trial Balance of X Co is set out below.

X Co

Trial Balance

	DR £	CR £
Credit Sales		30,000
Debtors (including B £500)	3,000	
Cash	10,000	

Show the entries necessary to record the following transactions:

1 May   X delivers a bill to A for credit sales of £200.

2 May   A pays but X mistakenly records the receipt as coming from B.

3 May   X discovers the mistake and corrects it.

4 May   B sends X a cheque for £500 in payment of the amount due.

5 May   Bank tells X that B's cheque has been dishonoured.

6 May   X writes off B's debt as bad.

(See overleaf for solution.)

Solicitors

Exercise 3A

Credit Sales

Date	Details	DR	CR	BAL
May 1	Balance			30,000CR
1	A		200	30,200CR

A

Date	Details	DR	CR	BAL
May 1	Credit Sales	200		200DR
3	Cash		200	—

Cash

Date	Details	DR	CR	BAL
May 1	Balance			10,000DR
2	B	200		10,200DR
3	B – correction of error		200[1]	10,000DR
3	A	200[1]		10,200DR
4	B	500		10,700DR
5	B – dishonoured cheque		500	10,200DR

[1] These entries cancel each other out. You could omit them completely and correct the error more simply by making a DR entry on B's account and a CR entry on A's account.

B

Date	Details	DR	CR	BAL
May 1	Balance			500DR
2	Cash		200	300DR
3	Cash – correction of error	200		500DR
4	Cash		500	—
5	Cash – dishonoured cheque	500		500DR
6	Bad Debts		500	—

Bad Debts

Date	Details	DR	CR	BAL
May 6	B	500		500DR

Chapter 4

FINAL ACCOUNTS – PREPARATION

4.1 PURPOSE OF FINAL ACCOUNTS

So far we have looked at the bookkeeping entries made by a firm to record its day-to-day business. These entries give the firm information on every single transaction carried out, for example payment of a gas bill, purchase of a fixed asset, delivery of a bill to a client, receipt of cash from a client in payment of costs.

This information is required so that periodically (usually once a year) the business can calculate its net profit and list its assets and liabilities. As we saw in Chapter 2, net profit is calculated on a Profit and Loss Account, assets and liabilities are listed on a Balance Sheet. These end of year accounts are referred to as 'Final Accounts'.

4.2 DIFFERENCES BETWEEN FINAL ACCOUNTS OF TRADING BUSINESSES AND PROFESSIONAL BUSINESSES

The Final Accounts of a trading business differ from those of a business providing professional services.

Both businesses have a Balance Sheet. A professional business has only a Profit and Loss Account. This Profit and Loss Account shows income from professional charges and any other sources (eg interest received, commission received) less its expenses. The difference between the two is its net profit.

A trading business has a preliminary account called a Trading Account.

This Trading Account shows income from sales less the cost of those sales (ie the cost of buying the trading stock). The difference between the two is the gross profit. The gross profit is then carried forward to start the Profit and Loss Account and the expenses of the business are deducted. The difference between the two is the net profit.

We will consider the preparation of the final accounts of a professional business first and then the preparation of the accounts of a trading business.

4.3 THE PROFIT AND LOSS ACCOUNT

4.3.1 The period covered

The accounting period will normally (but not necessarily) be one year. It is important that the Profit and Loss Account is headed with the period to which it relates.

> **Examples**
>
> Profit and Loss Account for ABC & Co for year ended 30 September [year]
>
> Profit and Loss Account for ABC & Co for 1 October [year] to 30 September [year].

4.3.2 Classification of items

The profit or loss calculated on the Profit and Loss Account is the result of subtracting expenses from income. It is, therefore, vital that you can accurately identify these items and distinguish them from assets and liabilities of the business. If necessary, re-read **2.1**.

Exercise 4A

Study the following list of items. Identify those which will appear on the Profit and Loss Account as income and those which will appear there as expenses.

Premises	Capital	Interest received	Stationery
Rent paid	Drawings	Interest paid	Creditors
Machinery	Profit costs	Insurance commission received	Debtors
Wages	Bank loan	Gas	
Repairs	Cash	Electricity	

Note: Those items which are neither income nor expenses will be assets or liabilities and will appear on the Balance Sheet.

Note: It is important to distinguish income receipts from capital receipts. A firm may sell its premises; the receipt of cash is a capital receipt and does not in itself affect the profitability of the firm. The firm has simply transformed one asset, premises, into a different sort of asset, cash. There will be changes on the firm's Balance Sheet but nothing will appear on the Profit and Loss Account. However, it may be that an asset is sold for more or less than the value recorded for that asset in the firm's accounts. The resulting gain or loss over the recorded value would represent a profit or loss and would affect the firm's profitability. That profit or loss would appear on the firm's Profit and Loss Account. See **5.3.2**.

Example

A professional partnership buys premises for £150,000. Two years later it sells them for £150,000. After the sale the Balance Sheet will show cash instead of premises. Nothing will be shown on the Profit and Loss Account in respect of the sale.

Had the premises been sold for £200,000, the gain of £50,000 over the recorded value of the premises would be shown on the Profit and Loss Account as additional income of the firm.

Had the premises been sold for £100,000, the resulting loss of £50,000 would have appeared on the Profit and Loss Account as an additional expense.

The disposal of assets is dealt with in more detail in Chapter 5.

4.3.3   Preparation

Once you have identified the income and expense accounts you will transfer the balances on those accounts to the Profit and Loss Account. The income and expense accounts will then have zero balances and will be closed. New accounts will be opened for the following period.

Expenses are transferred to the DR side of the Profit and Loss Account; income is transferred to the CR side of the Profit and Loss Account.

Note: As we will see later, the Profit and Loss Account is, in fact, usually set out vertically going down the page instead of in the normal tabular fashion. Rather than having a DR side and a CR side, it has a DR section set out below the CR section. However, we will not consider this form of presentation initially.

Example

Ann, a solicitor in sole practice, has the following income and expense accounts for the year 1 March [Year X] to 28 February [Year X]. The balances are transferred to the Profit and Loss Account and the ledger accounts for the current year are closed.

Ann, a firm
Extract from Trial Balance 28 February [Year X]

	DR	CR
Profit Costs		120,000
Interest Received		20,000
General Expenses	10,000	
Salaries	30,000	

The balance on the Profit and Loss Account, ie the difference between the income side and the expenses side (£100,000), will represent the net profit.

Profit and Loss Account for Ann for
year ended 28 February [Year X]

	DR	CR	BAL
Costs		120,000	120,000CR
Interest Received		20,000	140,000CR
Salaries	30,000		110,000CR
General Expenses	10,000		100,000CR

The balance on the Profit and Loss Account (£100,000 in the above example) is transferred to the capital account. If you think about it, you will see why. The net profit is 'owed' to the proprietor of the business; the capital account is the account which shows how much the business 'owes' the proprietor.

Example (continued)

Ann contributed £120,000 cash to the business when she started it. During the first year she withdrew £20,000 cash. At the end of the first year her net profit was £100,000. Her capital account will appear as follows:

Capital

	DR	CR	BAL
Cash – Original Contribution		120,000	120,000CR
Cash – Drawings	20,000		100,000CR
Net Profit for year		100,000	200,000CR

(1) Vertical presentation

The Profit and Loss Account is usually set out in what is called the 'vertical' form of presentation. As the name suggests, the income items and expense items are listed vertically and the total of expenses is deducted from the total of income. One of the reasons that this form of presentation has become popular is that it is thought easier for a lay person to understand information presented as a list instead of as a two-sided account.

Despite its unusual appearance, the vertical Profit and Loss Account remains part of the double entry system. An entry in the income section is equivalent to a credit entry and an entry in the expenses section is equivalent to a debit entry.

Example

We have redrafted Ann's Profit and Loss Account from the example above in the vertical form.

Profit and Loss Account for Ann for year ended 28 February [Year X]

Income	£	£
Profit Costs	120,000	
Interest Received	20,000	
		140,000
Expenses		
Salaries	30,000	
General Expenses	10,000	
		(40,000)
NET PROFIT		100,000

Exercise 4B

Prepare a Profit and Loss Account for Smith for the year ended 31 December [Year 10] based on the Trial Balance set out below. Use the vertical form of presentation.

Trial Balance as at 31 December [Year 10]

	£	£
Profit Costs		18,462
Wages and Salaries	14,629	
Motor Expenses	520	
Rent and Rates	2,820	
Stationery	111	
General Expenses (including Electricity)	105	
Fixtures and Fittings	6,500	
Motor Vehicles	6,200	
Debtors	1,950	
Creditors		1,538
Cash at Bank	1,654	
Petty Cash	40	
Drawings	895	
Capital		15,424
	35,424	35,424

4.4   THE BALANCE SHEET

4.4.1   The date of preparation

The Balance Sheet is a list of the assets and liabilities of the business. It lists assets and liabilities on the last day of the accounting period and is accurate only for that one day. It must be headed with that date.

Example

Balance Sheet for ABC & Co as at 31 December [year].

4.4.2   Assets and liabilities

As we saw in **4.3.3** above, income and expense accounts are closed at the end of the accounting period and the balances transferred to the Profit and Loss Account to calculate net profit. The remaining accounts represent assets and liabilities. These accounts are not closed. If a business has an asset or a liability on the evening of the last day of an accounting period, it will still have that asset or liability on the morning of the first day of the following accounting period. The balances on these accounts are carried down to start off the ledger accounts for the next period. The values of these assets and liabilities are listed on the Balance Sheet. Notice that the Balance Sheet is not an account and is not part of the double entry system. It is simply a list which summarises information already available to the proprietor in the accounts.

4.4.3   Preparation

The horizontal form of Balance Sheet lists liabilities on the left and assets on the right.

Example

A solicitor has the following balances on asset and liability accounts on 30 September [Year 10]. After taking into account the firm's net profit for the year the balance on the capital account is £110,000.

	£
Premises	50,000
Machinery	50,000
Debtors	10,000
Cash in office bank account	2,000
Creditors	2,000

The Balance Sheet would look as follows:

Balance Sheet as at 30 September [Year 10]

Liabilities	£	Assets	£
Capital	110,000	**Fixed Assets**	
		Premises	50,000
		Machinery	50,000
Current Liabilities		**Current Assets**	
Creditors	2,000	Debtors	10,000
		Cash	2,000
	112,000		112,000

Assets will always equal liabilities (unless an error has been made). This is because, when a business makes a profit its assets will increase, making the assets side heavier. However, the profit is owed to the proprietor and is, therefore, added to capital making the liabilities side heavier. Conversely, when the business makes a loss, both sides of the Balance Sheet will become lighter. The business will lose assets and will owe less to the proprietor.

(1) Order of items

By convention, items are listed in decreasing order of permanence (or, to put it another way, in increasing order of liquidity).

Thus, fixed assets are shown before current assets. Premises are always shown first in the list of fixed assets, and debtors are always shown before cash in the list of current assets. Fixed assets are those which are bought not for resale but to improve the efficiency of the business, for example premises, machinery. Current (or circulating) assets are short-term assets which turn from one into another.

[cash → trading stock or work in progress → debtors → cash]

On the liabilities side capital is always shown first, then long-term liabilities and, finally, current liabilities. Anything which is repayable more than 12 months from the date of the Balance Sheet is a long-term liability; anything repayable within one year is a current liability. Thus, a bank loan is normally a long-term liability and an overdraft (which is repayable on demand) is a current liability.

A Balance Sheet is set out below demonstrating the order of items:

Balance Sheet as at [date]

Liabilities	£	Assets	£
Capital	XX	**Fixed Assets**	
		Premises	XX
Long-term Liabilities		Machinery	XX
Bank loan	XX	**Current Assets**	
		Stock/Work in progress	XX
Current Liabilities		Debtors	XX
Creditors	XX	Cash	XX

(2) The capital account

As explained in *(1)* above, the balance on the capital account will be made up of the balance on that account at the start of the accounting period less any drawings made during the accounting period plus the net profit or minus the net loss made during the period. It is possible to show the figures making up the balance on the capital account as separate items on the Balance Sheet.

Example

Taking the figures from the previous example, assume that the capital balance of £110,000 was made up of an opening balance of £80,000, drawings of £30,000 and net profit of £60,000. This would be shown on the Balance Sheet as follows:

Balance Sheet as at 30 September [Year 10]

	£	£		£
Liabilities			**Assets**	
Capital				
Opening balance	80,000			
Net profit	60,000			
Drawings	(30,000)			
		110,000		

(3) *Vertical presentation*

The vertical form of Balance Sheet, as you might expect, lists assets and liabilities vertically down the page instead of side by side as on the horizontal form.

However, instead of listing all the assets and then all the liabilities (or vice versa), the vertical form of Balance Sheet subtracts current liabilities from current assets to give a figure for **net current assets**. The net current assets are added to fixed assets.

The result is that the assets section shows fixed assets plus net current assets. An illustration is given below, using the figures from the example above. Again, items appear in increasing order of liquidity.

Example

Vertical Balance Sheet as at 30 September [Year 10]

	£	£
Employment of Capital		
Fixed Assets		
Premises	50,000	
Machinery	50,000	
		100,000
Current Assets		
Debtors	10,000	
Cash	2,000	
Less Current Liabilities		
Creditors	(2,000)	
Net Current Assets		10,000
		110,000
Capital Employed		
Capital		
Opening balance	80,000	
Net profit	60,000	
Drawings	(30,000)	
		110,000

You may be wondering why net current assets are treated in this way. The reason is that the value of net current assets (often called 'working capital') is very important to a variety of people (eg the person running the business, lenders to the business and people thinking of investing in the business). The net current assets figure shows how likely the business is to run short of liquid funds. A business may have lots of assets and be very profitable but, if it has insufficient liquid assets, it may be wound up because it cannot pay a debt which has fallen due.

In the illustration above we showed the assets section first and the liabilities section second, labelling the sections 'Employment of Capital' and 'Capital Employed' respectively. However, it is perfectly possible to show it the other way round with the liabilities section first. Different titles are often used for the two sections of the vertical Balance Sheet. The assets section is often titled simply 'Assets' and the liabilities section is often labelled 'Financed By' or 'Represented By'.

(4)   Where do long-term liabilities appear?

Long-term liabilities can be included in the 'Capital Employed' section. However, it is now usual to deduct long-term liabilities from the total of the assets section. Thus, the vertical Balance Sheet shows in one section the total of fixed assets plus net current assets less long-term liabilities owed to outsiders and in the other section the total owed to the proprietor by the business. This has the advantage of highlighting the proprietor's investment in the firm.

Example

Taking the figures from the previous example assume that the business has just borrowed £100,000 from the bank on a five-year loan. The cash is in the bank at the moment although eventually the business will spend the cash on additional fixed assets. The Balance Sheet will appear as set out below.

Balance Sheet as at 30 September [Year 10]

	£	£
Employment of Capital		
Fixed Assets		
Premises	50,000	
Machinery	50,000	
		100,000
Current Assets		
Debtors	10,000	
Cash	102,000	
Less Current Liabilities		
Creditors	(2,000)	
Net Current Assets		110,000
		210,000
Less Long Term Liabilities		
Five-Year Bank Loan		(100,000)
		110,000
Capital Employed		
Capital		
Opening balance	80,000	
Net profit	60,000	
Drawings	(30,000)	
		110,000

(5) Client bank account

A firm of solicitors will have an additional asset – a bank account containing money held for clients. This asset will always be equalled by the amount the firm 'owes' its clients. The two items are normally shown as self-cancelling items after net current assets.

Example

	£	£
Net Current Assets		10,000
Client bank account	100,000	
Due to clients	(100,000)	

Exercise 4C

Prepare a Balance Sheet for Smith as at 31 December [Year 10] based on the Trial Balance set out in Exercise 4B. Use the vertical form of presentation.

4.5   TRADING BUSINESSES

4.5.1   Need for Trading Account

A trading business must produce a Trading Account as well as a Profit and Loss Account. The Trading Account calculates the difference between income from selling goods and the cost of goods sold. The result is called 'gross profit'. The Trading Account must be headed with the period to which it relates.

4.5.2   Preparation of Trading Account

The balance on the sales account will be transferred to the Trading Account as income. The balance on the purchases account will be transferred to the Trading Account as an expense. The sales and purchases accounts for the period in question will then be closed.

The balance on the Trading Account, ie the difference between the sales income and the cost of buying trading stock, will represent the gross profit. It will be carried down to start the Profit and Loss Account.

Example

A business, ABC & Co, has the following balances on its sales and purchases accounts for the year 1 January to 31 December Year 10. The balances are transferred to the Trading Account and the ledger accounts for Year 10 are closed.

ABC & Co
Extract from Trial Balance as at 31 December Year 10

	DR	CR
Sales		400,000
Purchases	280,000	

Trading Account for ABC & Co for year ended 31 December Year 10

		£
	Sales	400,000
Less	Cost of goods sold	(280,000)
	Gross profit	120,000

The gross profit is carried forward to start the Profit and Loss Account.

4.5.3   The 'cost of goods sold'

In the example of ABC & Co we took the balance on the purchases account as the cost of goods sold. Frequently, it will be necessary to make an adjustment to allow for the value of stock left over at the end of the year. We will consider this in more detail in Chapter 5.

Solutions

Exercise 4A

Expenses	Income
Rent paid	Profit costs
Wages	Interest received
Repairs	Insurance commission received
Interest paid	
Gas	
Electricity	
Stationery*	

* You may have wondered whether to classify stationery as an asset or as an expense item. It is correct to classify it as an expense since the purchase of stationery is recurrent and the benefit of it is normally exhausted relatively quickly. (Any stationery which is left over at the end of the accounting period will be shown on the Balance Sheet as an asset. See Chapter 5.)

The remaining items represent assets or liabilities which will appear on the Balance Sheet.

Exercise 4B

Profit and Loss Account for Smith for year ended 31 December [Year 10]

	£	£
Income		
Profit Costs		18,462
Expenses		
Wages and Salaries	14,629	
Motor Expenses	520	
Rent and Rates	2,820	
Stationery	111	
General Expenses	105	
		(18,185)
NET PROFIT		277

Exercise 4C

Balance Sheet for Smith as at 31 December [Year 10]

	£	£
Employment of Capital		
Fixed Assets		
Fixtures and Fittings	6,500	
Motor Vehicles	6,200	
		12,700
Current Assets		
Debtors	1,950	
Cash at Bank	1,654	
Petty Cash	40	
	3,644	
Less Current Liabilities		
Creditors	(1,538)	
NET CURRENT ASSETS		2,106
		14,806
Capital Employed		
Capital		
Opening Balance	15,424	
Net Profit	277	
Drawings	(895)	
		14,806

Chapter 5

ADJUSTMENTS

5.1 WHAT FIGURES FOR INCOME AND EXPENSES?

5.1.1 The concept of accruals

During the accounting period, entries are made on the ledger accounts as and when expenses are actually paid. Thus, if an electricity bill of £100 has been received but not yet paid, there will be no entries in the accounts.

The Final Accounts of most businesses are prepared rather differently on what is called the 'accruals basis'. The accruals basis requires that income and expenditure are recorded in the period **to which they relate** rather than that in which payment or receipt occurs. The Final Accounts must include all expenses which relate to the period irrespective of whether the expense has yet been paid or whether bills have yet been received. So far as income is concerned the accruals basis requires the Final Accounts to include all income 'earned' during the period, irrespective of whether cash has yet been received or whether bills have yet been delivered.

Conversely, if an expense has been paid in the current accounting period which actually relates to an earlier or later period, it will not be included in the current Final Accounts; neither will income received in the current accounting period which actually relates to an earlier or later period be included. Instead, such items will be included in the Final Accounts for the appropriate period.

Think of the process of determining which items relate to which period as 'matching'. You are trying to 'match' the expense to the period in which the benefit of the expense was obtained and to 'match' the income to the period in which the work producing the income was done.

The detail of what entries need to be made in the accounts will vary depending on the type of income or expense involved but the principle of 'matching' remains the same.

Exercise 5A

You are preparing Final Accounts for Smith & Co for the accounting year ending 31 December 1999. Decide which of the following items relate to the accounting year ending 31 December 1999.

(a) Electricity bill paid 10 January 1999 for period July–December 1998

(b) Electricity bill paid 10 July 1999 for period January–June 1999

(c) Electricity bill unpaid for period July–December 1999

(d) Stationery bill paid 30 November 1999. Three-quarters of the stationery purchased remains in the stationery cupboard on 1 January 2000.

(e) Rent for new premises paid in advance on 28 December 1999 for period January–March 2000

(f) Work done for clients during 1999 but not yet billed by 31 December 1999 is estimated at £15,000.

5.1.2 Outstanding expenses

As and when expenses are paid during an accounting period, entries are made on the cash account and on the relevant expense account.

By the end of an accounting period, a DR balance will have built up on each expense ledger account. An unpaid bill increases the amount of the expense correctly attributable to the accounting period and must be added to the DR balance on the expense account to increase it. The increased expense is then shown on Profit and Loss as the true expense for the current accounting period. The amount of the unpaid liability is shown on the Balance Sheet, as a current liability.

Note: The expense has been added to this year's profits but will not actually be paid until the following year. When it is paid the bookkeeper must make sure that the expense is not included a second time. He does this by carrying forward a CR entry to start the expense account for the following period. Having a CR entry already made on the expense account at the start of the period means that, when the expense is finally paid, the balance on the expense account will return to zero.

Adjustments will be made *after* the preparation of the Trial Balance at the end of the accounting period.

You will never be required to adjust the ledger accounts, but a full example of the entries is given below for completeness.

Example

On 31 December, AB & Co are preparing their Final Accounts for Year 1. There was a balance on the General Expenses account of £48,000 on 31 December Year 1 but there was an unpaid bill of £3,000. This bill was finally paid on 30 January Year 2.

On 31 December Year 1, before any adjustments, the General Expenses account looked like this:

General Expenses Year 1

	DR	CR	BAL
Dec 31 Balance			48,000DR

To make the adjustment for the outstanding expense the entries are as follows:

Entries:

> DR General Expenses ledger account for Year 1
> CR General Expenses ledger account for Year 2   } with the outstanding expenses

General Expenses Year 1

	DR	CR	BAL
Dec 31 Balance			48,000DR
31 Adjustment	3,000		51,000DR

General Expenses Year 2

	DR	CR	BAL
Jan 1 Adjustment		3,000	3,000CR

The Profit and Loss Account for Year 1 will show the new balance on the General Expenses account of £51,000.

The Balance Sheet will have an additional current liability of £3,000.

On 30 January Year 2 when the bill is paid the entries will be as follows:

Entries:

> CR Cash
> DR General Expenses ledger account Year 2

Cash					General Expenses Year 2			
	DR	CR	BAL			DR	CR	BAL
Jan			XX		Jan			
30 Electricity		3,000	XX		1 Adjustment		3,000	3,000CR
					30 Cash	3,000		—

You can see that, once the old bill is paid in Year 2, the balance on the General Expenses account for Year 2 returns to zero ready to start recording the Year 2 expenses.

Note: The Profit and Loss Account and Balance Sheet position is shown in the Specimen Accounts at **2.1.3**. The Profit and Loss Account shows the adjusted balance for General Expenses. The Balance Sheet has an additional current liability, accrued expenses of £3,000.

5.1.3 Prepayments

As and when expenses are paid during an accounting period, entries are made on the cash account and on the relevant expense account.

By the end of an accounting period a DR balance will have built up on each expense ledger account.

An amount paid in the current period, the benefit of which will not be received until the following period, reduces the amount of the expense correctly attributable to the current accounting period and should be deducted from the DR balance on the current period's account to reduce it. The reduced expense is then shown on Profit and Loss as the true expense for the current accounting period.

The amount of the prepayment is shown on the Balance Sheet as a current asset (usually after cash). The 'asset' is the benefit of the payment. It allows the business to use something in the future without any future payment.

Note: The amount of the payment in advance is carried forward as a DR entry to start the expense account for the following period.

This ensures that, although no cash payment will be made in the following period to reflect the expense, there will be a DR entry on the expense account to increase the expenses for the following period to the appropriate level.

You will never be required to adjust the ledger accounts, but a full example of the entries is given below for completeness.

Example

On 31 December, AB & Co are preparing their Final Accounts for Year 1. There was a balance on the rent paid account of £25,000 on 31 December Year 1 but £4,000 of it relates to Year 2. On 31 December Year 1, before any adjustment, the rent account looked like this:

Rent Paid Year 1			
	DR	CR	BAL
Dec			
31 Balance			25,000DR

To make the adjustment for the prepayment the entries are as follows:

Entries:

CR Rent Paid ledger account for Year 1
DR Rent Paid ledger account for Year 2 } with the prepayment

Rent Paid Year 1

	DR	CR	BAL
Dec			
31 Balance			25,000DR
31 Adjustment		**4,000**	21,000DR

Rent Paid Year 2

	DR	CR	BAL
Jan			
1 Adjustment	**4,000**		4,000DR

You can see that the rent account starts Year 2 with an expense of £4,000 already recorded.

Note: The Profit and Loss Account and Balance Sheet position is shown in the specimen Accounts at **2.1.3**. The Profit and Loss Account shows the adjusted balance for Rent Paid. The Balance Sheet has an additional current asset, prepayment £4,000.

5.1.4   Work in Progress

A firm of solicitors (or other business which provides services) will want to adjust its profit costs account at the end of the year to reflect the value of work in progress at that date.

As and when bills are delivered during the accounting period, the amount of profit costs will be recorded on the costs account and the client's ledger account. By the end of an accounting period, a CR balance will have built up on the profit costs ledger account. Some work will have been done but not yet billed.

The estimated value of work done but not yet billed increases the profit costs properly attributable to the current period and must be added to the balance on the costs account. The increased balance on the costs account must be shown on Profit and Loss. It is usual, however, to show the costs actually billed and the value of work in progress at the end of the year as two separate items which are added together on Profit and Loss.

The value of work in progress at the end of the year is shown on the Balance Sheet as a current asset. It is normally shown as the first of the current assets.

Note: The value of work in progress is carried forward as a DR entry to start the costs account for the following period.

This is to ensure that when the bills are delivered in the following period the value of work in progress which has already been attributed to the current accounting period is not attributed a second time to the following period.

It is normal to show the value of work in progress at the start of the year as a deduction on Profit and Loss from the value of bills delivered during the year.

Example

On 1 January Year 1 Jay & Co start a practice. During Year 1 bills are delivered for profit costs of £30,000.

On 31 December Year 1 estimated work in progress is £3,000.

During Year 2 bills are delivered for costs of £40,000.

On 31 December Year 2 estimated work in progress is £4,000.

During Year 3 bills are delivered for costs of £50,000.

On 31 December Year 3 estimated work in progress is £5,000.

The Profit and Loss Account for Years 1, 2 and 3 will look as follows:

Profit and Loss Account Year ended 31 December Year 1

	£	£
Costs Billed	30,000	
plus Work in progress at end of year	3,000	
		33,000

Profit and Loss Account for Year ended 31 December Year 2

	£	£
Costs Billed	40,000	
less Work in progress at start of year	(3,000)	
plus Work in progress at end of year	4,000	
		41,000

Profit and Loss Account for Year ended 31 December Year 3

	£	£
Costs Billed	50,000	
less Work in progress at start of year	(4,000)	
plus Work in progress at end of year	5,000	
		51,000

The Balance Sheet for 31 December Year 1 will show work in progress as a current asset of £3,000, that for Year 2 will show £4,000 and that for Year 3 will show £5,000.

Note: Although you would never be required to adjust the ledger accounts a full example is given below for completeness.

On 31 December Year 1, before any adjustment for work in progress at the end of Year 1, the costs account looked like this:

Costs Year 1

	DR	CR	BAL
Dec 31 Balance			30,000CR

To make the adjustments the entries are as follows:

Entries:

CR Work in progress at 31 December to costs ledger account Year 1
DR Work in progress at 31 December to costs ledger account Year 2

Costs Year 1

	DR	CR	BAL
Dec 31 Balance 31 Work in progress – end year		3,000	30,000CR 33,000CR

Costs Year 2

	DR	CR	BAL
Jan 1 Work in progress – start year	3,000		3,000DR

On 31 December Year 2, before any adjustment for work in progress at the end of Year 2, the costs account would look like this:

Costs Year 2

	DR	CR	BAL
Jan 1 Work in progress – start year	3,000		3,000DR
Dec 31 Costs billed during year		40,000	37,000CR

To make the adjustment the entries are as follows:

Entries:

CR Work in progress at 31 December to costs ledger account Year 2
DR Work in progress at 31 December to costs ledger account Year 3

Costs Year 2

	DR	CR	BAL
Jan 1 Work in progress	3,000		3,000DR
Dec 31 Costs billed during year		40,000	37,000CR
Work in progress – end year		4,000	41,000CR

Costs Year 3

	DR	CR	BAL
Jan 1 Work in progress – start year	4,000		4,000DR

On 31 December Year 3, before any adjustment for work in progress at the end of Year 3, the costs account would look like this:

Costs Year 3

	DR	CR	BAL
Jan 1 Work in progress – start year	4,000		4,000DR
Dec 31 Costs billed during year		50,000	46,000CR

To make the adjustments the entries are as follows:

Entries:

CR Work in progress at 31 December to costs ledger account Year 3

DR Work in progress at 31 December to costs ledger account Year 4

Costs Year 3

	DR	CR	BAL
Jan 1 Work in progress – start year	4,000		4,000DR
Dec 31 Costs billed during year		50,000	46,000CR
Work in progress – end year		**5,000**	51,000CR

Costs Year 4

	DR	CR	BAL
Jan 1 Work in progress – start year	**5,000**		5,000DR

The Specimen Accounts at **2.1.3** show a firm which billed £478,000 in profit costs but had £30,000 work in progress at the start of the year. It estimated the value of its work in progress at the end of the year as £40,000.

5.1.5 Adjustment for closing stock on Trading Account

When we calculated gross profit on the Trading Account earlier, we deducted the cost of goods sold from sales and we used the purchases figure to represent the cost of goods sold. However, the purchases figure does not by itself represent the correct value for cost of goods sold. It is necessary to make an adjustment for the value of stock purchased during the year and left unsold at the end of the year.

To see why this is so consider the following example.

Example

X starts a trading business. In Year 1, X purchases goods for £3,000. During the year, X sells goods for £7,000. At the end of the year, X has goods left over which cost £1,000 to buy and which X hopes to sell for £2,500.

To buy the goods *which X sold* cost X £3,000 less £1,000.

The Trading Account set out below shows this calculation:

Trading Account for X
Year 1

		£	£
Sales			7,000
Less Cost of Goods Sold			
	Purchases	3,000	
	less Closing Stock	(1,000)	
			(2,000)
	GROSS PROFIT		5,000

The 'closing stock' is an asset of the firm. It will be valued at the lesser of cost or realisable value and will be carried forward to start the next accounting period where it will be referred to as 'opening stock'. The value of opening stock will also have to be taken into account when calculating the cost of goods sold in the next accounting period.

In Year 2, X purchases goods for £5,000, sells goods for £12,000, and has goods left over at the end of the year which cost £2,000.

In Year 2, X has available for sale not just the goods purchased in Year 2 but also the stock purchased in Year 1 and left over. The value of opening stock will, thus, increase the cost of goods sold.

The Trading Account set out below shows this calculation:

Trading Account for X
Year 2

		£	£
Sales			12,000
Less Costs of Goods Sold			
	Purchases	5,000	
	plus Opening Stock	1,000	
	less Closing Stock	(2,000)	
			(4,000)
	GROSS PROFIT		8,000

You will see from the above example that the cost of goods sold is calculated as follows.

Purchases + Opening stock – Closing stock = Cost of goods sold

By convention, stock is valued at the *lesser* of acquisition or realisable value. It is, therefore, necessary to inspect the goods at the end of the accounting period to check for deterioration and pilferage. When you are analysing accounts always look critically at the figure given for closing stock. The value given may not be a realistic assessment of the value of the stock. Overvaluing stock is an easy way to make your profit figure look better. Look at the following example.

Example

In its first year of trading X & Co has sales of £20,000 and purchases of £10,000.

We have set out below the Trading Account on the basis that:

(a)   closing stock is valued at £1,000;
(b)   closing stock is valued at £7,000.

(a) Trading Account for X Co

Year 1

	£	£
Sales		20,000
Less Costs of Goods Sold		
Purchases	10,000	
less Closing Stock	(1,000)	
		(9,000)
GROSS PROFIT		11,000

(b) Trading Account for X Co

Year 1

	£	£
Sales		20,000
Less Costs of Goods Sold		
Purchases	10,000	
less Closing Stock	(7,000)	
		(3,000)
GROSS PROFIT		17,000

You will see that increasing the value for closing stock has the effect of increasing gross profit. Obviously, therefore, it is very important that the closing stock figure should be accurate. If it is not, the gross profit figure is also inaccurate.

The value of closing stock is an asset of a trading business and as such must be shown on the Balance Sheet. It is a current asset.

Exercise 5B

Study the Trial Balance of Daniel Deronda & Co set out below.

Trial Balance as at 31 December [Year X]

	DR	CR
	£	£
Sales		109,083
Purchases	89,621	
Opening stock	1,000	
Wages and salaries	14,629	
Motor expenses	520	
Rates	2,820	

Stationery	261	
General expenses (including electricity)	205	
Fixtures and fittings	2,500	
Motor vehicles	2,200	
Debtors	1,950	
Creditors		1,788
Cash at bank	1,654	
Petty cash	40	
Drawings	895	
Capital		5,424
Rent received		2,000
	118,295	118,295

(a)   Prepare the Final Accounts for Daniel Deronda & Co for the 12 months ending 31 December [Year X].

(b)   Prepare Final Accounts for Daniel Deronda & Co for the 12 months ending 31 December [Year X] taking into account the following adjustments.

(i)   Closing stock at 31 December was £2,548.

(ii)   The firm has received an electricity bill for £80 which it has not yet paid. There is unused stationery amounting to £20.

5.1.6   Other adjustments

The principle of 'matching' income and expenditure to the appropriate accounting period extends to all types of income and expenditure.

For example, a firm may receive some rent from a tenant in one accounting period which relates wholly or partly to a later period. Only the portion of rent which is correctly attributable to the current period will appear on the Profit and Loss Account.

5.1.7   Bad and doubtful debts

(1)   Bad debts

It was mentioned in Chapter 3 that a business will have to write off debts as bad from time to time.

   Entries:
      DR Bad Debts account
      CR Customer's ledger account

The bad debts account is an expense account. Some debts will be written off as bad during the accounting period. In addition, at the end of an accounting period, a business may review debtors to consider whether any further debts need to be written off as bad. The balance on the bad debts account will be shown on Profit and Loss as an expense reducing the net profit.

After writing off any further debts considered to be bad, the remaining debtors will be shown on the Balance Sheet as a current asset.

Exercise 5C

At the end of an accounting period you have already written off £1,500 debts as bad. Your remaining debtors amount to £20,000. You decide to write off a further £1,000 of debts as bad.

(a)   What figure will you show on the bad debts account?

(b)   What figure will you show on Profit and Loss for bad debts?

(c)   What figure will you show on the Balance Sheet for debtors?

---

(2)   Doubtful debts

At the end of an accounting period, a business will be shown as owed on paper a certain amount by debtors. However, the business will know from past experience that it never manages to collect all its debts. The percentage of debts which have to be written off normally remains fairly constant from year to year (although in times of recession a firm would expect the percentage of bad debts to rise). Thus, an accountant looking at a figure for debtors will know that over the next year a certain percentage will have to be written off as bad although no one will know precisely which debtors will turn out to be bad.

It would therefore be inaccurate to calculate net profit on the basis that all debtors will pay and inaccurate to include the full debtors figure on the Balance Sheet. An adjustment must be made for doubtful debts.

You will calculate the value of debtors you think will never pay. This is referred to as a 'Provision for Doubtful Debts'. You will DR the amount of this provision to the bad debts account and this will increase the figure for bad debts shown on Profit and Loss.

Note: The amount of provision will be carried down as a CR balance to start the bad debts account for the following period. The effect of starting the year with a CR balance on bad debts is that, when debts are written off as bad during the accounting period, there will be no expense to be taken to Profit and Loss until sufficient bad debts are written off to exhaust the credit balance on the bad debts account.

The ledger account is frequently referred to as a 'Bad **and Doubtful** Debts Account'.

The amount of the 'Provision for Doubtful Debts' will be shown on the Balance Sheet as a deduction from debtors.

The Specimen Accounts at **2.1.3** show a business which at the date of the Trial Balance had written off £15,000 of debts as bad and had £82,000 of debtors. It then decided to write off an additional debt of £2,000 and to make a provision for doubtful debts of 10% of remaining debtors.

Exercise 5D

The Trial Balance for Elliot & Co prepared on 31 December shows that debtors are £31,000 and that bad debts already written off are £4,000. The firm wants to write off as bad the debt of Jones who owes £1,000 and then to make a provision of 5% of debtors.

(a)   What figure will appear on the Profit and Loss account for **bad** debts? Do not include provision for doubtful debts in your answer to this part of the question.

(b)   What figure will appear on the Profit and Loss account for bad debts?

(c)   What figure will appear on the Balance Sheet for debtors?

(d)   Will Jones be shown as owing the firm money?

Exercise 5E

Freda is a solicitor in practice on her own. Her accounting period is 1 July to 30 June. As at 30 June [Year X] her bookkeeper prepares the following Trial Balance.

Trial Balance as at 30 June [Year X]

	£	DR £	CR £
Capital			30,000
Drawings		20,000	
Costs Bills delivered during year	80,000		
Work in progress at start of year	(4,000)		76,000
Premises		60,000	
Wages		20,000	
Electricity		5,000	
Stationery		2,000	
Travel Expenses		500	
Rates		2,200	
Cash – Office Bank Account		250	
Petty Cash		50	
Debtors		4,100	
Creditors			3,100
Bank Loan			5,500
Loan Interest		1,500	
Bad Debts		1,000	
Interest Received			2,000
Client Bank Account		100,000	
Due to Clients			100,000
		216,600	216,600

There are outstanding electricity expenses of £200 to take into account and stationery stock left over at the end of the year amounts to £300. Work in Progress at the start of the year is estimated at £7,000. A provision is to be made for doubtful debts of £175.

After the Trial Balance has been prepared the bookkeeper finds a cheque for £350 from a debtor in settlement of the debtor's account. This cheque was received the week before but not recorded in the accounts as the bookkeeper had temporarily overlooked it. The bookkeeper wishes to adjust the accounts to allow for the receipt of the money before preparing the accounts.

An employee of Freda's explains to the bookkeeper that she paid travel expenses of £25 from her own pocket the previous week and requires reimbursement. The bookkeeper gives the employee £25 from petty cash and adjusts the travel expenses account before preparing the Final Accounts.

For questions (1)–(5) below, tick which **one** of the alternative statements you think is correct.

(1) **In relation to the £200 outstanding electricity bill:**

   (a) The £200 will increase the amount shown on Profit and Loss for electricity. It will not appear on the Balance Sheet. ☐

   (b) The £200 will reduce the amount shown on Profit and Loss for electricity and will appear on the Balance Sheet as a current asset. ☐

   (c) The £200 will increase the amount shown on Profit and Loss for electricity and will appear on the Balance Sheet as a current asset. ☐

   (d) The £200 will increase the amount shown on Profit and Loss for electricity and will appear on the Balance Sheet as a current liability. ☐

(2) **In relation to the prepaid stationery stock of £300:**

   (a) The £300 will increase the amount shown on Profit and Loss for stationery. It will not appear on the Balance Sheet. ☐

   (b) The £300 will reduce the amount shown on Profit and Loss for stationery and will appear on the Balance Sheet as a current asset. ☐

   (c) The £300 will increase the amount shown on Profit and Loss for stationery and will appear on the Balance Sheet as a current asset. ☐

   (d) The £300 will increase the amount shown on Profit and Loss for stationery and will appear on the Balance Sheet as a current liability. ☐

(3) **The receipt of £350 in settlement of a debtor's bill will:**

   (a) Increase debtors. ☐

   (b) Reduce debtors. ☐

   (c) Reduce bad debts. ☐

   (d) Have no effect on debtors. ☐

(4) **The receipt of £350 as in (3) above will:**

   (a) Reduce cash. ☐

   (b) Increase profit costs. ☐

   (c) Increase cash. ☐

   (d) Reduce profit costs. ☐

(5) **The payment of £25 from petty cash to reimburse the employee for travel expenses will:**

   (a) Reduce cash. ☐

   (b) Increase current liabilities. ☐

   (c) Increase travel expenses. ☐

   (d) Reduce current liabilities. ☐

5.2   WHAT FIGURES FOR ASSETS?

5.2.1   Depreciation

(1)   Profit and Loss

Many fixed assets lose some of their value each year, for example cars, fixtures and fittings. This annual loss of value is a hidden expense of the business and must be shown on Profit and Loss as an item reducing net profit.

Example

X Co buys a car at the beginning of the year for £15,000. At the end of the year it is worth £13,000. The car has depreciated by £2,000. To look at it another way, it has cost X Co £2,000 to keep the car for a year. The Profit and Loss Account for the year must show an expense of £2,000.

---

(2)   Balance Sheet

The Balance Sheet must show the true value of the asset at the date of the Balance Sheet not the original purchase price. It is conventional to show the original purchase price with a deduction for the amount of depreciation incurred to date since the original purchase. This depreciation is referred to as 'accumulated depreciation'.

Example

X Co's accounting year ends on 31 December. X Co bought a car at the beginning of Year 1 for £15,000. Each year X depreciates the car by £2,000. By the end of Year 3 X Co will have depreciated the car 3 times (once at the end of Years 1, 2 and 3). Accumulated depreciation will therefore amount to £6,000. The Balance Sheet as at 31 December Year 3 would include the following item for cars:

Fixed Assets

	£	£
Car	15,000	
less Depreciation	(6,000)	
		9,000

Note 1: The £9,000 in the above example is referred to as the 'book value' of the car – its value in X Co's books or accounts.

Note 2: The Profit and Loss Account *each year* will record the loss in value over the one-year period. Thus, each year the depreciation expense shown on Profit and Loss will be £2,000.

Note 3: Each year the amount of accumulated depreciation shown on the Balance Sheet will increase by £2,000.

---

(3) Calculation

There are different methods of calculating the amount of depreciation, for example the 'straight line' method and the 'reducing balance' method.

On this course we will look only at the 'straight line' method.

A firm using the straight line method will decide on the likely life of an asset, for example 10 years, 4 years.

The loss in value is spread evenly over the projected life of the asset. Thus, if the projected life is 10 years, each year the asset will lose 10% of its original value. If the projected life is 4 years, each year the asset will lose 25% of its original value.

The reason that this method is called 'straight line' is that each year the same amount of depreciation is written off. If the asset is kept for the whole of its projected life, the value of the asset will eventually be reduced to zero.

Note: The 'reducing balance' method of recording depreciation requires the firm to write off a fixed percentage of the value of the asset as reduced by depreciation to date. This has the merit of recording the greatest drop in the value of the asset in the first year of the asset's life. Each year, less depreciation will be written off.

There are different ways of making the entries for depreciation. The simplest way is to DR the depreciation directly to the Profit and Loss Account as an expense and to CR a 'Provision for Depreciation' account. For brevity, we will refer to it as a 'Depreciation' account. This must be done *after* the preparation of the Trial Balance. The CR balance on the depreciation ledger account will be carried down to start the account for the following period.

The longer the asset is kept, the more depreciation will be written off and the bigger the carried forward CR balance on the depreciation account will be. Remember that the carried forward balance on the depreciation account represents accumulated depreciation from earlier years.

Entries:

DR Profit and Loss Account
CR Depreciation account   } Current year

The increased CR balance on the depreciation account will then be carried down to the depreciation account for the following year.

Example

X Co buys a machine in Year 1 for £10,000. X Co decides to depreciate it by 10% pa. Each year, after the preparation of the Trial Balance, £1,000 will be charged to Profit and Loss as an expense and £1,000 will be added to the balance on the depreciation account. The increased balance on the depreciation account will be shown on the Balance Sheet as a deduction from the value of the asset.

Thus, the Profit and Loss Account for each of the 10 years will appear as follows:

X Co
Profit and Loss Account Years 1–10

	£
Expenses	
Depreciation	**1,000**

However, the Balance Sheet for each of the 10 years will appear as follows:

X Co
Balance Sheet end of Year 1

	£	£
Machinery	10,000	
Depreciation	**(1,000)**	
		9,000

Balance Sheet end of Year 2

	£	£
Machinery	10,000	
Depreciation	**(2,000)**	
		8,000

Balance Sheet end of Year 3

	£	£
Machinery	10,000	
Depreciation	**(3,000)**	
		7,000

Balance Sheet end of Year 4

	£	£
Machinery	10,000	
Depreciation	**(4,000)**	
		6,000

This depreciation continues until, at the end of Year 10, the value of the machine is reduced to zero.

(4) *Date of purchase and sale*

It is common practice:

- to depreciate all assets held at the end of an accounting period for an entire accounting period irrespective of the point in the period at which the purchase was made;
- not to depreciate assets sold part way through an accounting period.

This has the merit of simplifying calculations.

Example

The accounting period of X Co is 1 January–31 December. In February X Co sells a car which it has owned for several years and purchases a replacement. It purchases a second car in November.

At the end of the accounting period on 31 December the new car will be depreciated for a full year. No depreciation will be recorded on the car sold.

Exercise 5F

A buys a car for her business for £20,000 on 1 July Year 1. Cars are depreciated by 10% pa using the straight line basis. A's accounting year ends on 31 December.

For questions (1) and (2) below indicate which **one** of the alternative statements you think is correct.

(1) (a)   The Profit and Loss Account for year ended 31 December Year 1 shows depreciation of £1,000. ☐

(b)   The Profit and Loss Account for year ended 31 December Year 2 shows depreciation of £2,000. ☐

(c)   The Profit and Loss Account for year ended 31 December Year 3 shows depreciation of £4,000. ☐

(d)   The Profit and Loss Account for year ended 31 December Year 4 shows depreciation of £6,000. ☐

(2) (a)   On 31 December Year 1 the book value of the car shown on the Balance Sheet is £20,000. ☐

(b)   On 31 December Year 1 the book value of the car shown on the Balance Sheet is £18,000. ☐

(c)   On 31 December Year 4 the book value of the car shown on the Balance Sheet is £14,000. ☐

(d)   On 31 December Year 4 the book value of the car shown on the Balance Sheet is £10,000. ☐

The Specimen Accounts at **2.1.3** show a firm which depreciates assets as follows:

- fixtures 5%
- computers 20%
- cars 20%

You can see that their Profit and Loss Account shows one year's depreciation, but that the Balance Sheet shows the original value of the asset less the total accumulated depreciation to date.

Exercise 5G

The following information is extracted from the accounts of Brown, a sole trader, in respect of the year ended 31 May [Year X].

		£
Sales		422,168
Purchases		292,350
Capital Account		58,125
Bank Loan		15,000
Drawings		33,600
Fixtures, Furniture and Office Equipment at cost		22,500
Accumulated depreciation on Fixtures, Furniture and Office Equipment at start of year		11,000
Motor Cars at cost		20,000
Accumulated depreciation on Motor Cars at start of year		8,000
Lease at cost		7,893
Creditors		90,970
Debtors		26,781
Cash at Bank (Office Account)		2,519
Petty Cash Balance		50
Interest Received		7,896
Opening Stock		14,322
Bad Debts		320
Miscellaneous Income		2,330
General Expenses		54,047

The following additional information is pertinent:

(a) Closing Stock is valued at £16,217.

(b) During the year, Brown purchased some reproduction antique furniture for use in the office. Due to an error made by the supplier, the amount paid by the firm in respect thereof, included the sum of £500 in payment for furniture for Brown's private use. No adjustment has yet been made in respect of this error.

(c) Miscellaneous Income includes the sum of £100 representing rent received in respect of the following year.

(d) Depreciation is to be charged (straight line basis) at the following rates:

Fixtures, Furniture and Office Equipment   5% per annum
Motor Cars   10% per annum

(e) In addition to the above adjustments, there are bills outstanding at the end of the year in respect of General Expenses which have not yet been accounted for, and these amount to £496.

(f) Additional bad debts amounting to £450 are to be written off.

For questions (1)–(9) tick which **one** of the alternative statements you think is correct.

(1) **With regard to the £450 written off as additional bad debts, the Profit and Loss Account will show:**

    (a) Bad debts of £320. ☐

    (b) Bad debts of £450. ☐

    (c) Bad debts of £770. ☐

    (d) Debtors of £26,781 – £770 = £26,011. ☐

(2) **With regard to the £450 written off as additional bad debts, the Balance Sheet will show:**

    (a) Bad debts of £450. ☐

    (b) Bad debts of £770. ☐

    (c) Debtors of £26,781 – £770 = £26,011. ☐

    (d) Debtors of £26,781 – £450 = £26,331. ☐

(3) **Closing Stock will be:**

    (a) Added to Purchases on Trading Account. ☐

    (b) Deducted from Purchases on Trading Account. ☐

    (c) Shown on the Balance Sheet as an addition to capital. ☐

    (d) Shown on the Balance Sheet as a deduction from capital. ☐

(4) **Opening Stock will be:**

    (a) Added to Purchases on Trading Account. ☐

    (b) Deducted from Purchases on Trading Account. ☐

    (c) Shown on the Balance Sheet as an addition to capital. ☐

    (d) Shown on the Balance Sheet as a current liability. ☐

(5) **The £500 for Brown's private furniture will:**

    (a) Be shown on Profit and Loss as an expense. ☐

    (b) Reduce the value of the furniture shown on the Balance Sheet. ☐

    (c) Increase Brown's capital balance. ☐

    (d) Not affect Brown's capital balance. ☐

(6) **The £100 of rent receivable relating to the following year will:**

    (a) Only increase miscellaneous income on Profit and Loss. It will not affect the Balance Sheet. ☐

    (b) Only reduce miscellaneous income on Profit and Loss. It will not affect the Balance Sheet. ☐

    (c) Increase miscellaneous income on Profit and Loss and be shown as a current asset on Balance Sheet. ☐

    (d) Reduce the miscellaneous income on Profit and Loss and be shown as a current liability on Balance Sheet. ☐

(7) **Depreciation on cars on Profit and Loss will be:**

    (a) £800. ☐

    (b) £8,880. ☐

    (c) £2,000. ☐

    (d) £10,000. ☐

(8) **Depreciation on cars shown on the Balance Sheet will be:**

    (a) £8,000. ☐

    (b) £2,000. ☐

    (c) £10,000. ☐

    (d) £8,800. ☐

(9) **Outstanding expenses of £496 will:**

    (a) Increase expenses on Profit and Loss. ☐

    (b) Reduce expenses on Profit and Loss. ☐

    (c) Have no effect on Profit and Loss. ☐

    (d) Have no effect on the Balance Sheet. ☐

5.2.2 Revaluation

Assets are recorded in the appropriate ledger account at their acquisition value. Each year in which an asset is retained, its acquisition value is brought forward to start the ledger account for the new accounting year. If the asset is being depreciated, a balance will be accumulating on the depreciation account but the acquisition value on the asset account will remain unchanged.

Over a period of time, the acquisition value of an asset may come to have little relationship to its current market value. When this happens a business may decide to alter the value of the asset on the ledger account. This is referred to as a 'revaluation'.

When an asset increases in value, the increase 'belongs' to the proprietor. Thus, you will want to adjust the capital account to show that more is owed by the business to the proprietor.

When an asset decreases in value by more than the amount of depreciation allowed the proprietor suffers a reduction in the amount 'belonging' to him. Thus, you will want to adjust the capital account to show that less is owed by the business to the proprietor. An example is set out below.

Entries:

If asset has increased in value:

DR Asset account

CR Capital account } with amount of increase

If asset has decreased in value:

CR Asset account

DR Capital account } with amount of decrease

Example

Premises were bought for £100,000. The balance on the capital account is £200,000. Premises are to be revalued by £50,000 to £150,000.

Premises

	DR	CR	BAL
Balance			100,000DR
Capital	50,000		150,000DR

Capital

	DR	CR	BAL
Balance			200,000CR
Premises		50,000	250,000CR

If the premises were to be *reduced* by £50,000.

Premises

	DR	CR	BAL
Balance			100,000DR
Capital		50,000	50,000DR

Capital

	DR	CR	BAL
Balance			200,000CR
Premises	50,000		150,000CR

Assets may be revalued before a major change in the structure of a business. For example, a sole practitioner might revalue assets before admitting a partner.

Such a revaluation ensures the asset values are up to date before the business commences in its changed form. It also ensures that, by increasing the capital balance, *before* admitting a partner, the original proprietor gets the sole benefit of increases in value of assets. The new partner will only get the benefit of increases in value occurring *after* he is admitted to the partnership.

Exercise 5H

Ruddle has been in practice as a solicitor for some years, and he decides to admit Trant into the firm as a partner with effect from 1 January Year 10, the name of the firm being Ruddle, Trant & Co.

The firm's accountant produces the following list of balances, for the year ended 31 December Year X.

		£
Capital account		
(at 1 January Year X)		100,000
Cash at Bank – Client account:		
Deposit account		660,000
Current account		47,896
Office account		6,427 (credit)
Petty Cash		50
Clients' Ledger balances:		
Office account		35,946
Client account		707,896
Drawings		55,500
Profit Costs		392,568
Opening Work in Progress		29,644
Interest Received		22,567
Sundry Creditors		20,463
Administrative and General Expenses		323,465
Freehold Premises		90,000
Furniture and Library at cost		15,000
Motor Cars at cost		39,420
Provision for Depreciation at start of Year X:		
Furniture and Library		4,500
Motor Cars		15,768
Bank Loan		26,732

(a) Ruddle decides that premises will be revalued by £160,000 on 31 December Year X before admitting Trant.

(b) Depreciation is to be charged at the following rates (straight line basis):

Furniture and Library   15% per annum
Motor Cars   20% per annum

(c) Interest Received includes the sum of £800 which had been paid into the office bank account by the bank in error. The money belonged to another customer of the bank and the error has not yet been rectified by them. You have made no entries as yet to correct the error.

For questions (1)–(6) below tick which **one** of the alternative statements you think is correct.

(1) **On the Balance Sheet prepared on 31 December Year X:**

   (a) Premises will be shown at their acquisition value of £90,000. ☐

   (b) Premises and capital will both be increased by £160,000. ☐

   (c) Premises will be increased by £90,000. ☐

   (d) The capital account of Ruddle will be increased by £90,000. ☐

(2) **On the Profit and Loss Account for year ended 31 December Year X the increase in value of premises will:**

   (a) Be shown as additional income. ☐

   (b) Be shown as additional expenses. ☐

   (c) Be shown as a deduction from expenses. ☐

   (d) Not be shown. ☐

Depreciation on furniture and library will be:

(3) (a) £2,250 on Profit and Loss. ☐

   (b) £1,500 on Profit and Loss. ☐

   (c) £4,500 on Profit and Loss. ☐

   (d) £450 on Profit and Loss. ☐

(4) (a) £4,500 on the Balance Sheet. ☐

   (b) £6,750 on the Balance Sheet. ☐

   (c) £2,250 on the Balance Sheet. ☐

   (d) £1,500 on the Balance Sheet. ☐

(5) **Depreciation on motor cars will be:**

   (a) £15,768 on Profit and Loss. ☐

   (b) £7,884 on Profit and Loss. ☐

   (c) £7,884 on the Balance Sheet. ☐

   (d) £15,768 on the Balance Sheet. ☐

(6) **The £800 received in error as interest received will:**

   (a) Reduce income on Profit and Loss. ☐

   (b) Increase income on Profit and Loss. ☐

   (c) Reduce cash on the Balance Sheet. ☐

   (d) Increase capital on the Balance Sheet. ☐

5.3   DISPOSAL OF A FIXED ASSET

5.3.1   Disposal at 'book' value

When an asset is sold the business will lose the asset and gain cash.

Exercise 5I

(1)   What changes would you need to make to the ledger accounts set out below to record the sale of premises for £180,000?

Premises	DR	CR	BAL
Balance			180,000DR

Cash	DR	CR	BAL
Balance			20,000CR

(2)   Would the transaction have any effect on:

  (a)   the Profit and Loss Account, and/or
  (b)   the Balance Sheet?

The loss of the asset and the receipt of cash must be recorded on the ledger accounts as in question (1) of **Exercise 5I**. Provided the asset is sold for exactly the value at which it is recorded in the accounts of the business no gain or loss over book value arises as a result of the transaction. The only effect of the sale will be on the Balance Sheet where there will be fewer fixed assets and more cash. Total assets on the Balance Sheet remain the same.

No entries are made on the Profit and Loss. This is because the Profit and Loss Account records *income* receipts and expenditure. The sale of an asset gives rise to a *capital* receipt and, thus, has no effect on Profit and Loss.

5.3.2   Disposal not at 'book' value

It is fairly unusual for an asset to be sold for exactly the amount recorded in the accounts. If the asset is sold for *more* than its book value, the excess will be a *profit* on the sale. The profit will be recorded on the Profit and Loss Account in the income section. If the asset is sold for *less* than its book value, there will be a loss on the sale. The loss will be recorded on the Profit and Loss Account in the expenses section.

Note that only the *excess or shortfall* over book value is recorded on Profit and Loss.

Exercise 5J

Premises recorded in the accounts at £170,000 are sold for £200,000.

(a)   What is the gain over book value?

(b)   What will be recorded on Profit and Loss?

(c)   What effect will the sale have on the Balance Sheet assuming the Balance Sheet is prepared immediately after the sale?

5.3.3   Disposal of an asset which has been depreciated

When a business has been depreciating an asset there will be an amount of accumulated depreciation on the depreciation ledger account relating to that asset. The 'book' value of the asset will be the value recorded on the asset's ledger account (normally its acquisition value) *less* the total depreciation accumulated to date. Before you can calculate whether the asset has been disposed of for more or less than book value it is therefore necessary to calculate what its book value is.

When the asset is disposed of the business must remove the value of the asset from the asset account *and* the amount of depreciation relating to it from the depreciation account so that no entries relating to the asset remain in the accounts.

Exercise 5K

A machine was bought for £10,000 in June Year 1. Machinery is depreciated by 10% per annum. The accounting year ends on 31 December. The machine is sold in November Year 5 for £4,000.

(a)   What is the book value of the machine at the date of sale?

(b)   What is the gain or loss over book value?

(c)   How much will be removed from the machinery account after the disposal?

(d)   How much will be removed from the depreciation account after the disposal?

After completing Exercise 5K successfully you will now be able to record the disposal of an asset which has been depreciated in the Final Accounts. You will never be required to make double entries to adjust the ledger accounts, but, for the sake of completeness, there follows, after the list of steps, the entries which would be made in the ledger accounts to record the disposal in the accounts of the business. If you wish to skip this section, go straight to **5.3.4**.

Steps necessary to deal with a disposal in relation to Profit and Loss and Balance Sheet

(a)   Reduce the asset account by the acquisition value of the asset disposed of.
(b)   Having calculated the amount of accumulated depreciation on the asset disposed of, reduce the depreciation account by that amount.
(c)   Deduct accumulated depreciation from the acquisition value of the asset to give book value of the asset. Compare book value with proceeds of sale to see whether a gain or loss over book value has been made.
(d)   Show the gain or loss on the Profit and Loss Account as income or as an expense as appropriate.

Entries on the ledger accounts
To record the disposal of an asset which has been depreciated you will need a temporary account called a 'disposal' account.

When an asset is disposed of, entries must be made on the asset account and on the depreciation account to remove from the ledger accounts all reference to the asset and the depreciation relating to it. The corresponding double entries will be made on the 'disposal' account. Any cash received on the sale will be recorded as a DR on the cash account and will be recorded as a CR on the disposal account. You will find that any balance on the disposal account will represent the gain or loss on the disposal. A gain will be represented by a CR balance on the disposal account and will be transferred to the income section of Profit and Loss. A loss will be represented by a DR balance on the disposal account and will be transferred to the expense section of Profit and Loss.

Entries:

(a)   DR proceeds of sale to cash account
      CR proceeds of sale to disposal account

(b)   CR acquisition value of asset to asset account
      DR acquisition value of asset to disposal account

(c)   DR accumulated depreciation on asset to depreciation account
      CR accumulated depreciation on asset to disposal account

(d)   If the balance on the disposal account is a DR balance, it represents a loss on the disposal. Transfer the balance to the expense section of Profit and Loss.

      CR Disposal account
      DR Profit and Loss Account (expense section)

(e)   If the balance on the disposal account is a CR balance, it represents a gain on the disposal. Transfer the balance to the income section of Profit and Loss.

Example

A business makes up its accounts to 31 December each year. It buys a machine for £10,000 in June Year 1 and sells it in November Year 5 for £3,000. The machine has been depreciated by 10% per annum (a total of 4 × £1,000). We will assume a DR balance on cash account of £2,000.

(a)

Cash

	DR	CR	BAL
Balance			2,000DR
Disposal	**3,000**		5,000DR

Disposal

	DR	CR	BAL
Cash		**3,000**	3,000CR

(b)

Machine

	DR	CR	BAL
Balance			10,000DR
Disposal		**10,000**	—

Disposal

	DR	CR	BAL
Cash		3,000	3,000CR
Machine	**10,000**		7,000DR

(c)

Depreciation

	DR	CR	BAL
Balance			4,000DR
Disposal	**4,000**		—

Disposal

	DR	CR	BAL
Cash		3,000	3,000CR
Machine	10,000		7,000DR
Depreciation		**4,000**	3,000DR

(d)   The balance on the disposal account of £3,000 represents a loss on book value of £3,000. This will be shown on the Profit and Loss Account as an additional item of expense.

Disposal

	DR	CR	BAL
Cash		3,000	3,000CR
Machine	10,000		7,000DR
Depreciation		4,000	3,000DR
Loss to PL		**3,000**	—

5.3.4 Disposal of one of a number of assets

In all the examples given so far, the asset account and depreciation account have been reduced to zero by the disposal. It is much more likely that a business will sell only one of a category of assets in a particular accounting period. In such a case there will be a balance remaining on the asset account and on the depreciation account. Remember that at the end of the accounting period you will depreciate the *remaining* assets at the appropriate rate.

Example

In March Year 1 you start a business and buy three machines for £10,000 each. You depreciate machinery by 10% per annum. Your accounting year ends on 31 December.

At the start of Year 4 the balance on the depreciation account was £9,000 (3 × £3,000). In June Year 4 you sell one machine for £8,000.

(a) Have you made a gain or loss over book value?

The asset has been depreciated by 10% three times (Years 1, 2 and 3). Therefore, its book value is:

£10,000 – £3,000 = £7,000

You have made a gain over book value of £1,000.

(b) There will be a gain of £1,000 in the income section of Profit and Loss.

(c) You must reduce the machines account by £10,000 and the depreciation account by £3,000.

(d) After making all the entries relating to the disposal the balance on the machines account is £20,000, representing the acquisition price of the two remaining machines. The balance on the depreciation account is £6,000 representing 3 years of accumulated depreciation of machines costing £20,000 at 10% per annum (3 × £2,000).

(e) On 31 December Year 4 the remaining machines must be depreciated by 10% per annum for the current year.

£20,000 at 10% = £2,000

Profit and Loss will show depreciation on machines of £2,000.

The Balance Sheet will show machines with an acquisition value of £20,000 and depreciation of £8,000. (This is accumulated depreciation of £6,000 + current depreciation of £2,000.)

Balance Sheet as at 31 December Year 4

Fixed Assets	£	£
Machines	20,000	
Depreciation	(8,000)	12,000

Exercise 5L

The bookkeeper of Smith, a sole trader, has prepared a trial balance for the year ended 30 April [Year X]. The following is an extract:

Extract from Trial Balance 30 April
Year X

	DR	CR
	£	£
Furniture and Office Equipment at Cost	40,600	
Accumulated Depreciation on Furniture and Office Equipment at start of year		20,000
Motor Cars at Cost	36,000	
Accumulated Depreciation on Motor Cars at start of year		9,000

After the above list of balances had been prepared, Smith and the office accountant decided that the following adjustments were necessary.

(a) Depreciation is charged (straight line basis) at the following rates:

Furniture and Office Equipment 10% per annum
Motor Cars 25% per annum

(b) A car was sold in February of the current year for £8,000. The car had been purchased in the previous year for £12,000. It is Smith's practice to charge a full year's depreciation on fixed assets in the year of acquisition, but not to charge depreciation in the year of disposal. The bookkeeper has not yet calculated the effect on the business of the sale and has not yet adjusted the accounts to allow for the effect of the sale.

(c) During the year, some minor repairs were carried out on various office machines, the cost (£600) being included in the amount shown above for furniture and office equipment. The bookkeeper decides to transfer £600 to an equipment repairs account before preparing the Final Accounts.

For questions (1)–(6) below tick which one of the alternatives you think is correct.

In relation to the disposal of the car:

(1) (a) £8,000 will be shown as income on Profit and Loss. ☐

(b) £8,000 will be shown as an expense on Profit and Loss. ☐

(c) £1,000 will be shown as income on Profit and Loss. ☐

(d) £1,000 will be shown as an expense on Profit and Loss. ☐

(2) (a) The balance on the cars account will be reduced by £8,000. ☐

(b) The balance on the cars account will be increased by £8,000. ☐

(c) The balance on the cars account will be increased by £12,000. ☐

(d) The balance on the cars account will be reduced by £12,000. ☐

(3) (a) The balance on the depreciation account will be reduced by £3,000. ☐

(b) The balance on the depreciation account will be increased by £3,000. ☐

(c) There will be no change to the cars account. ☐

(d) There will be no change to the depreciation account. ☐

In relation to depreciation on cars for the current year:

(4) (a) Depreciation charged to Profit and Loss will be £9,000. ☐

(b) Depreciation charged to Profit and Loss will be £900. ☐

(c) Depreciation charged to Profit and Loss will be £6,000. ☐

(d) There will be no depreciation charge to Profit and Loss. ☐

(5) (a) The accumulated depreciation shown on the Balance Sheet will be £6,000. ☐

(b) The accumulated depreciation shown on the Balance Sheet will be £15,000. ☐

(c) The accumulated depreciation shown on the Balance Sheet will be £12,000. ☐

(d) No accumulated depreciation will be shown on the Balance Sheet ☐

(6) **In relation to depreciation on furniture:**

(a) Depreciation charged to Profit and Loss will be £4,060. ☐

(b) Depreciation charged to Profit and Loss will be £4,000. ☐

(c) Depreciation charged to Profit and Loss will be £2,000. ☐

(d) Accumulated depreciation shown on the Balance Sheet will be £24,060. ☐

Solutions

Exercise 5A

(a) This expense relates to an earlier accounting period and will not be included in the Profit and Loss Account for the current year even though it is paid in the current period.

Note: The amount of the expense will have been included in the previous year's Profit and Loss Account.

(b) This expense relates to the current accounting year and will be included in the Profit and Loss Account for the current year.

(c) This expense relates to the current accounting year and will be included in the current Profit and Loss Account even though not yet paid.

The firm has an outstanding liability which must be shown on the Balance Sheet at the end of the year.

(d) The stationery bill should be apportioned. One-quarter of the stationery purchased has been used in the current accounting period; three-quarters will not be used until the following period.

Therefore, one-quarter of the bill should be shown as an expense on the current Profit and Loss Account and three-quarters should be carried forward as an expense to the Profit and Loss Account for the following period.

The value of the stock remaining is an asset of the firm and must be shown on the Balance Sheet as such.

(e) The rent has been paid in the current accounting period but the benefit will not be obtained until the following period.

Therefore, the whole of the expense should be carried forward to the Profit and Loss Account for the following period.

The firm has an asset, the right to occupy the premises for three months without further payment. The right of occupation is an asset and should be shown as a current asset on the Balance Sheet at the end of the year.

(f) The work has been done in the current accounting period and therefore the benefit of it should be attributed to the current accounting period. It will be included on the current Profit and Loss Account as additional income. The value of the work done will be shown as a current asset on the Balance Sheet at the end of the year.

Exercise 5B

(a)

Trading and Profit and Loss Account for Daniel Deronda & Co
for year ended 31 December [Year X]

			£	£
Sales				109,083
Less	**Cost of goods sold**			
	Purchases		89,621	
	Opening stock		1,000	
				(90,621)
Gross Profit				18,462
Income	Rent received			2,000
Expenses	Wages		14,629	
	Motor expenses		520	
	Rates		2,820	
	Stationery		261	
	General expenses (including electricity)		205	
				(18,435)
Net Profit				2,027

Balance Sheet for Daniel Deronda & Co
as at 31 December [Year X]

		£	£
Employment of Capital			
Fixed Assets			
	Fixtures and fittings	2,500	
	Motor vehicles	2,200	
			4,700
Current Assets			
	Debtors	1,950	
	Cash at bank	1,654	
	Petty cash	40	
Current Liabilities			
	Creditors	(1,788)	
Net Current Assets			1,856
			6,556

	£	£
Capital Employed		
Balance as at 1 January	5,424	
Drawings	(895)	
Net profit	2,027	
		6,556

(b) (i) The cost of goods sold must be found by adding £1,000 (opening stock) and deducting £2,548 (closing stock). Closing stock must be shown as a current asset.

   (ii) General expenses must be increased by the outstanding electricity bill of £80.

   The £80 must be shown on the Balance Sheet as a current liability.

   Stationery must be reduced by £20, which must be shown on the Balance Sheet as a current asset prepayment.

Trading Account for Daniel Deronda & Co
for year ended 31 December [Year X]

	£	£
Sales		109,083
Less **Cost of goods sold**		
Purchases	89,621	
plus Opening stock	1,000	
less Closing stock	(2,548)	
		(88,073)
Gross profit		21,010

Profit and Loss Account for Daniel Deronda & Co
for year ended 31 December [Year X]

	£	£
Income		
Gross profit		21,010
Rent Received		2,000
		23,010
Expenses		
Wages and salaries	14,629	
Motor expenses	520	
Rates	2,820	
Stationery	241	
General expenses	285	(18,495)
Net Profit		4,515

**Balance Sheet for Daniel Deronda & Co
as at 31 December [Year X]**

	£	£
Employment of capital		
Fixed Assets		
Fixtures and fittings	2,500	
Motor vehicles	2,200	4,700
Current Assets		
Stock	2,548	
Debtors	1,950	
Cash at bank	1,654	
Petty cash	40	
Prepayment	20	
	6,212	
Current Liabilities		
Creditors	(1,788)	
Accruals	(80)	
Net Current Assets		4,344
		9,044
Capital employed		
Capital		
Balance as at 1 January	5,424	
Net profit	4,515	
	9,439	
Drawings	(895)	
		9,044

Exercise 5C

(a)   £2,500. Bad debts *were* £1,500; you have now written off a further £1,000.

(b)   £2,500.

(c)   £19,000. The debtors on the last day of the accounting period, having already written off bad debts of £1,500, *were* £20,000. You then wrote off a further £1,000 which will reduce debtors to £19,000.

Exercise 5D

(a) £5,000. Bad debts were £4,000 but the firm writes off an additional £1,000.

(b) £1,500. Debtors were £31,000 *but* an additional £1,000 of debts were written off as bad. Once a debt is written off it ceases to be shown as an asset as part of the debtors figure. Thus, the debtors figure is reduced by £1,000 to £30,000. Five per cent of £30,000 is £1,500.

(c) The debtors figure has been reduced to £30,000 and this will be shown on the Balance Sheet. *However*, a provision of £1,500 has been made and this must be shown on the Balance Sheet as a deduction from £30,000:

Debtors	30,000
Provision	(1,500)
	28,500

Thus, the final value of debtors shown on the Balance Sheet will be £28,500.

(d) No. Jones will not be shown as a debtor of the firm. His account has been closed and no longer has a DR balance. Only people who are still expected to pay are shown as debtors of a firm. Once a debt is written off as bad, it ceases to be an asset of the firm.

Exercise 5E

(1) (d) Outstanding expenses increase expenses shown on Profit and Loss and are shown on the Balance Sheet as a current liability.

(2) (b) Prepaid amounts reduce expenses shown on Profit and Loss and are shown on the Balance Sheet as current assets.

(3) (b) The cash received from a debtor will increase cash and reduce debtors. It will have no
(4) (c) other effect.

(5) (c) The payment of petty cash to reimburse an employee for travel expenses will reduce *petty* cash and increase travel expenses (thereby reducing net profit). It will have no other effect.

Exercise 5F

(1) (b) Each year the Profit and Loss Account shows a charge for depreciation of 10% of the acquisition value. Thus, each year the charge is £2,000.

(2) (b) The book value shown on the Balance Sheet is acquisition value less accumulated depreciation to date. At the end of Year 1 there has been one charge to depreciation, hence the book value is £18,000. At the end of Year 4 there have been four charges to depreciation, hence the book value is £12,000.

Exercise 5G

(1) (c)   The full amount of bad debts written off during the year is shown on Profit and Loss (£320 + £450). Debtors do not appear on Profit and Loss. They are an asset.

(2) (d)   The debtors figure shown on the Trial Balance already reflects the fact that £320 has been written off. When an additional £450 is written off the debtors figure must be reduced further (£26,781 – £450). Bad debts do not appear on the Balance Sheet. They are an expense.

(3) (b)   Closing stock is subtracted from purchases on Trading Account and is shown on the Balance Sheet as a current asset.

(4) (a)   Opening stock is added to purchases on Trading Account. It is not shown as a separate item on the Balance Sheet.

(5) (b)   The adjustment has no effect on the Profit and Loss Account. The value of furniture held by the firm must be reduced on the Balance Sheet. Brown owes the firm £500 and this will be shown on the Balance Sheet by *reducing* the balance on his capital account by £500.

(6) (d)   This receipt is partly attributable to the following period. Thus, income shown on Profit and Loss for the current period must be reduced and the Balance Sheet must show that £100 is 'owed' to next accounting period as a current liability.

(7) (c)   The charge to depreciation shown on Profit and Loss is 10% of acquisition value:

$$\frac{10}{100} \times £20,000 = £2,000$$

(8) (c)   Accumulated depreciation must be shown on the Balance Sheet. This is depreciation already accumulated from previous years shown on the Trial Balance as £8,000 plus the current year's depreciation of £2,000.

$$£8,000 + £2,000 = £10,000$$

(9) (a)   Outstanding expenses increase expenses on Profit and Loss and are shown as a *current liability* on the Balance Sheet.

Exercise 5H

(1) (b)   Premises and capital accounts are both increased by £160,000.

(2) (d)   An increase in value resulting from a revaluation does not appear on Profit and Loss.

(3) (a)   Depreciation on furniture charged to Profit and Loss is 15% of the acquisition value shown on Trial Balance:

$$\frac{15}{100} \times £15,000 = £2,250$$

(4) (b)   Accumulated depreciation shown on the Balance Sheet is the total of accumulated depreciation from previous years plus current depreciation:

$$£4,500 + £2,250 = £6,750$$

(5) (b) Depreciation on cars charged to Profit and Loss is 20% of the acquisition value shown on Trial Balance:

$$\frac{20}{100} \times £39,420 = £7,884$$

Accumulated depreciation shown on Balance Sheet is:

$$£7,884 + £15,768 = £23,652$$

(6) (a) The £800 must be deducted from interest receivable since it is *not* income of the firm. It has not yet been removed from the bank account and, therefore, cash cannot be reduced. However, £800 is owed to the bank. Hence, there is an additional current liability.

Exercise 5I

(1) You will have no premises but more cash. Therefore you must reduce the balance on premises account and increase the balance on cash by £180,000.

Entries:
CR Premises £180,000
DR Cash   £180,000

(2) (a) It will have no effect on Profit and Loss. The Profit and Loss account records income receipts and expenditure. This is a capital receipt.

(b) There will be no premises on the Balance Sheet. Hence, fixed assets will be reduced. There will be more cash on the Balance Sheet. Hence current assets will be increased. Overall, total assets will remain the same.

Exercise 5J

(a) Book value was £170,000. The sale was for £200,000. Therefore, the gain over book value is £30,000.

(b) Only the excess over book value, £30,000, is recorded on Profit and Loss. Thus, the net profit of the business will be increased by £30,000.

(c) Premises will no longer be shown in the fixed assets section of the Balance Sheet. Fixed assets will, therefore, be reduced by £170,000.

Cash will be increased by £200,000. Overall, therefore, the assets of the business will have been increased by £30,000.

The Capital Employed section will also be increased by £30,000, since the net profit of the business goes up by £30,000 and net profit is shown in the capital employed section of the Balance Sheet representing an amount owed to the proprietor by the business.

An extract from the Profit and Loss Account is shown below:

Profit and Loss Account year ended [date]

	£	£
Income		
Profit Costs		xxx
Profit on Sale of Premises		30,000

Exercise 5K

(a)   The book value of the machine is acquisition value less depreciation to date. Acquisition value was £10,000.

Depreciation is £4,000. (The machine was depreciated on 31 December Years 1, 2, 3 and 4 but not on 31 December Year 5 since it had already been disposed of by that date.)

Book value is therefore £6,000.

(b)   The machine was sold for £4,000. Therefore, as compared with book value there is a loss of £2,000.

(c)   The acquisition value of the machine, £10,000, must be removed from the machinery account.

(d)   The accumulated depreciation on the machine, £4,000, must be removed from the depreciation account.

Exercise 5L

(1)   (d)   The car had been depreciated by 25% of £12,000 (ie £3,000) once on the previous year.

It was not depreciated on 30 April of the current year as it had already been sold.

Therefore, its book value at the time of sale was £9,000 and a loss of £1,000 was made. This must be charged to Profit and Loss as an expense.

(2)   (d)   The cars account will be reduced by the acquisition value of the car (£12,000).

(3)   (a)   The depreciation account will be reduced by the amount of depreciation already written off on the car (£3,000).

(4)   (c)   Depreciation charged to Profit and Loss will be 25% of the balance on the cars account which has been reduced by £12,000:

$$\frac{25}{100} \times £24,000 = £6,000$$

(5)   (c)   Accumulated depreciation will be the balance on the depreciation account reduced by £3,000 plus the current depreciation of £6,000:

$$(£9,000 - £3,000) + £6,000 = £12,000$$

(6)   (b)   The costs of repairs should have been charged to a repairs account and not included on the furniture account. Therefore, the balance on the furniture account will be reduced by £600.

Depreciation will be 10% of the reduced figure:

$$\frac{10}{100} \times £40,000 = £4,000$$

Accumulated depreciation shown on the Balance Sheet will be accumulated plus current depreciation:

$$£20,000 + £4,000 = £24,000$$

Chapter 6

PARTNERSHIPS

6.1 INTRODUCTION

In a partnership, capital is contributed by a number of different people (the partners) and the firm's profit is 'owed' to those partners. Separate records will have to be kept for each partner showing:

- the amount of capital contributed;
- the amount of profit 'owed' at the end of each year by the business to the partner;
- the amount of cash withdrawn from the business during the year by the partner.

The accounts of a partnership will have to show this information. There will, therefore, be some differences between the accounts of a sole practitioner and the accounts of a partnership.

Both trading and professional businesses can be run through the medium of a partnership. In this chapter for convenience we shall use a solicitor's firm for our illustrations.

6.2 HOW DO PARTNERSHIP ACCOUNTS DIFFER FROM A SOLE TRADER'S ACCOUNTS?

6.2.1 Capital accounts

(a) Each partner will have a capital account in his or her own name. This account will show the amount contributed by the partner.

Example

A and B set up a partnership and contribute £30,000 and £20,000 respectively as capital.

	A – Capital					B – Capital			
Date	Details	DR	CR	BAL	Date	Details	DR	CR	BAL
	Cash		30,000	30,000CR		Cash		20,000	20,000CR

The Balance Sheet will show separately the balance on each capital account.

Balance Sheet as at [date]

		£	£
Capital			
A		30,000	
B		20,000	
			50,000

(b) The capital account will also show the partner's share of an increase (or decrease) in value of an asset recorded in the accounts by way of revaluation.

The ratio in which partners are to share increases and decreases in the value of capital assets may be set out in the partnership agreement. If the partnership agreement is silent on this point, the partners will share capital increases and decreases in the ratio in which they agreed to share profits and losses.

Example

A and B in the previous example agreed that they would share increases and decreases in the capital value of assets in the ratio 2:1.

After a few years they agree to increase the value of premises by £90,000.

A – Capital

Date	Details	DR	CR	BAL
	Balance			30,000CR
	Revaluation			
	of premises		60,000	90,000CR

B – Capital

Date	Details	DR	CR	BAL
	Balance			20,000CR
	Revaluation			
	of premises		30,000	50,000CR

Note: The balance on the premises account will be increased by £90,000.

6.2.2   Profit sharing

A well-drawn partnership agreement should set out the profit sharing ratio. If it is silent the partners will share profits and losses equally.

A partnership agreement may provide that partners are to receive 'interest' on capital (common where capital contributions are unequal) and/or 'salaries' for partners (common where some partners are required to work longer hours than others).

In the case of a sole practitioner, interest paid to lenders and salaries paid to employees are expenses which reduce net profit for tax purposes. However, so-called 'interest' and 'salaries' allowed to partners are not regarded by the Inland Revenue as expenses for tax purposes. The Inland Revenue regards such items as 'preferential appropriations' of profit. In other words, the partners must calculate net profit without regard to 'interest on capital' and 'salaries due to partners'. The partners must then take that net profit figure and appropriate it to the various partners in accordance with the terms of the partnership agreement, appropriating 'interest' and 'salaries' first, and then any balance to the partners in the agreed profit sharing ratio.

Unless the partnership agreement provides otherwise 'salaries' and 'interest' must be appropriated to partners by the partnership irrespective of whether the net profit is sufficient to cover the amount due. The result may be to produce a loss for the year which must then be appropriated among all partners in the agreed profit sharing ratio. A well-drafted partnership agreement should, therefore, provide that salaries and interest are due only if profits are sufficient to cover them.

6.2.3   The appropriation account

The Profit and Loss Account of a partnership is prepared in exactly the same way as the Profit and Loss Account of a sole practitioner. However, as stated above, 'salaries' and 'interest' due to partners are not shown on the Profit and Loss Account.

The Profit and Loss Account is extended to an appropriation account on which the allocation of net profit among partners is shown.

Example

X and Y set up in partnership. X contributes capital of £5,000 and Y contributes £2,000.

The net profit for the year has been calculated at £21,700. The partnership agreement provides for interest on capital of 10% per annum, a salary for Y of £1,000 per annum and remaining profits to be divided 3:1.

Profit and Loss Account for X Y & Co year ended [date]

	£	£	£
Net Profit			21,700
Appropriations	**X**	**Y**	
Interest on Capital	500	200	700
Salary	–	1,000	1,000
Profits	15,000	5,000	20,000
	15,500	6,200	21,700

6.2.4 Current account

The appropriation of net profit is 'owed' to each partner. A sole practitioner credits net profit direct to the capital account. In the case of a partnership it is usual to have a separate current account for each partner to which the appropriation of net profit (including salary and interest) is credited and to which drawings are debited. The reason for separating capital and current accounts is that many partners are entitled to interest on capital contributed. It is, therefore, desirable to keep the capital contribution of each partner readily accessible and unaffected by subsequent appropriations of profits and drawings.

Example

Continuing the previous example, if X withdrew £10,000 and Y £8,000 during the first year their current accounts would appear as follows:

X – Current

	DR	CR	BAL
Appropriations		15,500	15,500CR
Drawings	10,000		5,500CR

Y – Current

	DR	CR	BAL
Appropriations		6,200	6,200CR
Drawings	8,000		1,800DR

The CR balance on X's current account shows that X has withdrawn less than his full entitlement to profit so the business 'owes' him £5,500. The DR balance on Y's current account shows that Y has withdrawn more than his full entitlement to profit and so Y owes the business £1,800.

A well-drafted partnership agreement should limit the drawings partners are free to make without the agreement of other partners.

6.2.5 The Balance Sheet

The capital and current account balances of each partner are shown separately on the Balance Sheet under the general heading of capital employed. A DR balance on a current account is subtracted from the other balances in the capital employed section.

Example

Continuing the previous example, the Balance Sheet will appear as follows:

Balance Sheet for X Y & Co as at [date]

		£	£
Capital Employed			
Capital	X	5,000	
	Y	2,000	
Current	X	5,500	
	Y	(1,800)	
			10,700

6.2.6 Details of movements on partners' current accounts

You will notice that in the previous example we showed only the final balances for the current accounts on the Balance Sheet. This is because the Balance Sheet would be very cluttered if full details of salaries, interest, profit shares and drawings were included, especially where there are several partners. It would be difficult to pick out the important figures. However, it is clearly desirable to provide information as to how the balances were arrived at. It is, therefore, usual to provide an appendix to the Balance Sheet which sets out the detailed picture of movements on partners' current accounts.

A common form of presentation is set out in the example below.

Example

Details of movements on current accounts

	A	B
	£	£
Balance at start of accounting period	2,000CR	2,000CR
Appropriations	40,000	34,000
Drawings	(22,000)	(18,000)
Closing balance	20,000CR	18,000CR

Exercise 6A

Parsley, Thyme and Sage are in partnership as solicitors. The partnership agreement provides for interest on capital of 10% per annum. Thyme is to receive a salary of £9,000 per annum and Sage a salary of £10,000 per annum. Remaining profits are to be shared in the ratio 2:2:1.

The Trial Balance of Parsley, Thyme and Sage extracted at 31 December [year X] is as follows:

Trial Balance [Year X]

		DR £	CR £
Capital:	Parsley		120,000
	Thyme		80,000
	Sage		10,000
Current:	Parsley		2,000
	Thyme		1,000
	Sage	4,000	
Bank loan			27,750
Premises		150,000	
Office machinery		35,000	
Provision for depreciation on machinery			5,000
Library		22,700	
Vehicles		18,000	
Provision for depreciation on vehicles			9,000
Costs: Work in progress at start			
of year	(20,000)		
Billed during year	250,000		230,000
Interest received			20,000
General expenses		135,300	
Interest paid on bank loan		3,750	
Bad debts		10,000	
Travel expenses		3,000	
Debtors		141,000	
Creditors			20,000
Office bank account		2,000	
Client bank account		400,000	
Due to clients			400,000
		924,750	924,750

The firm's policy is to depreciate cars by 10% pa and office machinery by 2% pa.

On 31 December [year X] after preparation of the Trial Balance but before preparation of the Final Accounts the following events occur:

(a) The bank informs the firm that an additional £250 interest has been credited to the firm's office bank account for the current year.

(b) Closing work in progress is estimated at £30,000.

(c) £1,200 is to be allowed to Sage in mileage allowance for the current year. The adjustment is to be effected on Sage's current account.

(d) Additional bad debts of £1,000 are to be written off and a provision for doubtful debts of 2½% of remaining debtors is to be allowed.

Prepare Final Accounts for the partnership for year ending 31 December [year X].

6.3   PARTNERSHIP CHANGES

The number of partners may change part of the way through an accounting period either because a new partner is admitted or because an old partner leaves. This will affect the accounts as follows:

- Any contribution or removal of capital will be recorded immediately and any drawings will be recorded as and when they occur.
- The Profit and Loss Account will be prepared for the whole accounting period in the normal way and a net profit figure produced for the whole accounting period in the normal way.
- The net profit will then be apportioned on a time basis to the period before and the period after the change.
- Two appropriation accounts will be prepared, one allocating the pre-change profit in accordance with the pre-change partnership agreement and one allocating the post-change profit in accordance with the post-change partnership agreement.

Exercise 6B

A and B are the partners in a firm of solicitors, AB & Co.

Their partnership agreement provides that partners are to receive interest on capital of 10 per cent per annum and that B is to receive a salary of £10,000 per annum (profits permitting). Remaining profits are to be divided in the ratio 3:2.

The following Trial Balance is extracted from the accounts at the end of the current accounting year.

Prepare Final Accounts including Movements on Partners' Current Accounts for the current year.

Note: The Specimen Accounts at **2.1.3** form the solution to this exercise.

AB & Co Solicitors
Trial Balance as at 31 December [Year X]

	£ 000s	£ 000s
Current Accounts		
A		2
B		3
Drawings		
A	30	
B	26	
Capital		
A		50
B		30
Leasehold Premises	218	
Fixtures	20	
Depreciation on Fixtures		12
Computers	50	
Depreciation on Computers		30
Cars	40	
Debtors	82	

	£	£
Office Bank Account	10	
Petty Cash	1	
Profit Costs Billed		478
Opening Work in Progress	30	
Interest Received		20
Insurance Commission Received		10
Salaries	98	
General Expenses	55	
Administrative Expenses	35	
Bad Debts	15	
Rent Paid	21	
Loan Interest	5	
Bank Loan		60
Creditors		39
Gain on Sale of Car		2
Client Bank Account	150	
Due to Clients		150
	886	886

The following matters need to be taken into account:

(1) Work in Progress at the end of the year is estimated at £40,000.

(2) The partnership wishes to write off an additional debt of £2,000 as bad and to make a Provision for Doubtful Debts of 10% of remaining debtors.

(3) There are prepaid General Expenses of £4,000 which relate to the following year.

(4) Depreciation is allowed on the straight line basis as follows:

Fixtures at 5%
Computers at 20%
Cars at 20%

Note: During the current year the partnership sold its previous car making a gain of £2,000 over its book value and acquired the present car for £40,000.

6.4 TAXATION OF PARTNERSHIPS

Each individual partner makes a tax return claiming personal allowances. The senior partner of the firm makes a return of partnership income. The Inland Revenue then makes a joint assessment to tax in the partnership name. This assessment is based on each partner's share of profit less reliefs and charges, and supplies the senior partner with information on the method of calculation so that the tax burden can be apportioned among its partners.

The tax liability does not appear on the Profit and Loss or Appropriation Account of the partnership. You will see when you come to look at company accounts that the position of companies is different. A company has its own tax liability which is shown on its Appropriation Account.

Solutions

Exercise 6A

Parsley, Thyme and Sage
Profit and Loss Account for year ended 31 December [year]

		£	£	£
Income				
	Costs Billed	250,000		
less	Work in progress at start of year	(20,000)		
plus	Work in progress at end of year	30,000		
			260,000	
Interest Received			20,250	
				280,250
Expenses				
	General expenses		135,300	
	Interest on bank loan		3,750	
	Bad debts		11,000	
	Provision for doubtful debts		3,500	
	Travel expenses		4,200	
	Depreciation: Cars	1,800		
	Office machinery	700	2,500	
				(160,250)
NET PROFIT				120,000

Appropriations

	Parsley	Thyme	Sage	
	£	£	£	
Interest	12,000	8,000	1,000	21,000
Salary	–	9,000	10,000	19,000
Profits	32,000	32,000	16,000	80,000
	44,000	49,000	27,000	120,000

Parsley, Thyme and Sage
Balance Sheet as at 31 December [year]

	£	£	£
Employment of Capital			
Fixed Assets			
Premises		150,000	
Cars	18,000		
less depreciation	(10,800)		
		7,200	
Machinery	35,000		
less depreciation	(5,700)		
		29,300	
Library		22,700	
			209,200
Current Assets			
Work in progress		30,000	
Debtors	140,000		
less provision	(3,500)		
		136,500	
Office bank account		2,250	
		168,750	
Current Liabilities			
Creditors		(20,000)	
Net Current Assets			148,750
Client bank account		400,000	
Due to clients		(400,000)	
			357,950
Capital Employed			
Capital: Parsley		120,000	
Thyme		80,000	
Sage		10,000	
			210,000
Current: Parsley		46,000	
Thyme		50,000	
Sage		24,200	
			120,200
			330,200
Less Long-Term Liabilities			
Bank loan			(27,750)
			330,200

Movements in Partners' Current Accounts

	Parsley	Thyme	Sage
Opening Balance	2,000	1,000	(4,000)
Mileage Allowance	—	—	1,200
Appropriations	44,000	49,000	27,000
	46,000	50,000	24,200

Chapter 7

COMPANY ACCOUNTS (1)

7.1 INTRODUCTION

The accounts of a company are prepared on exactly the same accounting basis as those of a sole trader or a partnership. There are, however, some differences in the form of the accounts because of the different legal nature of a company. We will look first at the way in which a company would record the raising of capital.

7.2 RAISING CAPITAL BY ISSUING SHARES

7.2.1 Issuing shares

When a company issues shares, the entries are the same as those made when a sole practitioner or partner introduces capital except that a share capital account is used. Thus, if a company issues shares for £100,000 in cash, the entries will be:

Cash

	DR	CR	BAL
Share Capital	100,000		100,000DR

Share Capital

	DR	CR	BAL
Cash		100,000	100,000CR

Question   Why do you think a company does not have a separate capital account for each shareholder?

Answer (1)   There could be an enormous number of different shareholders, so that having a separate capital account for each one would be unmanageable.

(2)   Since shareholders can sell their shares, the company would have to keep updating the names of the different capital accounts.

7.2.2 Issuing shares at par

A company may issue shares either at par or at premium. (It is not possible for shares to be issued at a discount; see Companies Act 1985, s 100.) Each share has a nominal or par (ie face) value, eg £1. The issue of shares at par means that the shares are 'sold' to the shareholder for their nominal value; the accounting entries would be the same as in the above illustration. If a Balance Sheet were drawn up at this stage, it would appear as follows:

Balance Sheet as at [date]

ASSETS	£
Cash	100,000

FINANCED BY	£
Share Capital	100,000

7.2.3 Issuing shares at a premium

The issue of shares at a premium means that the shares are 'sold' to the shareholders for more than their nominal value. Thus a share with a nominal value of £1 may be issued to a shareholder for £1.50; the premium is 50p. In such a case the entries are as follows:

Entries:

DR the cash account with the *total amount* received from the shareholder, ie the nominal value of the share *plus* the amount of the premium;

CR the share capital account with the *nominal value* only of the share; and

CR the share premium account with the amount of *the premium*.

Exercise 7A

A company issues £10,000 worth of shares, each with a nominal value of £1, at a premium of 10%. This means that the company will receive £11,000 from the shareholders (ie the premium is £1,000).

(a) What entries would appear in the accounts?

Cash

	DR	CR	BAL

Share Capital

	DR	CR	BAL

Share Premium

	DR	CR	BAL

(b) If a Balance Sheet were drawn up at this point, what would it look like?

Balance Sheet as at [date]

£   £

ASSETS

Cash

£   £

FINANCED BY

Share Capital

Share Premium

You will see that the premium forms part of the capital employed by the company, but is shown separately from the share capital account, which is limited to the nominal value of the shares (or, if less, their paid-up value). The premium represents a surplus on the issue of the shares. However, the surplus it represents cannot as a matter of law be returned to the shareholders during the lifetime of the company (except in exceptional cases). This is because of the company law rules on maintenance of capital. Therefore the balance on the share premium account generally remains unaltered unless it is used for one of a limited number of permitted purposes (eg writing off the expenses of forming the company).

7.2.4 Different types of shares

A company may issue shares of different types (ordinary, preference or deferred shares) and also shares of the same type carrying different rights (eg voting and non-voting ordinary shares). Preference shareholders are entitled, assuming that a dividend is in fact declared, to a share in any profit made by the company in priority to any other shareholders. If there is only a small profit, the preference shareholders may receive a dividend and the ordinary shareholders nothing.

Different classes of preference share may be issued.

- The shares may be 'cumulative', which means that if a dividend is not declared in any year the shareholders have the right to receive arrears of dividend as well as the current dividend before any amount is paid to the ordinary shareholders.
- 'Participating preference shares' give the right to participate in the distribution of any surplus profits after a stated percentage dividend has been paid to the ordinary shareholders and may also carry the right to share in any surplus assets on a winding-up.
- 'Redeemable preference shares' are those issued on terms that they will be repaid by the company at some time in the future. A company may also issue redeemable ordinary shares (Companies Act 1985, s 159).

The important point to appreciate is that whatever type of share is issued, the basic **entries** are precisely the same, even though the shares will be recorded in different ledger accounts and will be shown separately in the Balance Sheet.

Exercise 7B

A company issues 50,000 8% preference shares of £1 each and 200,000 £1 ordinary shares at par for cash.

(a) What entries would appear in the accounts?

Cash Account

Date	Details	DR	CR	BAL

Ordinary Share Capital Account

Date	Details	DR	CR	BAL

8% Preference Share Capital Account

Date	Details	DR	CR	BAL

(b) If a Balance Sheet were drawn up at this point, what would it look like?

Balance Sheet as at [date]

	£	£
ASSETS		
Cash		
FINANCED BY	£	£
8% £1 Preference Shares		
£1 Ordinary Shares		

7.2.5   The requirements of FRS4

The aim of Financial Reporting Standard 4 (FRS4) is to introduce greater consistency into the accounting treatment of 'capital instruments' (ie long-term debts and of share capital). It has been obligatory for companies to observe FRS4 in respect of periods ending on or after 22 June 1994.

It requires that the total of 'Shareholders' funds', by which it means share capital and reserves (but excluding minority interests – see below), be shown on the face of the Balance Sheet. Further, shares must be divided into 'equity' and 'non-equity'. Non-equity shares are shares which have a meaningful restriction on the rights which attach to them. The restriction may be as to the right to participate in profits or in assets on a winding up. Equity shares are those which have no such restriction. The accounts must distinguish the types of share and must include a summary of rights attaching (eg rights to dividends, when redeemable and for how much, what priority and what entitlement on winding up, what voting rights).

7.2.6   Company buying its own shares

The Companies Act 1985, ss 162–181 permit a company, provided various conditions are complied with, to purchase its own shares (in the case of a private company out of capital). Once purchased, the shares are cancelled and the issued share capital reduced by the nominal amount of the shares. However, except in the case of a private company purchasing out of capital, the overall share capital of the company is not reduced. This is because the shares must be purchased either from the proceeds of a new issue or from distributable profits. If new shares are issued, there is obviously no reduction in capital. If the shares are purchased from distributable profits, the company is required to make a transfer to a capital redemption reserve. This reserve (dealt with in more detail later in this section) is subject to the ordinary rules as to reduction of share capital.

7.3   RAISING CAPITAL BY BORROWING

7.3.1   Issuing debentures at par

If a company borrows money, it will commonly do so by issuing debentures. A debenture is a document evidencing a loan made to the company. Thus, if a company issues debentures of £50,000, this basically means that the company is borrowing £50,000.

To record borrowing £50,000 by issuing a 12% debenture, the accounts would appear as follows:

<table>
<tr><th colspan="5">Cash Account</th></tr>
<tr><th>Date</th><th>Details</th><th>DR</th><th>CR</th><th>BAL</th></tr>
<tr><td></td><td>12% Debenture</td><td>50,000</td><td></td><td>XXX XXX</td></tr>
</table>

<table>
<tr><th colspan="5">12% Debenture Account</th></tr>
<tr><th>Date</th><th>Details</th><th>DR</th><th>CR</th><th>BAL</th></tr>
<tr><td></td><td>Cash</td><td></td><td>50,000</td><td>50,000CR</td></tr>
</table>

A debenture differs from a share in that a debenture holder has no proprietary interest in the company (ie he is not a 'member' of the company), and the payment of interest on a debenture is not dependent on the making of profits by the company.

From the point of view of the company, this has advantages and disadvantages.

Exercise 7C

You are the major shareholder of Company X. You wish to raise additional capital of £50,000 and are trying to decide whether to issue more shares or to borrow.

What are the advantages and disadvantages of each course of action?

7.3.2 Issuing debentures at a discount

A company may issue debentures at par or at a discount. If debentures are issued at a discount, this means that the debenture holder pays less than the nominal value.

It is necessary to make entries regarding the discount both to record the expense incurred by the company in issuing the debenture and to ensure that the true liability of the company is shown in the debenture account, since the company will have to pay the full nominal value of the debenture on redemption.

7.3.3 The requirements of FRS4

The Companies Act 1985 only requires companies to show on the face of the Balance Sheet the division between amounts falling due within and after 12 months from the date of the Balance Sheet (ie to distinguish current and long-term liabilities). However, the accountancy profession has its own requirements. FRS4 requires a more detailed breakdown to be disclosed. Debts should be analysed between amounts falling due:

(a)   in one year or less, or on demand;
(b)   between one and two years;
(c)   between two and five years;
(d)   in five years or more.

If debts are convertible into shares, they should be treated as debts up until the date at which conversion takes place. However, convertible debts must be disclosed separately, together with details of the terms on which they may be converted.

FRS4 also deals with the procedure to be adopted when showing the cost of the debt in the accounts. However, this is beyond the scope of this book.

7.4 A COMPANY'S PROFIT AND LOSS ACCOUNT

A company, like a partnership, has an appropriation section at the end of its Profit and Loss Account. The whole account is often referred to as the 'Profit and Loss and Appropriation Account'. In essence, the Profit and Loss Account of a company is the same as that of a partnership. However, minor differences occur in the types of expense which may appear on a company's Profit and Loss Account. These differences flow from the fact that a company is a separate legal person with its own legal identity separate from its shareholders and directors. A salary paid to a director is, from the company's point of view, an expense incurred in earning profit and will therefore appear on the Profit and Loss Account as an expense; a 'salary' paid to a partner under the terms of the partnership agreement is merely a method of allocating the profit and will appear on the appropriation section of the account.

Exercise 7D

(a) Partner A in the partnership AB and Co is entitled under the terms of the partnership agreement to a salary of £10,000 pa. Where does this appear on the Profit and Loss and Appropriation Account?

(b) Director A of the company AB and Co Ltd is entitled to a salary of £10,000 pa. Where does this appear on the Profit and Loss and Appropriation Account?

7.5   THE USE OF THE APPROPRIATION SECTION OF A COMPANY'S PROFIT AND LOSS ACCOUNT

This shows the purposes for which profit will be used. There are three main purposes: taxation, dividends and retention of profits.

Usually, taxation and dividends items are not *paid* until after the end of the accounting period. However, the allocation of profit to cover these items will appear on the appropriation section of the account.

It is essential to appreciate that entries in the appropriation section of the Profit and Loss Account (whether of a partnership or company) do not involve the actual payment of money. All that is happening is that the 'book' profit as shown in the Profit and Loss section is being earmarked for various purposes. The question of paying out money for those purposes is a totally separate matter, and will be recorded on the ledger accounts and cash account of the company as and when payment is made.

The Companies Act 1985 requires accounts to be presented in one of a number of 'formats'. Pre-tax and post-tax profit must be shown.

Profits retained in previous years will be shown as an addition at the end of the Appropriation Account to show the increase in assets resulting from successful trading.

7.5.1   Taxation

The first item to be considered after the net profit has been ascertained is the company's liability to corporation tax on that profit. Until this has been provided for, the directors are in no position to make a decision on the declaration of a dividend. Corporation tax is not payable until 9 months after the end of the accounting period. Thus the company will show on its appropriation account that a certain amount of profit is needed to pay the company's tax bill. The amount due to the Inland Revenue will appear on the Balance Sheet as a current liability.

Example

A company has share capital of £20,000. In its first year of trading it has income of £60,000 and expenses of £50,000. It estimates that corporation tax of £2,500 will be payable.

(a) After providing for tax only £7,500 of profit will be left.

Profit and Loss Account for year ending [date]

	£	£
Net Profit before tax		10,000
Appropriated		
Tax		(2,500)
Post-tax profit		7,500

(b) The Provision for Tax will appear in the Current Liabilities section of the Balance Sheet as follows:

Balance Sheet as at [date]

	£	£
ASSETS		
Fixed Assets		xxxx
Current Assets	xxxx	
less Current Liabilities		
Creditors	(xxx)	
Provision for Tax	(2,500)	
Net Current Assets		xxx
		xxxx
	£	£
FINANCED BY		
Share Capital		xxxx

When the company *pays* its tax, the provision will disappear from the current liabilities section and cash will be reduced in the current assets section.

7.5.2 Dividends

A dividend represents a distribution of part of the net profit to the owners of the company (ie the shareholders). A company is most unlikely to distribute the whole of its profit after tax, either because it needs to retain some (eg for expansion) or because the profit is not actually available in the form of cash. Profit may be represented by any assets (eg stock, debtors or fixed assets).

The directors will decide how much dividend can in their opinion safely be distributed to the shareholders. The amount of this proposed dividend will be shown on the appropriation section of the Profit and Loss Account. The company cannot actually *pay* the dividend until the shareholders approve its size in the annual general meeting, which will take place after the end of the accounting period. Hence, the dividend will appear in the Balance Sheet prepared at the end of the accounting period as a current liability.

This is the timetable:

- Accounting period ends.
- Accountant draws up the final accounts.
- Board of directors consider the final accounts and decide how much dividend to recommend.
- Annual general meeting takes place at which the shareholders agree (or disagree) the size of the dividend.
- Company actually pays the dividend.

Example

The previous example showed a company which had a net profit of £10,000 and which had made provision for taxation of £2,500. Imagine now that the directors of the company recommend a dividend of £3,500. The appropriation section of the Profit and Loss Account will appear as follows:

Profit and Loss Account for year ending [date]

	£	£
Profit before tax		10,000
Appropriated		
Taxation	2,500	
Post-tax profit		7,500
Dividend	3,500	
Balance retained	4,000	

The directors therefore propose retaining £4,000 within the company.

The Balance Sheet set out below shows the proposed dividend.

Balance Sheet as at [date]

ASSETS	£	£
Fixed Assets		xxxx
Current Assets	xxxx	
less Current Liabilities		
Creditors	(xxx)	
Proposed dividend	(3,500)	
Provision for taxation	(2,500)	
Net Current Assets		xxx
		24,000
FINANCED BY		
Share Capital	20,000	
Retained Profit	4,000	
		24,000

The £4,000 ultimately retained within the company allows the directors to fund future expansion and cope with inflation; it is shown on the Balance Sheet as retained profit (otherwise known as a 'reserve': see **7.5.4**). In any event, since much of the profit will not be in the form of cash, it could not all have been distributed by way of dividend.

7.5.3 Interim dividends

A company may choose to pay a dividend (known as an 'interim dividend') during its accounting period. The amount of the interim dividend must be shown in the appropriation section of the Profit and Loss Account, since a portion of the company's profit has been allocated to this purpose. However, since an interim dividend has already been paid by the date of the Balance Sheet, it is not shown on the Balance Sheet as a liability. Only the amount of the final dividend needs to be shown as a liability.

Exercise 7E

A company pays an interim dividend of £12,000 during its financial year. When the final accounts for the year are subsequently drawn up, a post-tax profit of £65,000 is revealed and the directors decide to recommend a final dividend (ie in addition to the interim dividend) of £15,000. What will appear on the Profit and Loss Account and on the Balance Sheet in respect of the company's dividends?

Profit and Loss Account for year ending [date]

	£	£
Post-tax profit		65,000
less **Dividends:**		
Interim		
Final		

Balance Sheet as at [date]

	£	£
Current Liabilities		
Proposed Dividend		

7.5.4 What is a reserve?

Once provision has been made for taxation and dividends, the balance of the net profit is retained in the business.

This retained profit is referred to as 'reserved profit' or 'reserves'.

The retained profit is profit which could have been distributed to the shareholders had there been sufficient liquid funds within the company and had the directors decided to distribute it. The reserve is therefore 'owed' to the shareholders, and will be shown on the Balance Sheet as a liability. The amount of a reserve is normally shown on the Balance Sheet immediately after the share capital and the two figures together are referred to as 'shareholders' funds'.

Look at this company's appropriation account and the section of the Balance Sheet dealing with shareholders' funds:

Profit and Loss Account for year ending [date]

	£	£
Profit before tax		20,000
Appropriations		
Taxation	(5,000)	
Post-tax profit		15,000
Dividend	(8,000)	
Reserved profit		7,000
Profit brought forward from previous years		20,000
		27,000

Balance Sheet as at [date]

	£	£
Share Capital	25,000	
Reserves	27,000	

You will see on the Appropriation section of the Profit and Loss Account, the company shows an additional item, profit brought forward from previous years.

This additional item shows profit which could have been distributed to shareholders in previous years but which was required.

Adding together this year's retained profit and retained profit from previous years shows the shareholders the increase in the funds of the company from trading. The retained profits are often referred to as a 'Profit and Loss Reserve'.

The reason why a reserve has no direct equivalent in the accounts of a sole trader or partnership is that the only method by which shareholders can become entitled to profits in the form of cash is by declaration of a dividend.

In the case of a sole practitioner or partnership, however, the business is not a separate legal entity from its owner(s), so that any profit belongs immediately to the owner(s). Whether this profit can actually be drawn out of the business is a totally different matter and will depend (inter alia) on the availability of cash in the business. If profits of an unincorporated business remain undrawn, they will not be shown as 'reserves' in the Balance Sheet but will increase the capital account of a sole trader or, in the case of a partnership, the capital or current accounts of the partners.

In the case of a company, the balance of profit remaining after provision for tax has been made (ie net profit after tax) is, in theory, wholly available to the shareholders. The decision as to how much of the profit to recommend for withdrawal in this way is made not by the shareholders, however, but by the directors. In fact, only a part of this balance will be allocated to the shareholders by way of dividend. There are several reasons for this, including lack of available cash and the need to retain profits to provide for expansion or merely to maintain adequate working capital to cope with inflation. Whatever the reason for the non-distribution of the whole of the net profit, the profit retained will be added to reserves.

We will look in more detail at reserves in **7.5.6**.

7.5.5   Other appropriation account items

Although taxation, dividends and reserves represent the main allocations of profit, other items may occasionally appear in the appropriation section of a company's Profit and Loss Account, for example, 'write-offs'.

When the expression 'written off against profits' is used, what this in fact means is that a debit entry is made in the appropriation section, with a corresponding credit entry in the account of the item which is being written off.

Examples of items which may be dealt with in this way are goodwill purchased on the takeover of a business and company formation expenses.

Each of these items will initially appear as a debit balance in its respective account. When, for example, goodwill is purchased the entries will be DR goodwill account, CR cash. It is common practice, however, for the balance to be written off against profits in the appropriation section. This is because the 'asset' of goodwill is not a tangible asset and its value is, therefore, speculative. When the goodwill is written off, the entries made will be CR goodwill account, DR appropriation account. Similar entries would be made for other such 'assets' written off in this way.

7.5.6   Types of reserves

(1)   *General and specific reserves*

It is often difficult for people not directly involved in the management of the company (eg shareholders, employees) to understand why large amounts of profit are being retained within the company instead of being returned to the shareholders as dividends or being used to pay salaries for employees. It is quite common, therefore, for directors to indicate why profits are being retained by attaching labels to portions of retained profit, such as 'preference share redemption reserve', 'debenture redemption reserve'. However, it is important to realise the labels are for convenience only; the reserves remain undistributed profits *owed* to shareholders.

Exercise 7F

Study the following Balance Sheet. What changes will result when the debenture is redeemed?

Balance Sheet as at [date]

	£	£
ASSETS		
Fixed Assets		40,000
Current Assets		
Cash	25,000	
less Current Liabilities		
Creditors	(5,000)	
Net Current Assets		20,000
		60,000
Less LIABILITIES PAYABLE		
IN MORE THAN 12 MONTHS		
Debenture		(10,000)
		50,000
FINANCED BY	£	£
Share Capital	20,000	
Debenture Redemption Reserve	10,000	
Profit and Loss Reserve	20,000	
		50,000

---

(2)   *Capital and revenue reserves*

Capital reserves are reserves which, for legal or practical reasons, are not available for distribution by way of dividend. Although the Companies Act 1967 abolished the legal necessity for distinguishing between capital and revenue reserves in the Balance Sheet, it is still necessary to show a few capital reserves separately (eg a capital redemption reserve and a share premium account).

A capital reserve may be created by retaining profits for a specific purpose (eg the purchase of fixed assets) or it may arise through some activity unconnected with the earning of profits. Thus, when a company issues shares at a premium, it is required to show the surplus over the nominal value of the shares on a share premium account (see **7.2.3**).

When redeemable shares are redeemed, the company must make entries in its books to credit an amount equal to the nominal value of the shares to a capital redemption reserve, so that the capital of the company is not reduced.

A capital redemption reserve is required where a company buys back shares out of profits. To avoid reducing its capital, the company is required to transfer to a capital redemption reserve an amount equivalent to the nominal share capital bought back and cancelled.

Transfers to this reserve are also required where shares are purchased partly out of the proceeds of a fresh issue and partly from distributable profits and where a private company purchases shares out of capital. The precise rules as to the amount which needs to be transferred differ.

A revaluation reserve arises when a company decides to revalue its assets. As in the case of a partnership, if the value of assets shown in the Balance Sheet is increased, there must be a corresponding increase in the capital employed section of the Balance Sheet. Unlike a partnership, however, it is not the capital accounts which will record this increase; instead, a reserve account will be opened which will be credited with the revaluation increase. A revaluation reserve is a capital reserve. Having a capital reserve does not justify payment of dividends, since no profit has actually been realised as a result of the revaluation.

Example

A company decides to revalue its fixed assets. The revaluation produces a net increase of £100,000 over the assets' previous book value of £140,000. The Balance Sheet will therefore appear as follows:

Balance Sheet as at [date]

	(After Revaluation) £	(Before Revaluation) £
ASSETS		
Fixed Assets	240,000	(140,000)
Net Current Assets	180,000	(180,000)
	420,000	(320,000)
	£	£
FINANCED BY		
Share Capital	100,000	(100,000)
Capital Reserve (Revaluation)	100,000	–
Profit and Loss Reserve (Retained profits)	220,000	(220,000)
	420,000	(320,000)

Which items have changed?

A new reserve has been created, fixed assets have increased and net current assets remain unchanged.

Most reserves are revenue reserves. A revenue reserve may be created by retaining profits for a specific purpose (eg to even out dividend declarations over a number of years) or merely by retaining profit generally. In either case, the assets represented by the reserve profit can be used for the payment of dividends in future years, always assuming that the necessary cash is available. This last caveat is extremely important. A company may have made a large profit over the year's trading, but at the end of the year it may have no cash. The profit may be represented by increased stocks, debtors or fixed assets.

(3)   *Reserve funds*

As stated above, retaining profit for a particular purpose does not mean that the cash will be available for that purpose when it is required in the future. Although the value of the assets as a whole will have increased as a result of making a profit, the increase is likely to be in the form of extra fixed assets or trading stock, rather than extra cash. Therefore, in order the required amount of cash to ensure that available, it will be necessary at the same time as profit is retained within the business to set aside an equivalent amount of cash in a reserve fund (sometimes called a 'sinking fund'). This will be a fund of easily realisable investments which can be used when needed.

Exercise 7G

A company has issued debentures with a nominal value of £40,000 redeemable after 8 years. To cover the redemption of the debenture, the company decides to retain £5,000 of its net profit after tax each year for 8 years. To ensure it has cash available at the relevant time, it decides to create a sinking fund by purchasing £5,000 worth of government stocks each year.

The Balance Sheet of the company at the end of the first year would include the following:

Balance Sheet as at [date]

ASSETS	£
Fixed Assets	xxxxx
Debenture Redemption	
Sinking Fund	5,000
Net Current Assets	xxxxx
less Debenture	40,000
FINANCED BY	
Share Capital	xxxxx
Debenture Redemption	
Reserve	5,000
Profit and Loss Reserve	xxxxx

At the end of each succeeding year, the balances on both the reserve and sinking fund accounts would be increased by £5,000, so that by the time the debentures became redeemable, the Balance Sheet would include the following:

Balance Sheet as at [date]

ASSETS	£
Fixed Assets	xxxxx
Debenture Redemption	
Sinking Fund	40,000
Net Current Assets	xxxxx
less Debenture	40,000
FINANCED BY	
Share Capital	xxxxx
Debenture Redemption	
Reserve	40,000
Profit and Loss Reserve	xxxxx

How will the Balance Sheet change when the sinking fund investments are used to redeem the debenture?

(4)   Capitalisation of reserves

The result of retaining part of the net profit in the business is that after a number of years a company will have built up substantial reserves of undistributed profit. Although these reserves are in theory 'owed' to the shareholders, in reality they will be represented by fixed assets and net current assets, and there will not be sufficient cash to pay the shareholders everything 'owed'. To recognise this state of affairs, the company may decide to capitalise some of these reserves by making a bonus issue of shares to its members. The company will receive no cash in return for the shares, so instead of making a debit entry on the cash account, the debit entry will be made on the profit and loss reserve account.

Exercise 7H

A company with an issued share capital of £20,000 £1 ordinary shares and a profit and loss reserve of £25,000 decides to make a 'one for two' bonus issue (ie one bonus share for every two shares currently held).

(a)   What entries will be made to record this in the ledger account below?

Share Capital – £1 Ordinary

Date	Details	DR	CR	BAL
	Balance			20,000CR

Profit and Loss Reserve

Date	Details	DR	CR	BAL
	Balance			25,000CR

(b)   What changes will be made to the Balance Sheet of the company, after the bonus issue?

Balance Sheet

	(before)	(after)
	£	£
Share Capital	20,000	
Profit and Loss Reserves	25,000	

(c)   Will there be any changes to the assets section of the Balance Sheet?

The effect of a bonus issue is therefore that each shareholder will own a greater number of shares, but the value of each share will be less since the shares as a whole will still be represented by the same total value of assets. In addition, future dividends are likely to be declared at a lower rate, because a similar amount of net profit will have to be apportioned among a larger number of shares.

Exercise 7I

For questions (1)–(3), study the following extract from the appropriation account and Balance Sheet.

Profit and Loss Account for year ending [date]

	£
Profit before tax	**100,000**
Appropriated	
Tax @ 20%	(20,000)
Profit after tax	**80,000**
Dividend	(37,000)
Reserves	43,000

Balance Sheet as at [date]

Share Capital	100,000
Reserves	100,000

For questions (1) and (2), tick which one of the alternatives you think is correct.

(1) **Assume nothing has been written off against reserves. On last year's Balance Sheet, reserves would have been:**

    (a) £100,000. ☐

    (b) £143,000. ☐

    (c) £57,000. ☐

    (d) £43,000. ☐

Assume in addition to its final dividend of £37,000, the company had paid an interim dividend of £8,000 half-way through the accounting year:

(2)   (a) The Balance Sheet will show a liability for dividends of £45,000. ☐

    (b) The Balance Sheet will show a liability for dividends of £8,000. ☐

    (c) The Balance Sheet will show a liability for dividends of £37,000. ☐

    (d) The Balance Sheet will show none of the above. ☐

For questions (3) and (4), study the following Balance Sheet.

Balance Sheet as at [date]

	£	£
Fixed Assets		300,000
Current Assets		
Cash	300,000	
Others	100,000	
Current liabilities	(200,000)	
Net Current Assets		200,000
less Debenture		(100,000)
		400,000
Share Capital		
Ordinary		50,000
Redeemable Preference Shares		100,000
Debenture Redemption Reserve		100,000
Redeemable Preference Share Reserve		100,000
Profit and Loss Reserve		50,000
		400,000

Tick which one of the following alternatives you think is correct.

(3) **Assume you pay off the debenture:**

    (a) The debenture redemption reserve will disappear. ☐

    (b) Reserves will be reduced by £100,000. ☐

    (c) A capital reserve of £100,000 will be created. ☐

    (d) Cash will be reduced by £100,000. ☐

(4) **Assume you redeem the preference shares:**

    (a) The redeemable preference share reserve will disappear. ☐

    (b) The capital of the company will be reduced by £100,000. ☐

    (c) The company must create a capital redemption reserve of £100,000. ☐

    (d) Assets will not be reduced. ☐

For question (5), study the following extract from a Balance Sheet.

Balance Sheet as at [date]

	£
Share Capital £1 ordinary	50,000
Reserves	550,000
	600,000
Assets	600,000

(5) **Assume the company decides to make a 'two for one' bonus issue against reserves. Which one of the following alternatives is correct?**

    (a) Assets will be reduced by £100,000. ☐

    (b) Reserves will increase by £100,000. ☐

    (c) Reserves will be reduced by £100,000. ☐

    (d) Share capital will be increased by £50,000. ☐

Solutions

Exercise 7A

(a)

Cash

	DR	CR	BAL
Share Capital	10,000		10,000DR
Share Premium	1,000		11,000DR

Share Capital

	DR	CR	BAL
Cash		10,000	10,000CR

Share Premium

	DR	CR	BAL
Cash		1,000	1,000CR

(b)

Balance Sheet as at [date]

ASSETS	£	£
Cash		11,000
FINANCED BY	£	£
Share Capital	10,000	
Share Premium	1,000	11,000

Exercise 7B

(a)

Cash

	DR	CR	BAL
8% Preference Share Capital	50,000		50,000DR
Ordinary Share Capital	200,000		250,000DR

Ordinary Share Capital

	DR	CR	BAL
Cash		200,000	200,000CR

8% Preference Share Capital

	DR	CR	BAL
Cash		50,000	50,000CR

(b)

Balance Sheet as at [date]

ASSETS	£
Cash	250,000

FINANCED BY	£	£
8% £1 Preference Shares	50,000	
£1 Ordinary Shares	200,000	250,000

Exercise 7C

Shares	**Debentures**

Shares

Advantages

(i)   Dividends need only be paid if profits are sufficient.

(ii) Shares are not normally bought back by the company, so once issued, the company has no further capital liability to the shareholder during the lifetime of the company.

Disadvantage

(i)   Your majority shareholding will be diluted (unless the new shares are non-voting, but such shares may not be attractive to purchasers).

Debentures

Advantages

(i)   Once the fixed rate of interest has been paid, any surplus profits are available to shareholders.

(ii) Debenture holders have no vote at meetings, so your majority position is safe.

Disadvantages

(i)   The fixed rate of interest *must* be paid even when profits are poor.

(ii) The debenture will have to be redeemed, so cash will have to be made available.

Exercise 7D

(a)   On the appropriation section. A partner's 'salary' is merely a preferential appropriation of profit (ie it represents what the parties have decided to do with their net profit, not an item of expense which reduces the net profit).

(b)   On the Profit and Loss Account. The directors are quite separate from the company. Salaries paid to directors are true expenses which reduce the net profit of the company.

Exercise 7E

Profit and Loss Account for year ending [date]

	£	£
Post-tax profit		65,000
less **Dividends**		
Interim	(12,000)	
Final	(15,000)	

Balance Sheet as at [date]

	£	£
Current Liabilities		
Proposed Dividend		15,000

Exercise 7F

Balance Sheet as at [date]

	£	£
ASSETS		
Fixed Assets		40,000
Current Assets		
Cash	15,000	
less Current Liabilities		
Creditors	(5,000)	
Net Current Assets		10,000
		50,000

	£	£
FINANCED BY		
Share Capital	20,000	
Debenture Redemption Reserve	10,000	
Profit and Loss Reserve	20,000	
		50,000

Cash has been reduced by £10,000. The debenture of £10,000 has disappeared. Notice that the debenture redemption reserve has remained on the Balance Sheet. This is because it is merely undistributed profit 'owed' to the shareholders. Nothing has been distributed to the shareholders, so this 'liability' remains. The company may decide to relabel the reserve.

Exercise 7G

	£
ASSETS	
Fixed Assets	xxxxx
Net Current Assets	xxxxx
	xxxxx

	£
FINANCED BY	
Share Capital	xxxxx
Debenture Redemption Reserve	40,000
Profit and Loss Reserve	xxxxx
	xxxxx

Note that the debenture liability has disappeared, as has the sinking fund. However, the reserved profits remain as they have not been returned to shareholders.

Exercise 7H

(a)

Share Capital	DR	CR	BAL
Balance			20,000CR
Bonus Shares		10,000	30,000CR

Profit and Loss Reserve	DR	CR	BAL
Balance			25,000CR
Bonus Shares	10,000		15,000CR

(b)

Balance Sheet as at [date]

	(before) £	(after) £
Share Capital	20,000	30,000
Profit and Loss Reserve	25,000	15,000
	45,000	45,000

(c)   No. Assets have neither been received nor disposed of.

Exercise 7I

(1) (c) This year's reserved profits will be added to accumulated reserves. As the result is £100,000, last year's reserves must have been £100,000 less £43,000, ie £57,000.

(2) (c) Since the interim dividend has already been paid, it will have no effect on the Balance Sheet, which shows liability *to pay* dividends in the future.

(3) (d) Reserves are retained profits and cannot be reduced unless distributed to shareholders, used to write off allowable items or capitalised. The effect of repaying the debenture will be to remove a liability (the debenture) and to remove cash.

(4) (c) Because a company is not normally allowed to reduce its capital, it must create a capital reserve when shares are redeemed. The preference share redemption reserve does not disappear (see answer to question (4)). Assets will be reduced, since cash will leave the company.

(5) (c) Each shareholder will receive two shares for every one share held. Therefore, the company will issue 100,000 £1 shares. Share capital will increase by £100,000. Reserves will be reduced by £100,000. Assets will not be affected.

Chapter 8

COMPANY ACCOUNTS (2)

This chapter deals with additional items which you might encounter on a company balance sheet.

8.1 CONSOLIDATED ACCOUNTS

8.1.1 Parents and subsidiaries

It is very common for a company which is expanding its business activities either to acquire control of other companies or to compartmentalise parts of its own organisation so that each part can be run as a separate company (this is sometimes described as 'ring fencing' hazardous parts of the company's business undertaking).

The resulting business combinations are referred to as 'groups'. The controlling company is referred to as the 'parent' and the controlled company as the 'subsidiary'.

As early as 1948, it was realised that shareholders in the parent company needed additional financial statements to show the combined results of all the companies in the group if they were to be able to assess performance of their company.

Whenever a company becomes a 'parent', the Companies Act 1985 requires that, in addition to preparing the normal final accounts of each of the companies in the group, it must produce:

- a consolidated Balance Sheet showing the financial state of the parent company and its subsidiary undertakings; and
- a consolidated Profit and Loss Account showing the profit or loss of the group.

Thus, although each company retains its own legal identity and must prepare its own final accounts, the requirements as to group accounts reflect the commercial reality that the group as a whole is a single unit. (There are certain exceptions to the requirement that consolidated accounts be produced, see **8.1.2**.)

8.1.2 Statutory definition of a 'parent'

Sections 229 and 230 of the Companies Act 1985 (as amended by the Companies Act 1989) require group accounts to be prepared by a 'parent undertaking'. Section 258 defines the term as follows.

An undertaking is a parent to its subsidiary if:

(1) it holds a majority of voting rights in its 'subsidiary'; or
(2) it is a member of the 'subsidiary' and can appoint or remove directors who are able to exercise a majority of the voting rights at board meetings; or
(3) it is a member of the subsidiary with sole control, pursuant to an agreement with other shareholders or members of a majority of voting rights in it; or
(4) it has the right to exercise a dominant influence over the subsidiary by reason of provisions in its memorandum, articles, or a control contract; or
(5) it has a minimum stake in the subsidiary (generally, at least 20%) and either, actually exercises a dominant influence over the subsidiary or, is managed on a unified basis with the subsidiary.

There is no obligation to produce group accounts where *the group* comes within the definition of 'small' or 'medium-sized'. Also, an intermediate parent company which is itself included in consolidated accounts does not generally have to produce group accounts; it must, however, file a copy of these consolidated accounts with the Registrar of Companies together with its own accounts.

8.1.3 'Shares' or 'assets' takeovers

Sometimes, instead of buying shares in the other company, the acquiring company buys the *assets* of the other, which may well then be wound up (having sold all its assets, it now has only cash left). The difference between the two methods is that in the case of a 'shares takeover', the acquiring company becomes a 'parent' whereas, with an 'assets takeover', the companies remain quite separate.

Thus only a 'shares' takeover gives rise to a group of companies, and in the rest of this section we shall not consider an 'assets' takeover further.

8.1.4 FRS6 mergers

According to FRS6, a 'merger' is a business combination which results in the creation of a new reporting entity, formed from the combining parties in which the shareholders of those parties come together in partnership. No party obtains control or is seen to be dominant. The accounts of the new entity are prepared on a different basis to that on which the consolidated accounts of a parent and subsidiary are prepared. A combination meets the definition of a merger only if it satisfies the five criteria set out in paras 6–11 of FRS6 and Sch 4A, para 10 of the Companies Act 1985.

Merger accounting is not dealt with further in this book.

8.1.5 The consolidated Balance Sheet

(1) Elimination of inter-company items
The consolidated Balance Sheet must show the assets and liabilities of the group as a whole.

It will not show an item owed by one company to the other as this is merely an internal matter.

Example

Company A buys all the shares in Company B for £10,000, thereby getting the use of all Company B's assets which are valued at £10,000. Company A has an asset – its investment in Company B – which will be recorded on its Balance Sheet at the price paid. Company B has a liability – it owes the value of its share capital and its retained profits to its only shareholder, Company A.

Company A's asset and Company B's liability cancel each other out. Therefore, when preparing the consolidated Balance Sheet for the group, these inter-company items are excluded from the consolidated Balance Sheet.

The consolidated Balance Sheet for a group will show:

* the share capital and accumulated reserves of the parent;
* the current year's reserved profits for both companies as calculated on the current consolidated Profit and Loss Account;
* the assets of both companies excluding the parent's investment in the subsidiary;
* any liabilities owed by the companies to outsiders excluding the share capital and reserves owed by the subsidiary to the parent.

(2)   Goodwill and capital reserves

In the previous example, the parent company acquired the shares of the subsidiary for exactly the value of its assets. Sometimes a parent company may pay more for the shares in the subsidiary than the apparent value of the subsidiary's assets. Sometimes the parent may pay less.

A parent company which pays more for its subsidiary's shares than the book value of the assets warrants is paying an additional amount for 'goodwill'. Goodwill is classified as an intangible fixed asset.

Example

Parent acquires all the shares of Child for £12,000. The book value of Child's assets is only £10,000.

Parent has paid £2,000 for goodwill.

The 'extra' paid by the parent for the goodwill represents an asset which is not cancelled out by the subsidiary's liability and so it must be shown on the consolidated Balance Sheet.

Goodwill is classified as an intangible fixed asset and, because of its intangible nature, companies often write off its value. They can either do this against profits over a period of time or against reserves as soon as the goodwill is acquired.

A parent company which pays less for its subsidiary's share than the book value of the assets warrants is making a profit (albeit unrealised). Because the parent has made a profit on the transaction, the subsidiary's liability does not cancel out the parent's asset so the profit must be shown on the consolidated Balance Sheet. A profit owing to the shareholders but not distributed to them is a reserve. In this case the reserve is described as a 'capital' reserve and will appear as such on the consolidated Balance Sheet.

8.1.6   The consolidated Profit and Loss Account

This must show the income and expenses of the group as a whole. It will not show the dividend paid by the subsidiary to the parent as this is merely an internal matter.

The consolidated Profit and Loss Account for the group will show:

- the income of the parent and subsidiary excluding any dividend paid by the subsidiary to the parent;
- the expenses of the parent and subsidiary;
- the appropriation of profit excluding any dividend paid by the subsidiary to the parent.

8.1.7   Minority interests

One of the situations where a company becomes a 'parent' is where one company holds more than half in nominal value of the equity share capital of another company, with corresponding voting rights. It is therefore quite common for a 'group' to exist where part of the share capital of a subsidiary company is owned by shareholders who are not otherwise connected with the group. There is still a requirement that consolidated accounts be produced, but they will have to reflect the interest of the minority shareholders.

(1)   The Balance Sheet

The consolidated Balance Sheet will include the whole of the subsidiary's assets and outside liabilities. It will specify the interest of the minority shareholders, who for this purpose are treated as outside creditors.

FRS4 requires that minority interests be analysed into equity and non-equity interests. The values can be shown in the notes to the accounts, but the wording of the Balance Sheet must disclose that non-equity interests have been included. In the following example, we assume that the minority interests are equity interests.

Example

L Ltd is a company with assets of £95,000 financed by share capital of £40,000 and reserves of £50,000. It acquires 60% of the issued share capital in M Ltd for £9,000. M Ltd has assets of £15,000. The remaining 40% of the issued share capital (£6,000) remains in the ownership of outsiders.

The consolidated Balance Sheet for the group will appear as follows:

Consolidated Balance Sheet for L and M Group

			£	£
ASSETS				
Fixed Assets:	**L Ltd**		52,000	
	M Ltd		11,000	
Net Current Assets:	**L Ltd**		34,000	
	M Ltd		4,000	
				101,000
FINANCED BY				
Share Capital			40,000	
Reserves			55,000	
Interest of Minority Shareholders			6,000	
				101,000

You will see that the consolidated Balance Sheet shows *all* the assets of the two companies. This is correct, as the group has the use of all the assets. The interest of the minority shareholders appears as a liability.

(2)   *The Profit and Loss Account*

The existence of a minority shareholding in a subsidiary company will affect the entries appearing in a consolidated Profit and Loss Account for the group.

It is necessary to calculate the proportion of the subsidiary's net profit after tax which is attributable to the minority shareholders. This is then deducted before appropriations are made for dividends and reserves.

Example

N Ltd owns 60% of the issued share capital in P Ltd. N Ltd is therefore entitled to 60% of any dividend paid by P Ltd and 60% of any retained profit. The remaining 40% of each belongs to the minority shareholders. The pre-tax profit for N Ltd is £50,000 and for P Ltd is £41,000. Taxation for N Ltd is £20,000 and for P Ltd is £16,000. Post-tax profits are £30,000 and £25,000 respectively. N Ltd pays a divided of £19,000. P Ltd pays a dividend of £10,000.

The consolidated Profit and Loss Account will record the combined net profit of the two companies and the combined taxation of the two companies, and will show as a deduction the amount attributable to the minority shareholders, ie £10,000 (40% of the post-tax profit of

£25,000). The only item in respect of dividends which appears on the consolidated Profit and Loss Account is N Ltd's dividend to its own shareholders (£19,000).

The final item is the item for reserves. This is arrived at by adding together the reserves of N Ltd and the portion of the reserves of P Ltd shown in its Profit and Loss Account as due to N Ltd, ie 60% of P Ltd's total reserves of £15,000, which amounts to £9,000.

Consolidated Profit and Loss Account

		£	£
Profit before tax	N Ltd	50,000	
	P Ltd	41,000	
			91,000
Taxation	N Ltd	20,000	
	P Ltd	16,000	
			(36,000)
Net Profit after Tax			55,000
Amount attributable to minority shareholders			(10,000)
Dividend			(19,000)
Reserves	N Ltd		(17,000)
	P Ltd		(9,000)

8.2 DEFERRED TAXATION

Provision for taxation appears in the appropriation section of the Profit and Loss Account and in the Balance Sheet as a current liability (see **8.1**). Frequently, company accounts also include an item called 'provision for *deferred* tax' in this section of the final accounts. What is a provision for deferred taxation?

8.2.1 The concept

Accountants like to spread expenses evenly over the period to which they relate. Straight line depreciation is an example of this (see Chapter 5).

The Inland Revenue is not concerned with matching income and expenses to the appropriate period in the same way. Depreciation is not regarded as a deductible expense for tax purposes, so the tax liability of a company must be calculated on its net profit before deducting depreciation. Thus, net profit and taxable profit may be very different figures.

Companies are allowed to deduct capital allowances when calculating their taxable profit. The rules on the amount which can be deducted vary according to the policies of the government in power.

In some tax years companies have been allowed large 'first year' capital allowances on the cost of purchasing fixed assets. In years when this is possible it gives the company a great deal of tax relief in the year in which the allowance is claimed, resulting in a low tax bill and large post-tax profits for that year. Once the allowance has been claimed there will be little or no tax relief for later years which means bigger tax bills and, therefore, smaller post-tax profits for those years.

A distorting effect on a company's post box profit is produced by the fact that the benefit of the capital allowance on the purchase of an item of plant or machinery is usually greater *initially* than the figure treated as an annual accounting expense for depreciation. (Correspondingly, in later years it is generally less.) In simple terms, one might say that, from an accounting point of view, too much tax relief is being allowed initially and, as a result, too much tax will be charged in later years.

Accountants would describe such a situation by saying that a timing difference exists.

8.2.2   Object of deferred tax accounting

The object of deferred tax accounting is to restate the tax liability shown on the Profit and Loss Account as though timing differences did not exist and to iron out the distortions which they produce.

Accountants deal with timing differences by creating a provision for tax in a year in which they consider too little tax is being charged and then using that provision in later years to reduce the burden of the tax charged against current profits. The non-accountant may feel this to be an interesting but superfluous adjustment. However, this is not the case. Consider the following.

Example

You are looking at the accounts of a business. You find that the post-tax profit in 1998 is very high while the post-tax profit in 1999 is very low. Would this decrease in profitability alarm you?

Clearly, at first sight, a slump in profitability *would* alarm you, since it suggests a slump in trading profit.

However, there might be an explanation not linked to declining trading profit. It is possible that in 1998 the business received large capital allowances, which reduced its tax liability and thus increased its post-tax profit. In 1999 the business may have received lower capital allowances which increased its tax liability, thus reducing its post-tax profit.

It is clearly unsatisfactory that the figure for post-tax profit, which is used by many as a yardstick for a company's performance, should be liable to such fluctuations.

Furthermore, even if the reduction in capital allowances is the explanation for the fall in profit, there might still be some cause for alarm. Has the business got sufficient cash to pay its tax bill? Have the people running the business foreseen the increase in tax, and budgeted appropriately?

8.2.3   Items which may require or reduce a provision for deferred taxation

Accounting for deferred tax is regulated by a statement of standard accounting practice, SSAP 15 (as amended). The following items are dealt with.

(1)   Short-term timing differences
For taxation purposes, the 'cash' basis is normally used to prepare accounts. This means that income and expenses are treated as relating to the period in which they are receivable or payable.

For accounting purposes, the 'accrual or earnings' basis is normally used. This means that income is treated as relating to the period in which it is earned and expenses to the period in which the benefit of the item was enjoyed.

Thus an item dealt with in one period for tax purposes is dealt with in another period for accounting purposes, resulting in a 'timing' difference. Such timing differences normally reverse themselves in the next accounting period. It is none the less generally accepted that full provision for deferred taxation should be made in respect of them.

(2) *Capital allowances*

The precise amounts which can be claimed vary according to the tax rules in force at the time.

(3) *Revaluation surpluses on fixed assets*

Assets which have increased in value substantially carry the risk of a heavy tax charge on the increase; however, no tax charge actually arises until a gain is realised on a disposal for which no roll-over or similar relief is available. Provision should be made at the time the business decides that in principle it intends to dispose of the asset.

(4) *Trading losses*

Where such losses can be regarded as 'recoverable', they may reduce the amount of provision needed.

8.2.4   A basic illustration

First, consider how, in the absence of deferred tax accounting, the accounts of the following business (AB Ltd) would appear. For convenience, the example assumes an unchanging corporation tax rate of 40% for all of the years mentioned, and also that 100% capital allowances were available to the company. These assumptions highlight the problems caused by timing differences and make the illustration easier to follow.

Example

AB Ltd is a company which in recent years was making (after depreciation and other overheads) a profit of £10,000 per annum. Assume that in the first year covered by the example, it bought a machine for £10,000. The machine has an expected working life of 4 years, so that (calculated on the straight line basis) depreciation is for accounting purposes being treated as an annual expense of £2,500.

Since depreciation does not, however, qualify as a deductible expense for tax purposes, the £2,500 will have to be added back to determine the profit on which tax is payable.

The company took a 100% capital allowance in the year of acquisition in respect of the machine.

You will see from the example that the capital allowance has a distorting effect on the post-tax profit figures, because the tax relief is taken in the first year and not spread over the machine's working life.

Year	**Taxable profit**	**Tax @ 40%**	**Post-tax profit**
	£	£	£
1	12,500		
	less allowance (10,000)		
	2,500	1,000	9,000
2	12,500	5,000	5,000
3	12,500	5,000	5,000
4	12,500	5,000	5,000

Over the 4-year period, the company pays £16,000 in tax. If this were spread evenly over the 4-year period, the company would pay £4,000 per annum. From the point of view of accountants, who like to spread expenses evenly over the periods to which they relate, this means that in Year 1 the company paid £3,000 too little in tax. This is referred to as an 'originating difference'. In each of the next 3 years, the company pays £1,000 too much. This is referred to as a 'reversing difference'.

To iron out this distortion, AB Ltd should create in Year 1 a provision for deferred tax equal to the amount of tax 'saved' as a result of the excess tax relief (the originating difference). This provision would be shown on the Profit and Loss Account in Year 1, and would have the effect of reducing the post-tax profit for that year. In subsequent years, the provision would be used, and therefore shown on the Profit and Loss Account as a deduction from the taxation figure. This would have the effect of increasing the post-tax profit for subsequent years.

Example

The Profit and Loss Account for Year 1 should show the actual tax paid, as well as a provision for the amount of tax saved as a result of the excessive relief.

(a)   Using the figures from the example above, it will be necessary to create a provision of £3,000 for Year 1:

Profit and Loss Account for Year 1

	£	£
Net Profit		10,000
Tax	1,000	
plus Provision	3,000	
		(4,000)
Post-tax Profit		6,000

In subsequent years, the account will have to show the actual tax paid of £5,000 per annum. However, part of the provision created in Year 1 on the Profit and Loss Account will be used to reduce the amount finally shown as charged against profits.

(b)   Each year £1,000 of the provision will be used to reduce the amount of tax charged in the Profit and Loss Account.

Profit and Loss Account for Years 2, 3 and 4

	£	£
Net Profit		10,000
Tax	5,000	
less Provision	(1,000)	
		(4,000)
Post-tax Profit		6,000

The deferred tax account

The provision created in Year 1 in the previous example will be credited to a deferred tax account. Roughly speaking, the balance on that account represents an expectation of paying tax in the future. The provision will be shown on the Balance Sheet as a long-term liability.

In subsequent years, the balance on the deferred tax account will be reduced as the provision is used.

8.2.5 Deferred tax and changes in rates of taxation

It is necessary to adjust the amount of provision made in the light of changes to the prevailing tax rates.

The arithmetical calculation of the amount of the provision can be complex and is not something a solicitor would expect to do.

8.2.6 Difficulties with deferred taxation: SSAP 15 (as amended)

Many companies do not make full provision for deferred tax. This is because they consider that throughout the life of the company tax relief in some form or other will continue to be obtained so that the company will never have to face a completely unrelieved bill. This is accepted by the accountancy profession. Thus, companies are not required to account for deferred taxation on items if there is a reasonable probability that future originating differences will outweigh the effect of reversals.

8.2.7 Significance for solicitors

It is obvious that the actual calculation of the annual deferred tax charge is extremely complex. Accountants must calculate the actual amount of the originating difference for the year, then make allowance for any items of deduction and finally judge whether some or all of future reversals will be outweighed by future allowances. In addition, they must consider the impact of changes in the rates of corporation tax. Thus, a provision which originally was adequate may have become either inadequate or too great, and may therefore require adjustment.

As a solicitor, when looking at a set of accounts, you will probably not want (or be able) to check the actual calculation. However, you should certainly be concerned if no provision at all has been made, since this may mean that the business will face heavy tax bills in the future without any provision. This would mean a dramatic fall in post-tax profits. You should also ask whether correct accounting practice has been followed in calculating the amount of provision.

Chapter 9

HOW TO READ ACCOUNTS

9.1 THE PURPOSES OF READING ACCOUNTS

In broad terms, the purposes of reading the accounts of a business are:

- to assess its current performance; and
- to predict its future prospects.

Certain questions come immediately to mind, for example:

- Is the present level of profitability satisfactory?
- Is the profitability likely to improve in the future?
- Can the business meet its current liabilities?
- Will it be able to meet its current liabilities next year and the year after?
- Are investors in the business receiving a satisfactory return on their investment?
- Will they be doing better or worse in 5 years' time?

9.2 WHO WILL WANT TO READ ACCOUNTS AND WHY?

The following people are likely to be interested in reading accounts:

- **Investors** — To assess the level of risk and return.
- **Managers** — To make sure that the business is performing to its potential.
- **Lenders** — To ensure that the debt will be repaid and the business can pay interest.
- **Inland Revenue** — To assess the profits for tax.
- **Potential purchasers** — To consider whether the business is worth buying.
- **Employees** — To negotiate terms and conditions of employment.

Bear in mind that not all of those interested will be able to get full information about the business they are assessing. Obviously, managers will be able to get all the necessary information, but how much an investor will be able to find out will depend largely on how much of an investment is involved – the larger the amount, the more influence a potential investor will have when demanding information.

9.3 THE LIMITATIONS OF ACCOUNTS

You must be able to understand what is in the accounts, but looking at accounts alone may provide a misleading picture of the state of a business. Accounts are only produced after events have occurred.

Furthermore, accounts can only produce information of a financial nature. Thus, a Balance Sheet will only list assets purchased by the business. It will not indicate the health or otherwise of labour relations, despite the fact that many people would regard good staff relations as a very important asset. A poor trade reputation would be regarded by many people as a liability but it has no place on a financial statement.

There may also be matters entirely beyond the control of management, such as a declining market for the firm's products. In other words, the accounts provide only part of the information needed in the analysis of the position of a business.

9.4   WHAT INFORMATION DO YOU NEED?

It is important to have a general picture of the firm that you are investigating.

- It is large or small?
- Is it growing or contracting?
- What is the nature of its business?
- Does it operate in an expanding or declining market?
- Does it depend heavily on a particular product or products?

The questions which you should ask depend on the circumstances and are largely a matter of common sense.

9.4.1   Public companies

A public company must prepare an annual report. The report has two main purposes:

(a) It complies with the requirements of the Companies Act 1985 to produce certain information and accounts.

(b) It gives the company an opportunity to promote itself, to its shareholders, to prospective investors and to analysts.

As you read any company's report, be very aware of the need to question and check everything.

- Are any of the figures in the accounts not clear? Is there an explanation in the Chairman's Statement or the Directors' Report? Do the notes help?
- Is the chairman expressing over-optimistic hopes in his statement? Do they look as though they can be supported by the company's current financial position? Do they look sensible in the light of the economy here and abroad?

It is unlikely, although not impossible, that you would find a direct lie in a company's report but you should always look at the information critically to see whether a particular proposal or intention looks as if it can be justified.

Some of the items in a report are included because they must be, while some are included because the company wants to include them. The following must be included in any public company's report:

- Directors' Report;
- Auditors' Report;
- Balance Sheet – company and group;
- Profit and Loss Account – company or, if there is a group, then group only;
- Cash Flow Statement – company or, if there is a group, then group only;
- Notes giving the required information;
- Details of directors' interests.

Other items are optional, but you would generally be surprised if the following were not there in some form:

- Chairman's Statement. What is there to hide?
- Ten-year record missing? Has the company not been performing consistently in the long term?

In a sense, reading a company report is something which lawyers are well trained to do – you check and question everything before accepting it as true.

Remember, when you are reading the report, that there are other sources of information as well. Keep an eye on newspaper reports, television news, etc.

9.4.2   Partnerships and sole practitioners

There will be no published accounts for partnerships and sole practitioners. Even so, you should get copies of the accounts they produce and study them.

Be aware that the requirements as to the format and content of reports which apply to companies do not apply to unincorporated bodies to anywhere near the same extent.

In these circumstances, you must get as much information about the business as you can. Find out the following:

- Are its premises in a suitable area?
- Does it seem to be busy?
- Is it dealing in something which is going to provide an income in the long term?
- What sort of reputation does it have locally?
- What can you find out about the proprietors?

You can then look at the accounts in the light of that information. When your analysis raises further questions you can get down to detailed discussions of the problems with the proprietors or their advisers.

Obviously, the amount of information you can get will depend on what your relationship is, or is to be, with the business.

9.5   PRELIMINARY STEPS

As well as obtaining as much general information about the business as you can there are a number of preliminary steps you should take before launching into a detailed analysis of the accounts. These involve, in part, checking the accuracy and reliability of the figures presented and, in part, building up a general picture of the business and the market in which it operates, so that the information extracted can be considered in a proper context. What might be normal for a small business might be very unusual for a large one. A particular level of profitability may be commendable in a time of recession but disappointing in a period when business generally is 'booming'.

Common preliminary steps are as follows.

- **Obtain the accounts for several years.**   If you are going to make a realistic assessment of a business it is important that you obtain its accounts for several years rather than for the previous year alone. One year's accounts will reveal important information – the extent of borrowings, the value of fixed assets, the amount of unpaid bills, the value of stock in hand – but it is difficult to reach reliable conclusions without making comparisons with earlier years.
- **Check the date of the Balance Sheet.**   A business can choose a Balance Sheet date to suit itself. If the business is seasonal then a Balance Sheet drawn up at one date could include figures which would show the business in a much more favourable light than a Balance Sheet drawn up at another date.

Example

A business manufactures Christmas decorations. It sells the decorations to department stores in September. A Balance Sheet drawn up in September would show a healthy cash balance and probably substantial debtors. By contrast, a Balance Sheet drawn up in July would show substantial stock, a high creditors figure and, probably, a large overdraft.

Always consider whether you have to take the date of the Balance Sheet into account when you are analysing the figures.

- Check the method of valuing fixed assets.
- When were the assets last valued? Freehold premises purchased 20 years earlier for £5,000 may still be shown in the Balance Sheet at that value. Their current value will probably be quite different.
- Has provision been made for depreciation? If so, what method has been used?

In the case of a company, you will be looking for the answers to these and other questions in the notes and the statement of accounting policies included in the company's published accounts. If you are dealing with a partnership or sole trader you should ask for that information from the partners or proprietor.

Exercise 9A

What will be the effect on the Profit and Loss Account and on the Balance Sheet if values for fixed assets and depreciation are inaccurate?

- **Check how the closing stock is valued.** The normal method is to value stock at the lower of cost or current market value. If you want to do the job thoroughly, you should inspect the stock. It may be that it includes items which are no longer readily saleable. For example, in the fashion trade, a business may have purchased a whole stock of items some months ago, which are now out of fashion. They could still be appearing in the accounts under 'Stock' at cost price when in fact their current market value is little or nothing.

Exercise 9B

How will the Profit and Loss Account and the Balance Sheet be affected if the wrong figure for stock is included?

- **Analyse the figure given for debtors.** Will all the debts really be paid? Has a provision been made for bad debts? It is quite possible for a business not to write off bad debts so that the debtors figure appears larger than the amount of cash which the business can readily expect to receive.

Exercise 9C

Why might a business prefer not to write off bad debts? What else is affected apart from the Balance Sheet?

Are there any dangers in a business having a large number of debtors?

- **Look for unusual or exceptional items or major changes.** The picture given by the Profit and Loss Account and Balance Sheet for a particular year can sometimes be distorted because of some exceptional event or major change either in circumstances or in accounting policy.

Example

A business may have borrowed a substantial amount to invest in new plant or machinery. In the short term profit may be reduced because there has been no time to use machinery to increase profits, yet interest charges will already have been incurred. However, in the long term there may be prospects of rapid growth in future years.

Fixed assets such as land and buildings may have been revalued for the first time in many years. This will make the Balance Sheet look quite different but in reality nothing has changed.

You will have to take all these matters into account, particularly if you are going to make comparisons with previous years.

9.6   SOME GENERAL CONSIDERATIONS

9.6.1   Profitability and solvency

The two main questions which people ask when reading the accounts of a business are:

- Is the business profitable?
- Is the business solvent?

Profitability is not the same as solvency. The Profit and Loss Account shows whether the business has made a profit. The Balance Sheet shows whether it is solvent.

The fact that the accounts reveal that a profit has been made does not necessarily mean that the money is in the bank.

The Trading and Profit and Loss Accounts of a business will record sales and levels of professional charges which in turn will determine the amount of profit, but although the goods may have been sold or bills delivered, payment may not yet have been received. Thus, although the Profit and Loss Account may show a large profit, the Balance Sheet may record a high figure under debtors and there may be no cash in the bank.

Alternatively, the business may have sold goods or delivered bills and been paid; however, it may have purchased expensive new premises paying cash. The result is that while the Profit and Loss Account will show a profit, there is no money in the bank.

In either example, if the proprietors relied on the Profit and Loss Account to try to withdraw large amounts of cash they would find they could not because there was no money in the bank.

It is therefore a misconception to think that if a business is profitable it must be solvent (ie able to pay its debts). This is not so. Obviously, a business which is unprofitable is not likely to be solvent for long, but just because a business is profitable it does not necessarily mean that it is able to pay its debts at once. A profitable business may be driven into liquidation if it is unable to pay its debts as they fall due.

Exercise 9D

The accounts of a business show that it has made a large profit, but that it has no cash. In fact it has a large overdraft. How many possible factors can you think of to account for the lack of cash?

Accounts for Solicitors

9.6.2 Treatment of bank overdrafts

It is necessary to decide how to deal with a bank overdraft, particularly if this is substantial. It will normally appear in the Balance Sheet as a current liability because, in theory at least, it is repayable on demand. The reality may be quite different. The business may maintain a high overdraft indefinitely and finance its activities from it. Unless the business runs into difficulties the bank will not take steps to call in the money owing.

As a current liability, the bank overdraft will not appear as part of the capital employed in the business. Instead, it will be deducted from the current assets. If, however, it is a source of long-term finance, it should be treated as such in calculating the return on capital which the business is achieving. Again, in calculating whether a business can pay its debts by examining the ratio of current or liquid assets to current liabilities, a totally misleading picture may emerge if no distinction is made between the bank overdraft and ordinary trade creditors.

9.6.3 The impact of inflation

It is necessary to make allowance for the impact of inflation. If profits are increasing at the rate of 5% per annum when inflation is running at 8% per annum, then in real terms profits are falling. One way of dealing with inflation is by production of so-called current cost accounts which are adjusted for inflation but because there is disagreement over the way these should be produced, analysts will normally use figures from the historic cost accounts and then make allowance for inflation when analysing the ratios.

Solutions

Exercise 9A

Effect on Profit and Loss Account:
Depreciation is charged as an expense on the Profit and Loss Account. If the depreciation is understated the profit, therefore, will be artificially high.

The reverse will be true if the depreciation is overstated.

Effect on Balance Sheet:

Depreciation
The figure for fixed assets will be unreliable if depreciation is inaccurate. The figure for capital owing to the proprietors will also be unreliable as it is increased by the profit calculated on the Profit and Loss Account.

Fixed assets
If assets are overstated, the Balance Sheet will appear healthier than it really is. If assets are understated, the business may appear to be producing a high profit from its capital but since capital is understated this will be misleading. If the business is a company, understating its assets will make it vulnerable to takeover.

Exercise 9B

Effect on Profit and Loss Account:
Closing stock reduces the figure for cost of goods sold. If cost of goods sold is low then gross and net profit will appear to be high.

Thus, an overstated closing figure increases profit figures.

Effect on Balance Sheet:
Closing stock will be shown as a current asset. An inaccurate figure will affect the ratio between current assets and current liabilities.

Exercise 9C

Debtors are shown in the Balance Sheet as current assets. A high debtors figure will increase the apparent value of the assets. It will affect the ratio between current assets and current liabilities.

The Profit and Loss Account will also be affected. Bad debts are written off in Profit and Loss as expenses. The profit figure will be overstated if insufficient debts are written off as bad or doubtful.

The business could have cash flow problems if the debtors do not pay. The business could be particularly vulnerable if a large proportion of the debts are owed by a single debtor as that debtor may become insolvent and unable to pay.

Exercise 9D

You should have considered at least the following:

- excessive drawings by proprietors/dividends paid to shareholders;
- purchases of fixed assets out of cash received;
- failure to collect debts;
- excessive stock levels;
- dishonesty of staff.

PART II

ACCOUNTS FOR A SOLICITOR'S PRACTICE

Chapter 10

THE SOLICITORS' ACCOUNTS RULES

10.1 INTRODUCTION

While reading this chapter you should keep a copy of the Solicitors' Accounts Rules 1998 in front of you. These replace the Solicitors' Accounts Rules 1991 and incorporate the Accountants' Report Rules 1991.

The Rules are divided into 7 sections and include explanatory notes. These notes are part of the Rules.

10.2 PRINCIPLES

The main principles of the Solicitors' Accounts Rules are set out in Rule 1. They include the following:

- to keep other people's money separate from money of the solicitor or the practice;
- to keep other people's money safe in a bank or building society account identifiable as a client bank account;
- to use each client's money for that client's matters only;
- to keep proper accounting records to show accurately the position with regard to the money held for each client;
- to account for interest on other people's money.

In this chapter we will look at the way in which the Rules put these principles into practice.

The existence and enforcement of the Rules reduces the risk of accidental or deliberate misuse of client money. However, the Rules also demonstrate to the public that the profession is determined to police itself and to protect clients from the risks of accidental or deliberate mishandling of their money.

10.3 WHO IS BOUND BY THE RULES?

The Rules apply to sole practitioners, partners, assistant solicitors, in-house solicitors, directors of companies recognised by The Law Society under AJA 1985 and registered foreign lawyers. In practical terms they also bind anyone else working in a practice, such as cashiers and non-solicitor fee earners. Non-compliance by any member of staff will lead to the principals being in breach of the Rules, since the principals of a practice are required by Rule 6 to ensure compliance.

The case of *Weston v The Law Society* (1998) *The Times*, July 15 is a salutary reminder of how careful a partner in a firm must be. The Court of Appeal confirmed that it was appropriate to strike off a solicitor where no dishonesty was alleged but the solicitor in question was guilty of breaches of the Rules through his partners' activities of which he was unaware.

Lord Bingham referred to the 'duty of anyone holding anyone else's money to exercise a proper stewardship in relation to it'.

The Rules do not apply to solicitors employed by bodies such as local authorities or when carrying out judicial functions, such as acting as a coroner (Rule 5).

The 1998 Rules for the first time extend the application of the Rules (though only to a limited extent) to solicitors acting as:

- liquidators;
- trustees in bankruptcy;
- Court of Protection receivers;
- trustees of occupational pension schemes;

and to solicitors who hold client money jointly with a client, another solicitors' practice or a third party. Solicitors acting in such capacities are bound by some of the record keeping requirements contained in Rules 32 and 33.

10.4   CATEGORIES OF MONEY

10.4.1   Three categories

Rule 13 divides money into one of three categories:

- client money;
- controlled trust money;
- office money.

10.4.2   Client money

A client is a person *for whom the solicitor acts*.

Client money is money held or received for a client *plus* all other money which is not controlled trust money or office money.

Note that the definition of client money goes beyond holding money for 'a client'. If the solicitor holds money for someone who is not a client; for example, as stakeholder, bailee, agent, donee of a power of attorney, liquidator, trustee in bankruptcy or Court of Protection receiver, the money is client money.

Client money includes money received as 'an advance' or 'generally on account of costs' but not money received for costs in payment of a bill or agreed fee. This is an important distinction.

Exercise 10A

(a)   Solicitors deliver a bill to Client A for professional charges of £460. The client sends the solicitors a cheque for £460.

Is the £460 client's money or office money?   *office* ✓

(b)   Solicitors ask Client B for £200 generally on account of costs. The client sends the solicitors a cheque for £200.

Is the £200 client's money or office money?   *client* ✓

Where a solicitor receives money to cover disbursements which have not yet been paid, the money will normally be client money. (There is a limited exception to this; see **10.6.2** below.)

10.4.3   Controlled trust money

Controlled trust money is money held or received for a controlled trust. A controlled trust arises when a solicitor is the sole trustee of a trust or a co-trustee only with one or more of his/her partners or employees (see Rule 2(2)(h)). There is no outside trustee to scrutinise such trusts and so The Law Society singles them out for special treatment. Money subject to a trust which is not a controlled trust will be client money.

10.4.4   Office money

Office money is money which belongs to the solicitor or the practice. It includes the following:

- Interest earned on client money placed on a general deposit (solicitors are entitled to keep such interest under Solicitors Act 1974 – see post);

- Money received for profit costs and VAT where a bill has been delivered or a fee agreed (Rule 19(2) and (5));
- Money received to reimburse the solicitor for disbursements already paid on behalf of clients;
- Money received for disbursements which the solicitor has not yet paid but for which the solicitor has incurred liability, eg where a solicitor has an account at the Land Registry and pays monthly for searches.

However, money received for unpaid 'professional' disbursements is not office money. Professional disbursements are fees of counsel, experts, interpreters, translators, process servers, surveyors, estate agents. Money received in advance for such payments is classified as client money.

The reason for the distinction between the types of unpaid disbursements is that professional disbursements often amount to large sums of money, whereas items such as search fees are normally small. It would not be right for solicitors to be allowed to keep large sums in the office bank account which are actually due to other people.

Example

A solicitor acts for a client in connection with a land dispute. The solicitor carries out a Land Registry search. The Land Registry charges the price of the search to the solicitor's account. The solicitor also instructs counsel to advise and receives counsel's invoice for the advice.

The solicitor then sends the client a bill showing the solicitor's profit costs, the Land Registry search fee and counsel's fee. The client sends a cheque in payment. The amount representing the profit costs and the unpaid Land Registry search fee is office money, but the amount representing the unpaid counsel's fee is client money.

Note: A solicitor cannot be his/her own client for the purposes of the Rules so if the practice conducts a transaction for a partner any money received is office money. However, if the money is held for the partner *and another person* (eg a spouse) it will be client money.

Exercise 10B

Gibson and Weldon are solicitors in partnership together.

(a) Gibson asks Weldon to deal with the purchase of a house for her. Shortly before completion, Gibson gives Weldon the balance of the purchase price required for completion. Is the firm holding client money? *NO ~ OFFICE* ✓

(b) Gibson is selling her house. Weldon is acting. The buyer pays a deposit to the firm to hold as stakeholders. Is the deposit client money? *yes* ✓

10.5 USE OF THE CLIENT BANK ACCOUNT

10.5.1 Requirement for client bank account

Rule 14(1) requires a solicitor to keep at least one client bank account. The account must be in the name of the firm and include the word 'client' in the title. It must be kept at a bank or building society in England and Wales. A firm need only have one client bank account but will often choose to have more than one (for example, a current account and one or more deposit accounts).

10.5.2　Use of client bank account(s)

The primary rule relating to the use of the client bank account is Rule 15. It states that, *except as provided otherwise*:

- Client money and controlled trust money *must* without delay be paid into the client bank account (Rule 15(1)).
- *Only* client money or controlled trust money may be paid into a client bank account (Rule 15(2)).

Note: 'Without delay' is defined by Rule 2(2)(z) as on the day of receipt or on the next working day.

10.5.3　Use of client bank account for other money

Rule 15(2)(a) allows a solicitor to use office money to open a client bank account or to maintain it at an agreed level.

Examples

(1)　Smith and Brown are about to start practising in a partnership. As a preliminary, they need to open a client bank account and an office bank account. As yet they are holding no client money, so they are allowed to use their own office money to open a client bank account.

(2)　Smith and Brown have agreed with the bank that the balance on the client bank account will not be allowed to fall below £10,000. They will be allowed to pay in office money as and when required to maintain that balance.

A bank might impose such a condition in return for allowing the firm to operate an overdraft on its office bank account.

Rule 15(2)(b) allows a solicitor to advance money to a client or controlled trust where the firm holds insufficient money in the client bank account and needs to make a payment for that client. The money advanced becomes client money or controlled trust money and subject to the ordinary rules applying to such money. (This is not really an example of using the client bank account for other money as the money advanced becomes client or controlled trust money.)

Rule 15(2)(c) allows a solicitor to pay office money into the client bank account to replace money withdrawn improperly.

Example

A junior employee withdraws money from the bank account for a client not realising that the firm is holding no money for that client.

As soon as the mistake is discovered the firm should rectify it by paying office money into the client bank account.

Note: An efficient firm will organise a system which makes such a mistake impossible.

Rule 15(2)(d) allows a solicitor to pay office money into the client bank account in lieu of interest which could have been earned on client or trust money had the money of the client or controlled trust been placed on deposit.

Solicitors often receive cheques from clients containing a mixture of office and client money or controlled trust money.

Rule 20 provides that the money can be 'split' between the office and client bank account. Alternatively, the whole amount can be paid into the client bank account.

Example

Client X sends a cheque made up of £235 in payment of the solicitor's professional charges and VAT and £12,000 required to complete the purchase of her house. The whole £12,235 can be paid into the client bank account. The £235 can then be transferred from the client bank account to the office bank account at a later stage.

Note: It would be a breach of the Rules to pay the £12,000 of client's money into the office bank account.

Alternatively, it would be permissible to 'split' the cheque and pay £235 into the office bank account and £12,000 into the client bank account.

Where the cheque is not split the office money element must be transferred out within 14 days of receipt.

Note: Rule 19 and Rule 21 provide further ways of dealing with some types of mixed payments (see **10.6** post).

10.5.4   Situations where client money can be withheld from the client bank account

(1) Rule 16(1)(a) provides that client money can be held outside the client bank account (for example in the solicitor's safe or in a non-client bank account) but only where the client gives written instructions to the solicitor or where the solicitor confirms the client's instructions in writing.

   Note: The money is client money and the record keeping requirements of Rule 32 must be complied with.

(2) Under Rule 16(1)(b) the client may instruct the solicitor to place the money in a bank or building society account opened in the name of the client or some other person designated by the client. The instruction must be in writing or acknowledged in writing.

   Note: Once the money is paid into such an account, it ceases to be client money and is not subject to the record keeping requirements of Rule 32.

(3) Rule 17 provides that client money can be withheld in the following circumstances:

   (a) cash is received and is paid without delay in the ordinary course of business to the client or, on the client's behalf, to a third party;

   (b) a cheque or draft is received and is endorsed over in the ordinary course of business to the client or, on the client's behalf, to a third party;

   (c) money is withheld on instructions under Rule 16;

   (d) money is received for unpaid professional disbursements and is dealt with under Rule 19(1)(b) (see post);

   (e) money is received for unpaid professional disbursements from the Legal Aid Board and is dealt with under Rule 21 (see post);

   (f) money is withheld on the written authorisation of The Law Society (only rarely will such authorisation be given and the Society is able to impose a condition that the solicitor pay the money to a charity which gives an indemnity against any later legitimate claims to the money).

Note: Even though client money is withheld from the client bank account, dealings with it must be recorded in accordance with Rule 32

10.5.5   Situations in which controlled trust money can be withheld from the client bank account

Rule 18 provides that controlled trust money can be withheld from the client bank account in the following circumstances:

(a)   where cash is received and without delay paid in cash in the execution of the trust to a beneficiary or third party;

(b)   where a cheque or draft is received and without delay is endorsed over in the execution of the trust to a beneficiary or third party;

(c)   where a trustee in accordance with the trustee's powers pays the money into an account of the trustee which is a non-client bank account or properly retains cash;

(d)   where (as in Rule 17(f)) The Law Society gives written authorisation.

Note: In situations (a)–(c) the record keeping requirements of Rule 32 must be complied with.

10.5.6   When can money be taken out of the client bank account? (Rule 22)

How much can be spent?

The solicitor must not withdraw more money from the client bank account than is being held there for a particular client (or controlled trust) (Rule 22(5)). For example, if a solicitor holds £500 for Client A and £300 for Client B in the client bank account, the solicitor can spend only £300 from the client bank account for Client B.

There is one limited exception provided by Rule 22(6). This allows the solicitor to make an excessive payment from the client bank account for a particular client or controlled trust *but only where* the solicitor holds sufficient money in a separate designated client bank account and immediately transfers sufficient money from the separate designated client bank account to the general client bank account.

Rule 22(8) states that a client bank account must not be overdrawn except in limited circumstances the most important of which is where a controlled trustee overdraws a separate designated client account for a controlled trust by making payments (eg for IHT) before selling sufficient trust assets to cover the payments.

For what purposes can money be withdrawn from the client bank accounts?

Client money can be withdrawn where it is:

- properly required for a payment to or on behalf of the client (or person for whom the money is held);
- properly required for payment of a disbursement on behalf of the client;
- properly required in full or partial reimbursement of money spent by the solicitor on behalf of the client – money is 'spent' when a cheque is dispatched or where liabilities dealt with by an account are incurred, eg search fees, taxi fares;
- transferred to another client account (eg a separate designated account);
- withdrawn on the client's instructions: the instructions must be in writing or be confirmed by the solicitor in writing;
- a repayment to the solicitor of money advanced by the solicitor to the client to fund a payment (under Rule 15(2)(6));
- money which has been paid into the account in error – it must be withdrawn 'promptly' (Rule 22(4));
- money withdrawn on the written authorisation of The Law Society.

Controlled trust money can be withdrawn in similar circumstances.

Office money can be withdrawn where it:

- was paid in to open or maintain an account and is no longer required;
- is properly required to pay a solicitor's 'costs' and the solicitor has delivered a bill or other written notification;
- was paid into the client bank account under Rule 19(1)(c) and needs to be withdrawn within 14 days (see below);
- was part of an unsplit cheque;
- was paid into the account in breach of Rules – it must be withdrawn 'promptly' (Rule 22(4)).

Note: Where a solicitor wants to transfer money for costs, the solicitor must deliver a bill or other written notification and must transfer the money within 14 days (Rule 19(2) and (3)).

How is the money withdrawn?

A withdrawal must be authorised by a suitable person; for example, a solicitor with a current practising certificate (see Rule 23(1)).

If the money is withdrawn in favour of the solicitor, the payment from the client bank account must be by cheque in favour of the solicitor or by transfer into the office bank account. It must not be in cash or a cheque in favour of a third party.

Example

A solicitor is owed £100 in profit costs by Client A and owes £100 to a tradesman. The solicitor is holding £500 of A's money in the client bank account.

Provided the solicitor delivers a bill or other written confirmation of costs, the solicitor can withdraw £100 of the money held for A from the client bank account.

However, it cannot be withdrawn in cash or by way of a cheque in favour of the tradesman. It must either be a cheque in favour of the solicitor or a transfer to the office bank account.

10.6 SPECIAL RULES ON DEALING WITH MONEY RECEIVED IN PAYMENT OF A BILL (RULES 19 AND 21)

Rule 19 is quite complicated and you need to study it carefully.

When a solicitor receives money in payment of a bill the solicitor has various options. These are set out below.

10.6.1 Determine the composition of the receipt without delay and deal with it appropriately (Rule 19(1)(a))

You need to remember Rule 13, which sets out the Rules on classification of money:

- In particular remember that *money* received *to repay* the solicitor for disbursements already paid is *office money*.
- Money received to cover the cost of *unpaid disbursements* where the solicitor has incurred liability to pay is *office money unless* the disbursements are *'professional disbursements'*.
- Money received for *unpaid professional disbursements* even where the solicitor has incurred liability to pay is *client money*.

When a solicitor is proceeding under Rule 19(1)(a), a receipt which is entirely office money will be paid into the office bank account.

A receipt which is entirely client money (for example, money for unpaid professional disbursements) will be paid into the client bank account.

A receipt which is a mixture of office and client money will be split or all paid into the client bank account.

Rule 19(b)–(d) goes on to give alternatives.

10.6.2 Receipts consisting of office money and client money in the form of unpaid professional disbursements for which the solicitor is liable (Rule 19(1)(b))

The solicitor can place the entire amount in the office bank account *provided* by the end of the second working day, following receipt, the solicitor either pays the professional disbursements or transfers the amount required for the disbursement to the client bank account.

The effect of this option is to make life a little easier for solicitors. Where a receipt consists only of these two elements, the whole amount can be paid into the office bank account. This reduces the number of transfers made between client and office bank account.

Note: This option cannot be used if liability for professional disbursements has not yet been incurred; nor where the receipt includes other client money.

10.6.3 Any receipt irrespective of its composition (Rule 19(1)(c))

A solicitor can always elect to pay any receipt irrespective of its composition into the client bank account. Any office money element *must* be transferred out of the client bank account within 14 days of receipt.

10.6.4 Receipts from the Legal Aid Board (Rule 19(1)(d))

These can be dealt with under Rule 21 which provides two special dispensations for payments made by the Board:

(a) A payment on account by the Board in anticipation of work to be carried out can be placed in the office bank account, provided the Board gives written instructions that it should be done.

(b) A payment by the Board for profit costs can be placed in the office bank account even when it is mixed with client money for unpaid disbursements or professional disbursements provided the disbursements are paid or the money for them transferred to the client bank account within 14 days of receipt.

Exercise 10C

A firm delivers a bill which consists of the following items:

	£
Firm's Professional Charges	200
VAT	35
Court Fees (Paid)	80
Land Charges Search (unpaid)*	20
Counsel's Fees (unpaid)*	470
	805

*The solicitor has incurred liability for these items.

What options are available to the firm when dealing with the receipt of £805?

10.7 DEPOSIT INTEREST

10.7.1 When must interest be paid?

Rule 24(1) provides that where a solicitor has chosen to open a separate deposit bank account designated with the name of the client (or controlled trust) any interest earned on that account must be accounted for to the client.

Rule 24(2) provides that where a solicitor has chosen to hold client money in the general client bank account, the solicitor must account for a sum in lieu of interest calculated in accordance with Rule 25 (see post) *unless* one of the conditions set out in Rule 24(3) is met.

The conditions set out in Rule 24(3) are:

(a)　The amount of interest calculated is £20 or less.

(b)　The amount held and the period for which it is held falls into the de minimis table set out below:

Amount not exceeding £	Time not exceeding weeks
1,000	8
2,000	4
10,000	2
20,000	1

Note: If the solicitor holds an amount exceeding £20,000 for a week or less it may still be fair and reasonable for interest to be paid.

(c)　The money is held for counsel's fees and counsel has requested a delay in settlement.

(d)　The money is held for the Legal Aid Board.

(e)　The money held in the client bank account represents a sum advanced by the solicitor under Rule 15(2)(b) to cover a disbursement for which there was insufficient client money available.

(f)　There is an agreement that interest shall not be paid.

10.7.2 How is interest calculated?

Solicitors must aim to obtain a reasonable rate of interest on separate designated deposit accounts and must account for a fair sum in lieu of interest on money held in a general client bank account. The sum in lieu of interest need not reflect the highest rate of interest available but it is not acceptable to look only at the lowest rate of interest available. It should be calculated at a rate not less than the higher of:

* the rate payable on a separate designated client account for the amount held;
* the rate payable on the relevant amount if placed on deposit on similar terms by a member of the business community.

10.7.3 Factors affecting choice of method

When the solicitor opens a separate designated deposit bank account the bank calculates the amount and pays the amount of interest earned. When one is not opened, the solicitor has to calculate the appropriate amount and pay it from the office bank account. It might seem therefore that it is always preferable to open a separate designated deposit account. However, this is not so.

A solicitor who opened a separate designated deposit bank account for every client for whom money was held would end up with an enormous number of different bank accounts which would be administratively inconvenient.

A solicitor is allowed under the Solicitors Act 1976 to put client money held in a general client bank account on deposit and keep any interest earned over and above what is required to be paid under the Rules. In general, the more money placed in a deposit account, the higher the rate of interest the solicitor is able to earn. This is likely to encourage the solicitor to use the second method.

10.7.4   Money of controlled trusts

The rules on interest do not apply to controlled trusts. The general law requires a solicitor to act in the best interest of a trust and not to profit from his position as a trustee. Thus, a solicitor should obtain the best rate of interest possible for a controlled trust and account to the trust for all interest earned. The options are therefore either:

(1)   to put the money of a controlled trust into a separate designated deposit account; or

(2)   to set up a general client bank account just for money of controlled trusts. The interest earned is office money and will be paid into the office bank account in the ordinary way but the solicitor must then allocate it to each controlled trust without delay.

The solicitor must be careful not to obtain an indirect benefit from the controlled trust money, eg by getting a higher rate of interest on other money because of the addition of the trust money.

10.8   WHAT RECORDS MUST A SOLICITOR KEEP?

10.8.1   Importance of records

The Law Society is just as concerned that solicitors should keep the correct records as that they should do the correct things. It is impossible to check what is happening if records are inadequate.

10.8.2   The basic records

Rule 32 sets out the basic requirements for everyday transactions.

(1)   A solicitor must at all times keep properly written up records to show dealings with:

- Client money held or paid by the solicitor.
  Note: This includes money withheld from the client bank account under Rule 16.
- Controlled trust money held or paid by the solicitor.
  Note: This includes money held in a non-client bank account.

(2)   All dealings with client money (and controlled trust money) must be recorded:

- in a client cash account or in a record of sums transferred from one client ledger account to another; and
- on the client columns of a client ledger account.

(3)   If separate designated client accounts are used:

- a combined account must show the total amount held in separate designated client accounts; and
- the amount held for each client must be shown either in the deposit column of a client ledger or on the client columns of a client ledger kept specifically for showing money held in a separate designated client account for each client.

(4) All dealings with office money relating to any client or controlled trust matter must be appropriately recorded in an office cash account and on the office side of columns of a client ledger account.

Solutions

Exercise 10A

(a) Office money. It is a specific payment of a bill.

(b) Client's money. It is generally on account of costs.

Exercise 10B

(a) No. The only person entitled to the money (until completion) is a partner in the firm.

(b) Yes. The partner in the firm is not the only person entitled to the money. The money is held jointly for both buyer and seller awaiting the event.

Exercise 10C

First identify the composition of the receipt.

- Professional charges and VAT – office money.
- Paid court fees – office money.
- Unpaid search fee – office money (liability has been incurred).
- Unpaid counsel's fee – client money (professional unpaid disbursements).

(1) Under Rule 19(1)(a) and Rule 20 the receipt can be split. The office money element is paid into the office bank account; the client money element into the client bank account. Alternatively the whole amount is paid into the client bank account but the office money element must be transferred out within 14 days.

(2) The whole amount can be paid into the office bank account under Rule 19(1)(b) provided the counsel's fee is paid or the money required for it is transferred to the client bank account by the end of the second working day following receipt.

Chapter 11

SIMPLE ENTRIES FOR SOLICITORS

11.1 THE TWO SETS OF ACCOUNTING RECORDS

In order to control dealings with client money, a more sophisticated set of accounts is needed for a firm of solicitors than for most other businesses. It is essential that all the records of 'client money' (client bank account) are clearly separated from the records of the ordinary 'office money' dealings of the firm.

One way of understanding the system is to think of yourself carrying on two separate businesses with two separate sets of accounts. Thus, you would need one set (Set A) for the first business – say the business which handles client money – and another set (Set B) for the second – say the firm's ordinary business accounts. This explains the reason for one of the fundamental bookkeeping rules for solicitors. The two sets of accounts are entirely separate. Thus, you cannot enter a debit on one set of accounts (Set A) and a credit on the other set (Set B).

11.2 THE FORMAT OF THE ACCOUNTS

11.2.1 Requirements

The rules do not specify any particular type of accounting system, and a solicitor can therefore choose any of the various systems on the market which enable the recording requirements of Rule 32 to be satisfied. These range from a conventional card system to sophisticated, computerised systems, but they all have one thing in common – they are based on the principles of double-entry bookkeeping.

11.2.2 The dual cash account

Anyone running a business will want to keep a cash account to record dealings in each bank account. A solicitor is *required* by Rule 32(2) to keep a cash account for dealings with the client bank account and by Rule 32(4) to keep a separate cash account for dealings with the office bank account. Thus, the solicitor will need (at least) two separate cash accounts. To ease the administrative burden of actually moving from a cash account in one place to another cash account in a different place and back again, the normal format is to have the two individual cash accounts on the same page next to one another. One set of columns for 'Date' and 'Details' will do for both accounts.

Cash account: office

Date	Details	DR	CR	BAL

Cash account: client

Date	Details	DR	CR	BAL

Cash account

Date	Details	Office account			Client account		
		DR	CR	BAL	DR	CR	BAL

11.2.3 The dual ledger account for each client

To comply with Rule 32(2) and (4) there must be one ledger account for each client to show dealings with office money on behalf of that client and another ledger account to show dealings with client money for that client. As with the two cash accounts, it is usual to combine the two ledger accounts to show them side by side.

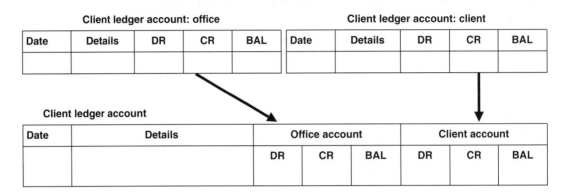

11.3 RECEIPTS

First decide whether you are receiving office money or client's money. The receipt can then be recorded in the correct section.

The entry in the cash account is a DR entry.

The corresponding CR entry is in the ledger account of the client from whom, or on whose behalf, the money is received.

If the receipt is into the office bank account, it will reduce the amount the client owes the firm (ie it will reduce the DR balance). If the receipt is into the client bank account, the resulting CR balance on the ledger account shows that the firm 'owes' the client money, ie the client is a *creditor* of the firm.

Example

Client Jones owes firm £100. (This means there is a DR balance on the office columns of Jones's ledger account.) Solicitor receives £20 from client Jones. Solicitor decides that it is a receipt of office money.

DR Cash account
CR Jones ledger account } Office section

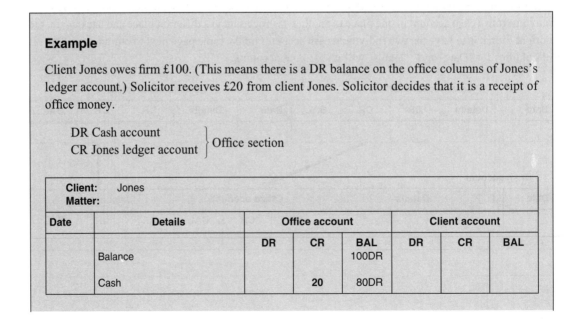

Cash account								
Date	Details	Office account			Client account		
		DR	CR	BAL	DR	CR	BAL
	Balance			xxx			xxx
	Jones	20		xxx			

Example

Solicitor receives £300 from client Brown. Solicitor decides that it is a receipt of client money:

DR Cash account
CR Brown ledger account } Client section

Client: Brown Matter:								
Date	Details	Office account			Client account		
		DR	CR	BAL	DR	CR	BAL
	Cash					300	300CR

Cash account								
Date	Details	Office account			Client account		
		DR	CR	BAL	DR	CR	BAL
	Balance						xxx
	Brown				300		xxx

11.4 PAYMENTS

First, decide whether you are making the payment from the office or client bank account so that the payment can be recorded in the appropriate cash account.

The entry on the cash account is a CR entry.

The corresponding double entry is a DR in the ledger account of the client on whose behalf the payment is made.

If the payment is made from the office bank account the resulting DR balance will show that the client owes the firm money, ie is *a debtor*. If the payment is made from the client bank account it will reduce the amount held for the client (ie it will reduce the CR balance).

Remember that under Rule 22(5) a payment cannot be made from the client bank account unless the firm is holding sufficient funds in the client bank account for that client.

Example

Solicitor pays court fees of £40 on behalf of client Black. The solicitor holds no client money for Black so must make the payment using office money:

CR Cash account
DR Black ledger account } Office section

Client: Black
Matter:

Date	Details	Office account			Client account		
		DR	CR	BAL	DR	CR	BAL
	Cash	40		40DR			

Cash account

Date	Details	Office account			Client account		
		DR	CR	BAL	DR	CR	BAL
	Balance			xxx			
	Black		40	xxx			

Example

Solicitor is holding client money of £500 for client White. Solicitor makes a payment of £500 for client White.

The solicitor holds sufficient client money for White to be able to make the payment using client money.

CR Cash account
DR White ledger account } Client section

Client: White
Matter:

Date	Details	Office account			Client account		
		DR	CR	BAL	DR	CR	BAL
	Balance						500CR
	Cash				500		–

Cash account

Date	Details	Office account			Client account		
		DR	CR	BAL	DR	CR	BAL
	Balance						xxx
	White					500	xxx

Exercise 11A

You act for Smith. Record the following events on Smith's ledger account and on the cash account.

Note: Assume that the balances on the cash account are office £1,000 DR, client £20,000 DR. Assume the balances on Smith's ledger account are zero.

June

1	Smith sends £1,000 generally on account of costs.

Note: This is a receipt of client money because it is not in payment of a bill for profit costs nor in reimbursement of an expense.

2   Firm pays £100 on Smith's behalf.

Note: This can be paid from the client bank account since sufficient funds are available.

4   Firm pays £900 on Smith's behalf.

Note: This can be paid from the client bank account since sufficient funds are available.

6   Firm pays £200 on Smith's behalf.

Note: This must be paid from the office bank account since no funds are held for Smith.

8   Firm pays £400 on Smith's behalf.

Note: This must be paid from the office bank account since no funds are held for Smith.

10   Smith sends firm £600 in reimbursement of expenses incurred.

Note: Subject to Rule 19(1)(c), this must be paid into the office bank account since it is a receipt of office money.

11.5 PROFIT COSTS

When the solicitor sends a bill to the client, it will include an item for professional charges. The solicitor will want to make entries in the accounts to show that the client now owes the firm money.

Note: At this stage there is no movement of cash so no entry is made in the cash account.

On the client ledger account, the bookkeeper must make DR entries for profit costs and VAT. The entries must be made in the office section (even if the solicitor holds client's money). This is because the purpose of the DR entries is to show that the client has incurred a debt to the firm.

The corresponding CR entries are made on the profit costs account and Customs & Excise account respectively.

Example

Solicitor sends a bill for £400 profit costs plus £70 VAT to client Smith:

     DR Smith ledger account £400
     DR Smith ledger account £70

     CR Costs account £400
     CR Customs & Excise account £70

(See Chapter 13 for details of VAT – Value Added Tax.)

Client: Smith
Matter:

Date	Details	Office account			Client account		
		DR	CR	BAL	DR	CR	BAL
	Costs	400		400DR			
	VAT	70		470			

Costs

Date	Details	DR	CR	BAL
	Smith		400	400CR

Customs & Excise

Date	Details	DR	CR	BAL
	Smith		70	70CR

Exercise 11B

Prepare the cash account and client ledger account for X to record the following events.

Solicitor acts for X in a litigation matter. The balances on the cash account are office £1,000DR, client £1,000DR. The balances on X's ledger account are zero.

June

1   X sends solicitor £200 on account of costs.
    Note: This is a receipt of client money because it is not in payment of a bill nor in reimbursement of an expense.

2   Solicitor pays court fees £20.
    Note: This can be paid from the client bank account since sufficient funds are available.

5   Solicitor pays expert witness £180.
    Note: This can be paid from the client bank account since sufficient funds are available.

7   Solicitor pays another expert witness £150.
    Note: There is no client money available. The payment must be made from the office bank account.

10 Matter is settled. Solicitor receives a cheque from the defendant for £5,000 in full and final settlement. This cheque is made out to the firm.
    Note: The firm has received client money. (Had the cheque been made out to the client the firm would simply have forwarded it to the client. It would not have been possible to pay the cheque into a bank account in the firm's name.) The solicitor could split the cheque and take £150 in reimbursement of the expense incurred. However, we will pay it all into the client bank account.

12 Solicitor sends client a cheque for £5,000.
    Note: This is a payment of client money.

14   Solicitor sends X a bill. Profit costs £200. VAT £35. Solicitor asks for the amount necessary to reimburse him for expenses incurred.

16   X sends solicitor amount requested on 14 June.

        Note: X will send £385 (£235 + £150) and this will be a receipt of office money. Subject to Rule 19(1)(c), it must be paid into the office bank account.

Solutions

Exercise 11A

Client:	Smith							
Matter:								

Date	Details	Office account			Client account		
		DR	CR	BAL	DR	CR	BAL
June							
1	Cash. On a/c costs					1,000	1,000CR
2	Cash				100		900
4	Cash				900		—
6	Cash	200		200DR			
8	Cash	400		600			
10	Cash		600	—			

Cash account							

Date	Details	Office account			Client account		
		DR	CR	BAL	DR	CR	BAL
June	Balances			1,000DR			20,000DR
1	Smith. On a/c costs				1,000		21,000
2	Smith					100	20,900
4	Smith					900	20,000
6	Smith		200	800			
8	Smith		400	400			
10	Smith. Reimbursement expenses	600		1,000			

Exercise 11B

Client:	X
Matter:	Litigation

Date	Details	Office account			Client account		
		DR	CR	BAL	DR	CR	BAL
June							
1	Cash. On a/c costs					200	200CR
2	Cash. Court fees				20		180
5	Cash. Expert witness				180		—
7	Cash. Expert witness	150		150DR			—
10	Cash. Settlement					5,000	5,000
12	Cash. To client				5,000		—
14	Costs	200					
	VAT	35		385			
16	Cash. Amount due		385	—			

Cash account							

Date	Details	Office account			Client account		
		DR	CR	BAL	DR	CR	BAL
June	Balance						
				1,000DR			1,000DR
1	X. On a/c costs				200		1,200
2	X. Court fees					20	1,180
5	X. Expert witness					180	1,000
7	X. Expert witness		150	850			
10	X. Settlement				5,000		6,000
12	X. Amount sent					5,000	1,000
16	X. Amount requested	385		1,235			

Chapter 12

SOLICITORS' ACCOUNTS – TRANSFERS

12.1 THE TWO TYPES OF TRANSFER

The first type of transfer involves the bank moving money from one bank account to another. It occurs when the solicitor instructs the bank to transfer money from the client bank account to the office bank account, or from the office bank account to the client bank account. The solicitor must make entries on the firm's internal cash accounts and client ledger to reflect the fact that money has actually moved between bank accounts.

The second type does not involve the bank moving money from one bank account to another. It occurs when a solicitor who is holding money in the client bank account for one client is instructed to stop holding the money to the order of the first client and to start holding it to the order of a second client. This type of transfer is called an inter-client transfer. To comply with the Rules and to keep the solicitor's internal records accurate, the solicitor must make entries on the ledger accounts of the two clients to show how much is held for each. No entries are made on the firm's internal cash account since there has been no movement of cash in the firm's bank accounts.

12.2 TRANSFERS BETWEEN CLIENT BANK ACCOUNT AND OFFICE BANK ACCOUNT

12.2.1 Why might such a transfer occur?

(1) A solicitor can transfer client money from the client bank account to the office bank account to reimburse the solicitor for money spent by the solicitor on behalf of the client. It is not necessary for the solicitor to deliver a bill of costs before making the transfer. Money is 'spent' for this purpose when the solicitor incurs liability for the expense, eg by charging an amount for taxi fares or search fees to the firm's account.

The money in the client bank account is client money until the solicitor decides to make reimbursement so there is no requirement to make the transfer within 14 days of incurring liability for the expense.

Note: Similar Rules apply to controlled trust money.

(2) A solicitor can transfer money from the client bank account to the office bank account for the solicitor's own professional fees including any VAT element, provided a bill has been sent (or a fee agreed in accordance with Rule 19(5));

(3) A solicitor can transfer office money to the client bank account in the circumstances set out in Rule 15:

- to open or maintain the client bank account;
- to advance money to a client or controlled trust where the solicitor needs to make a payment on behalf of the client or trust and insufficient client or trust money is available (once advanced the money becomes client or controlled trust money);

- to replace money withdrawn in error;
- in lieu of interest.

12.2.2 Recording the transfer

This is done in two parts, as follows.

(1) The solicitor records the withdrawal of money from the client bank account:

CR cash account
DR client's ledger account } Client section

(2) The solicitor records the receipt of money into the office bank account:

DR cash account
CR client's ledger account } Office section

Example

You act for Green. On 10 April you receive £800 from Green on account of costs to be incurred. On 26 April you send Green a bill for £400 plus £70 VAT. On 28 April you transfer £470 from the client bank account to the office bank account.

Entries are as follows.

(1) The £800 is client's money. It will be paid into the client bank account and recorded in Green's ledger account and in the cash account.

Client: Green
Matter: Miscellaneous

Date	Details	Office account			Client account		
		DR	CR	BAL	DR	CR	BAL
Apr 10	Cash. From Green. On account.					800	800CR

Cash account

Date	Details	Office account			Client account		
		DR	CR	BAL	DR	CR	BAL
Apr 10	Green				800		xxx

(2) When the bill is sent the entries for costs and VAT will be DR entries on Green's ledger account (remember that costs and VAT are always debited in the *office* section).

The CR entries will be on the costs and Customs & Excise account which we have not shown.

Client: Green Matter: Miscellaneous		Office account			Client account		
Date	Details	DR	CR	BAL	DR	CR	BAL
Apr 10 26	Cash. From Green. On account. Costs VAT	**400** **70**		400DR 470		800	800CR

Cash account		Office account			Client account		
Date	Details	DR	CR	BAL	DR	CR	BAL
Apr 10	Green				800		xxx

(3) The withdrawal from client account will look like this:

Client: Green Matter: Miscellaneous		Office account			Client account		
Date	Details	DR	CR	BAL	DR	CR	BAL
Apr 10 26 28	Cash. From Green. On account. Costs VAT Cash. Transfer from client account	400 70		400DR 470	 470	800	800CR 330

Cash account		Office account			Client account		
Date	Details	DR	CR	BAL	DR	CR	BAL
Apr 10 28	Green Green				800	470	xxx

(4) The receipt into office account will look like this:

Client: Green Matter: Miscellaneous		Office account			Client account		
Date	Details	DR	CR	BAL	DR	CR	BAL
Apr 10 26 28	Cash. From Green. On account. Costs VAT Cash. Transfer from client account Cash. Transfer to office account	400 70	 **470**	400DR 470 — 	 470	800	800CR 330

Cash account							
Date	**Details**	**Office account**			**Client account**		
		DR	**CR**	**BAL**	**DR**	**CR**	**BAL**
Apr							xxx
10	Green				800		
28	Green					470	
	Green	470					

Note: For the sake of convenience, the withdrawal from the client bank account and the receipt into the office bank account are often shown on the same line like this:

Client: Green **Matter:** Miscellaneous							
Date	**Details**	**Office account**			**Client account**		
		DR	**CR**	**BAL**	**DR**	**CR**	**BAL**
Apr							
10	Cash. From Green. On account.					800	800CR
26	Costs	400		400DR			
	VAT	70		470			
28	Cash. Transfer from client account to office account		470	—	470		330

Cash account							
Date	**Details**	**Office account**			**Client account**		
		DR	**CR**	**BAL**	**DR**	**CR**	**BAL**
Apr							xxx
10	Green				800		
18	Green. Transfer from client to office account	470				470	

12.3   INTER-CLIENT TRANSFERS

12.3.1   What is happening?

Sometimes, a solicitor who is holding money in the client bank account for Client A stops holding that money for Client A and starts holding it for Client B. An example would be where A owes B money and asks the solicitor to hold the money for B. No money is taken out of the client bank account. The solicitor is simply complying with the requirement in Rule 1(g) to show accurately the position with regard to the money held for each client.

12.3.2   Requirements

The transfer must comply with Rule 30. This means that the solicitor can only make the paper entries if the money could have been:

*   withdrawn from the client bank account on the instructions of the first client under Rule 22(1); and
*   paid into the client bank account on the instructions of the second client under Rule 15.

If the transfer is a 'private loan' the solicitor must have the prior written authority of both clients. This is not necessary if the transfer is for other purposes, eg a gift or in discharge of a debt. A private loan is any loan other than one provided by an institution which provides loans on standard terms in the normal course of its activities.

12.3.3 Recording the transfer

The transfer must be shown in the client ledger account:

DR Client ledger account of first client
CR Client ledger account of second client

In addition, to comply with Rule 32(2), it is necessary to keep a separate record. This will usually be referred to as a 'transfer journal' or a 'transfer sheet'.

Example

You are instructed by Anne Brown to collect a debt of £10,000 from White & Co. You write to White & Co requesting payment. On 7 August you receive a cheque from White & Co for £10,000 in payment of the debt.

You already act for Anne's sister, Jane Brown, who is buying a flat. On 9 August, Anne tells you that she is making a gift of £1,000 to Jane and asks you to hold £1,000 of her money to the order of Jane. You make the necessary inter-client transfer.

Entries are as follows.

(1) When the £10,000 is received it is client money held to the order of Anne. It will be recorded like this:

Cash account								
Date	Details	Office account			Client account		
		DR	CR	BAL	DR	CR	BAL
Aug 7	Anne Brown				10,000		xxx

Client: Anne Brown Matter: Debt collection								
Date	Details	Office account			Client account		
		DR	CR	BAL	DR	CR	BAL
Aug 7	Cash. From White & Co. Debt					10,000	10,000CR

(2) When Anne instructs you to hold £1,000 to the order of Jane, there will be no entry on the cash account. There will be the following entries on the ledger accounts of Anne and Jane:

Client: Anne Brown Matter: Debt collection								
Date	Details	Office account			Client account		
		DR	CR	BAL	DR	CR	BAL
Aug 7	Cash. From White & Co. Debt					10,000	10,000CR
9	Jane Brown. Transfer (TJ)				1,000		9,000

Client: Jane Brown							
Matter: Litigation							
Date	Details	Office account			Client account		
		DR	CR	BAL	DR	CR	BAL
Aug 9	Anne Brown. Transfer (TJ)					1,000	1,000CR

There will be a record on the transfer journal. You can include the initials 'TJ' in the details columns of the client ledger but this is not essential. It *is* essential to give the name of the ledger account where the other part of the double entry is made.

Exercise 12A

You are a solicitor. The following events occur:

February

1   You receive £800 generally on account of costs from your client Dean.

4   You pay a court fee of £100 (no VAT) on behalf of your client Wade.

5   You receive £7,000 on behalf of your client Will. It is a debt collected.

8   You agree to act for Simon. You ask for £300 generally on account of costs. Dean tells you that he is prepared to lend Simon the money for this. Dean and Simon instruct you in writing to make the necessary transfer.

11   You send a bill to Will. Your costs are £440 plus £77 VAT. You transfer the costs from the client bank account to the office bank account.

13   You send a bill to Wade for £200 plus £35 VAT. Will, who is Wade's uncle, instructs you to transfer an amount sufficient to pay Wade's indebtedness to you from the amount you are holding for Will. It is a gift from Will to Wade.

14   You send Dean a bill for £600 plus £105 VAT. You transfer the remaining money held for him in the client bank account in part payment of the bill.

Explain the application of the Rules to each transaction and prepare the clients' ledger accounts and the cash account.

(See overleaf for solution.)

Solutions

Exercise 12A

1 February	The money is client money. You must pay it into the client bank account (Rule 15).

1 February   The money is client money. You must pay it into the client bank account (Rule 15).

4 February   You are holding no money for Wade, so you must pay the money out of the office bank account (Rule 22(5)).

5 February   The money is client money. You must pay it into the client bank account (Rule 15).

8 February   Rule 30 applies. Written instructions are needed for a private loan from one client to another (Rule 30(2)). The money could be withdrawn from the client bank account on Dean's instructions (Rule 22(1)) and could be received into client bank account on Simon's instructions (Rule 15). Thus Rule 30 is satisfied and the inter-client transfer can be made. A record must be made in the transfer journal (Rule 32(2)).

11 February   **The bill**   DR Will's ledger account office section with costs and VAT. CR costs account and HM Customs & Excise ledger account respectively.

                 The transfer   The withdrawal from the client bank account and transfer to the office bank account is allowed by Rule 22(3)(b).

13 February   **The bill**   DR Wade's ledger account office section with costs and VAT. CR costs account and Customs & Excise ledger account respectively.

                 The transfer   Rule 30 is not satisfied. The money could be withdrawn from the client bank account on Will's instructions, but it could not be paid into the *client* bank account on Wade's instructions because it is being received specifically in payment of your bill. This is, therefore, office money and, as such, should be paid into the office bank account. You must therefore pay the money out of the client bank account on behalf of Will and receive it into the office bank account on behalf of Wade.

14 February   **The bill**   Entries as above.

                 The transfer   Rule 22(3)(b) applies. The entries are the same as those on 11 February.

                 Note: When Dean pays the balance, the money received will be office money and must be paid straight into the office bank account (unless it is dealt with under Rule 19(1)(c)).

The accounts are shown below.

Client: Dean
Matter: Miscellaneous

Date	Details	Office account			Client account		
		DR	CR	BAL	DR	CR	BAL
Feb							
1	Cash. From Dean.						
	Generally on account					800	800CR
8	Simon. Transfer (TJ)				300		500
14	Costs	600		600DR			
	C&E: VAT	105		705			
	Cash. Transfer from client						
	to office account		500	205	500		—

| Client: | Wade | | | | | | |
| Matter: | Miscellaneous | | | | | | |

Date	Details	Office account			Client account		
		DR	CR	BAL	DR	CR	BAL
Feb							
4	Cash. Court fee	100		100DR			
13	Costs	200		300			
	C&E: VAT	35		335			
	Cash. Transfer from Will		335	—			

| Client: | Will | | | | | | |
| Matter: | Miscellaneous | | | | | | |

Date	Details	Office account			Client account		
		DR	CR	BAL	DR	CR	BAL
Feb							
5	Cash. Debt collected					7,000	7,000CR
11	Costs	440		440DR			
	C&E: VAT	77		517			
	Cash. Transfer costs from						
	client to office account		517	—	517		6,483
13	Cash. From client to						
	office account for Wade				335		6,148

| Client: | Simon | | | | | | |
| Matter: | Miscellaneous | | | | | | |

Date	Details	Office account			Client account		
		DR	CR	BAL	DR	CR	BAL
Feb							
8	Dean. Transfer (TJ)					300	300CR

Cash account							

Date	Details	Office account			Client account		
		DR	CR	BAL	DR	CR	BAL
Feb							xxx
1	Dean				800		
4	Wade		100				
5	Will				7,000		
11	Will	517				517	
13	Will					335	
	Wade	335					
14	Dean	500				500	

Chapter 13

VALUE ADDED TAX

13.1 GENERAL PRINCIPLES

VAT involves two distinct aspects: output tax (charged by a business to its customers) and input tax (charged to the business by its suppliers). A business registered for VAT charges its customers output tax and then accounts to HM Customs & Excise for tax. In other words, it acts as an unpaid tax collector. It will normally be possible for such a business to deduct input tax charged to the business from the amount accounted for to HM Customs & Excise. See **13.1.2**.

13.1.1 Output tax

VAT is chargeable on the supply of goods or services where the supply is a taxable supply and is made by a taxable person in the course or furtherance of a business carried on by him (Value Added Tax Act (VATA) 1994, s 4(1)). Each element of this definition will be considered further below.

The person making the supply is liable to account to HM Customs & Excise for the amount of tax which he charges.

(1) Supply of goods
This comprises all forms of supply whereby the whole property in goods is transferred, including a gift of goods.

(2) Supply of services
This is anything which is not a supply of goods, but is done for a consideration. Note that a gratuitous supply of services is not a supply for VAT purposes, in contrast to a gift of goods.

(3) Taxable supply
This means any supply of goods or services other than an exempt supply. Exempt supplies are listed in VATA 1994, Sch 9, and include supplies of land (except for commercial purposes), insurance, postal services, finance, health services and burial and cremation.

Taxable supplies may be divided into two categories:

(1) those which are chargeable at the standard rate of 17.5%; and
(2) those which are chargeable at a zero rate. Zero-rated supplies are listed in VATA 1994, Sch 8, and include supplies of food, water, books, international services and transport.

Zero-rated and exempt supplies are similar in that no VAT is actually charged in either case by the supplier to his customer.

However, they must be carefully distinguished since only a person who makes taxable supplies is able to recover input tax, ie the VAT charged to him by his suppliers.

A solicitor supplying legal services will be making a standard-rated supply. Legal services include profit costs and *some* disbursements (see below). A solicitor supplying insurance will be making an exempt supply.

(4) Taxable person

A person is a taxable person if he *is* or *is required to be* registered under the Act. A person must register if, broadly, the value of his taxable supplies (*not* his profit) in the preceding 12 months exceeded a figure specified in each year's Budget, currently £51,000. A firm of solicitors will virtually always have to be registered.

Notice that voluntary registration is permitted. A person may register voluntarily in order to recover input tax charged to him.

(5) Business

VAT is chargeable by a taxable person only on taxable supplies made in the course or furtherance of a business carried on by him.

'Business' includes any trade, profession or vocation, but the term is not limited to these activities since it also covers, for example, the provision by certain clubs and associations of facilities to members.

Furthermore, although the services of an employee are not generally taxable, the Act provides that where a person, in the course of carrying on a trade, profession or vocation, accepts any office, any services supplied by him as holder of the office shall be treated as supplied in the course of a business carried on by him and are therefore chargeable with VAT.

A solicitor who is a taxable person must charge VAT not only on his supplies of professional services but also on any other supplies he makes in the course of his business, eg the sale of redundant office equipment.

13.1.2 Input tax

Where VAT is charged on the supply to a taxable person of any goods or services for the purposes of his business, he may generally deduct such tax from the amount of output tax for which he is liable to account to HM Customs & Excise (s 25(2)). Since input tax charged to a taxable person is recoverable by him, it follows that VAT is not an expense of a person who makes only taxable supplies, whether at the standard or zero rate.

A person who makes only exempt supplies is not a taxable person and so is unable to recover any input tax.

Example

A, an undertaker, and B, a bookseller, each buy stationery for £200 + £35 VAT. The bookseller can recover the VAT, therefore the expense to be charged to the Profit and Loss Account is only £200. The undertaker cannot recover the VAT and, therefore, the expense to be charged to the Profit and Loss Account is £235.

Where a taxable person makes both taxable and exempt supplies, he is then partly exempt and may only recover a proportion of the input tax charged to him. A solicitor who supplies insurance may find himself in this position.

Where the exempt supplies made by a taxable person fall within certain de minimis limits, they can be ignored, with the result that all his input tax is recoverable.

13.1.3 Value of supply

Where a supply is fully taxable, VAT at the rate of 17.5% is payable on the value of the supply. If the consideration is in money, the value of the supply is such amount as, with the addition of the total tax payable, is equal to the consideration (s 19(2)).

If a price or fee is agreed, this will be deemed to include VAT unless expressly stated to be tax exclusive.

Exercise 13A

A solicitor agrees to provide a legal service for client X for £200. How much will be recorded as profit costs and how much as VAT?

13.1.4 Time of supply

The importance of the time of supply (or tax point) is that it decides the quarter at the end of which a taxable person becomes liable to account for output tax on a particular supply. It also determines the quarter in which a taxable person can claim input tax on a taxable supply made to him. The basic tax points are as follows:

- **Goods** When the goods are removed or made available to the purchaser (s 6(2)).
- **Services** When the services are completed (s 6(3)).

These basic tax points will be varied in the following cases:

- If within 14 days after the basic tax point the supplier issues a tax invoice, the date of the invoice will become the tax point unless a longer period has been agreed with HM Customs & Excise (s 6(5) and (6)). In the case of solicitors, HM Customs & Excise have approved a general extension of the 14-day period to one of 3 months, so that, provided solicitors deliver their bills within 3 months of completion of their services, the date of each bill will be the tax point.
- If, before a basic tax point arises, the supplier issues a tax invoice or receives payment, the supply will, to the extent covered by the invoice or payment, be treated as taking place at the date of the invoice or payment (s 6(4)).

13.1.5 Tax invoices

Such invoices are of vital importance to a taxable person since they are evidence of his right to recover the input tax on a supply made to him, ie without such an invoice he will generally be unable to claim an input credit, irrespective of whether or not he has made payment to the supplier.

A taxable person making a taxable supply to another taxable person must, within 30 days after the time of supply (or within such longer period as HM Customs & Excise allow), provide him with a tax invoice which must state the following particulars:

- an identifying number;
- the date of the supply, ie the tax point;
- the supplier's name, address and VAT registration number;
- the name and address of the person to whom the supply is made;
- the type of supply, eg sale, loan, hire;
- the description of the goods or services supplied;
- the quantity of goods or the extent of the services and the amount (excluding VAT) payable for each description;

- the total amount payable (excluding VAT);
- the rate of cash discount;
- the rate and amount of tax charged.

13.1.6   Collection and accounts

Accounting for VAT will generally be by reference to quarterly accounting periods. Within one month after the end of each quarter, a taxable person must send a completed return form to HM Customs & Excise together with a remittance for the tax due. The amount payable, ie total output tax charged less deductible input tax, is obtained from a statutory VAT account which is required to be kept by every taxable person for each tax period. Apart from these details of the tax due, the return form must also contain a list of the tax exclusive value of all outputs, and also the total of all inputs exclusive of tax.

There are proposals to move from a quarterly to a yearly accounting system.

Example

(a)   During an accounting period, a firm of solicitors sends bills charging total profit costs of £200,000 plus output tax of £35,000. In the same period, the firm buys office equipment for £40,000 plus input tax of £7,000.

The firm accounts to HM Customs & Excise as follows:

	£
Output tax charged	35,000
less input tax suffered	(7,000)
Payable to C&E	28,000

(b)   During an accounting period, a retailer sells food for £50,000 plus output VAT at the zero rate. In the same period, the retailer buys equipment for £10,000 plus input tax of £1,750.

The retailer accounts to HM Customs & Excise as follows:

	£
Output tax charged	0
less input tax suffered	(1,750)
Recovered from C&E	1,750

Note: In both these examples the supplier can recover the input tax paid because the supplier is making taxable supplies, even though, in the case of the retailer, they are at the zero rate.

(c)   A funeral director sends bills for burial and cremation totalling £150,000. No VAT is charged as these are exempt supplies. During the same period, the funeral director buys equipment for £15,000 plus input tax of £2,625.

The funeral director is not a taxable person and so does not account to HM Customs & Excise. Therefore, the funeral director cannot recover the input tax paid.

13.2   VAT AND THE SOLICITOR

13.2.1   Professional charges

Solicitors must charge VAT on their supply of services.

Example

Bill	£
Professional charges	100.00
VAT @ 17.5%	17.50
Total	117.50

Entries: The solicitor will need a ledger account in the name of HM Customs & Excise, as well as a costs account and a ledger account in the name of the client.

   CR   Costs
   CR   Customs & Excise
   DR   Client ledger (office section) with costs and VAT as separate amounts

Client: Matter:							
Date	Details	Office account			Client account		
		DR	CR	BAL	DR	CR	BAL
	Costs	100		100DR			
	VAT	17.50		117.50			

13.2.2   What are disbursements?

As a matter of convenience for the client, solicitors frequently pay expenses (eg court fees) on behalf of the client. Such expenses are often referred to as 'disbursements'. It would be unduly harsh if HM Customs & Excise treated such items as part of the supply of services and required the solicitor to charge VAT on such expenses. HM Customs & Excise do not regard 'disbursements' as part of the solicitor's supply of services. However, an item can only be treated as a 'disbursement', if it is what HM Customs & Excise regard as a disbursement.

Payments may be treated as disbursements if all the following conditions are satisfied.

- The solicitor acted as agent for his client when paying the third party.
- The client actually received and used the goods or services provided by the third party to the solicitor. This is the condition which usually prevents the solicitor's own travelling expenses, telephone bills, postage, etc, being treated as disbursements for VAT purposes.
- The client was responsible for paying the third party.
- The client authorised the solicitor to make payment on his behalf.
- The client knew that the goods or services would be provided by a third party.
- The solicitor's outlay must be separately itemised when invoicing the client.
- The solicitor must recover only the exact amount paid to the third party.

Thus, it can be seen that many payments made by a solicitor on his client's behalf can be regarded as disbursements for tax purposes.

Items normally and necessarily part of the service rendered by the solicitor to his clients, eg telephone charges, postage and photocopying charges are overheads of the business, and HM Customs & Excise require solicitors to charge VAT on them. As a general rule, travelling expenses incurred by a solicitor are not disbursements and must be included as part of the solicitor's overall charge. This view was upheld in the case of *Rowe & Maw v C&E Commissioners* [1975] STC 340. The court held that the cost of fares incurred by the solicitor was incurred for the solicitor not for the client. Many firms do not include a separate item on the bill for post, fares, photocopying and telephone but include them in the figure charged for profit costs.

In such a case, since VAT is charged on profit costs, VAT will inevitably be charged on the post, fares, photocopying and telephone element. Where a separate mention is made of such elements the firm must remember to charge VAT on the separate elements.

The Law Society's view is that it is not normally appropriate to make a separate charge for such items, although there may be exceptional cases where it is appropriate to do so.

Example

(1) You send a bill to your client Wright. The following is an extract:

'Professional charges ...

[Details of the work are set out]

	£
Profit costs	800
VAT @ 17.5%	140
Post, fares and telephone calls	40
VAT @ 17.5%	7

In Wright's ledger account, it is simplest to DR £840 as profit costs and £147 as VAT.

(2) Alternatively, the bill could have appeared as follows:

'To professional charges ...

[Details of the work are set out]

	£
Profit costs	840
VAT	147

13.2.3   The treatment of disbursements

The solicitor simply passes on the cost to the client. The payment may be for an item which is non-taxable or which includes its own VAT.

(1)   Non-taxable

These are payments for something not subject to VAT such as exempt supplies and supplies not in the course of business, eg court fees, stamp duty, land registry fees, search fees, etc.

The solicitor can pay these out of the client bank account if there is sufficient money in the client bank account. Otherwise they are paid out of the office bank account.

In neither case does the solicitor pay VAT to the supplier or charge the client VAT when obtaining reimbursement.

(2) *Taxable*

These are payments made by the solicitor to a taxable person in respect of taxable supplies (eg counsel, surveyor, accountant, estate agent, etc). The payment made by the solicitor will include a VAT element. That VAT element must be passed on to the client. The solicitor does not charge the client any additional VAT.

There are two methods of doing this. The choice depends on whether the original supplier addressed the invoice to the solicitor or to the client. If addressed to the solicitor, the **'principal'** method must be used; if addressed to the client, the **'agency'** method must be used.

- **Agency method**
  If the invoice is addressed to the client, the supply is treated as made to the client. The solicitor simply acts as the agent, handing over the money on behalf of the client. If there is sufficient client money standing to the credit of the client, the payment can be made from the client bank account; otherwise it must be made from the office bank account.

  The solicitor does not separate the fee and VAT on the ledger account or cash account, but instead debits the tax inclusive amount as a global sum. If the payment is made out of office money then the solicitor will seek reimbursement of the tax inclusive amount, again without separating the fee and the VAT.

  The solicitor must send the supplier's tax invoice to the client, if asked. If the client is registered for VAT and the supply is in the course or furtherance of a business, the invoice can be used by the client to recover the input tax.

Example

A solicitor pays an expert witness's bill on behalf of a client. The bill is for £1,000 plus £175 VAT. The invoice is addressed to the client and is paid using the agency method.

The solicitor simply pays the total sum of £1,175 and does not distinguish between the fee and the VAT. Whether the payment was made out of office money or client money the solicitor will charge the client £1,175, again without distinguishing between fee and VAT.

If the expert gave the invoice to the solicitor, the solicitor must send the client the expert's original invoice. The invoice is addressed to the client and so the client can claim an input if the client is registered for VAT.

- **Principal method**
  If the invoice is addressed to the solicitor, the supply is treated as made to the solicitor in the first instance. The solicitor therefore pays the supplier's fees together with the input tax charged from the office bank account.

  The solicitor then resupplies the item to the client at the VAT exclusive price. The solicitor will charge output tax on the firm's professional charges *and* on the disbursement.

  If the client is entitled to a tax invoice the solicitor will provide one to cover both the professional charges and the disbursement.

Example

A solicitor receives an expert witness's invoice for £200 plus £35 VAT. The solicitor pays:

	£
Expert's fee	200
plus input tax	35
	235

The solicitor records the fee and the VAT as separate items on the cash account.

The VAT is recorded on the HM Customs & Excise account. The tax exclusive amount is recorded on the client ledger account.

When the solicitor later charges the client his own profit costs of £400 the bill will include:

	£
Expert's fee	200
Profit costs	400
plus output tax (£35 + £70)	105

Once again, the fee and the VAT are separate items.

Note: A disbursement paid on the principal method must be paid out of the office bank account, even if there is client money available. This is because the supply is treated as made to the solicitor and not to the client.

The solicitor can transfer money from the client to the office bank account to reimburse himself once the expense is paid.

(3)   A summary

As students generally find principal method disbursements difficult to deal with, we have included the following summary:

(1)   Identify that the disbursement is to be treated on the principal basis – if the invoice is addressed to the solicitor it will be treated on the principal basis.

(2)   CR tax inclusive amount to cash account office section – it is common, but not essential, to show the two elements separately.

(3)   DR VAT to Customs & Excise ledger.

DR VAT exclusive amount to client ledger office section.

Make a memorandum note in the 'Details' column of the client ledger of the amount of VAT which must be added to the VAT charged to the client when bill is delivered.

(4)   When bill is delivered add the VAT on the principal method disbursement to the VAT on the profit costs and make the normal entries for delivery of a bill.

DR, client ledger office section, with VAT and costs as two separate amounts.

CR, the costs account and Customs & Excise account, with costs and VAT respectively.

(4)   Counsel's fees – concessionary treatment

A concessionary treatment for counsel's fees was agreed between Customs & Excise, The Law Society and the Bar when VAT was first introduced, and was published in [1973] *Gazette*, 4 April.

The agent (usually a solicitor or accountant) may treat counsel's advice as supplied directly to the client and the settlement of the fees as an agency method disbursement. Counsel's VAT invoice may be amended by adding the name and address of the client and inserting 'per' before the agent's own name and address. The fee note from counsel will then be recognised as a valid VAT invoice in the hands of the client. Where the agent considers that the services of counsel, if supplied directly to the client, would be outside the scope of UK VAT, he may certify the counsel's fee note to this effect and pay only the net of VAT fee.

Normally, the tax point for counsel's services will be determined by payment and not delivery of a fee note. On payment, counsel's clerk will add the VAT number of counsel and other particulars required under reg 13 of the VAT Regulations 1995 to constitute a document as a VAT invoice so that the receipted fee note is a VAT invoice. This will usually be made out to the solicitor (so that the solicitor can claim input tax credit). However, if the solicitor alters the fee note so that it is addressed to the client (and input tax credit can be taken by his client) the solicitor should keep a photocopy of the VAT invoice, passing the original amended receipted fee note to the client. This is in case the fee note needs to be dealt with in the taxation of costs.

Exercise 13B

You act for Barton in connection with a tax dispute. The following events occur:

July
8   You receive £1,000 from Barton on account of costs to be incurred.
10   You pay a court fee of £100 out of client's money.
22   You pay accountant's fee of £400 plus £70 VAT. The invoice was addressed to you.
29   You pay counsel's fee of £600 plus £105 VAT. The invoice was addressed to Barton.

August
7   You send Barton a bill and VAT invoice. Your costs are £800 plus appropriate VAT.
9   You transfer the £195 remaining in the client bank account to the office bank account in part payment of your costs.
11   You receive from Barton a cheque for the balance of the costs outstanding.

Prepare the cash account and client ledger account for Barton together with the relevant entries on the ledger account for HM Customs & Excise.

Exercise 13C

You act for Avis in a boundary dispute. The following events occur.

November
5   You pay a court fee of £100 on Avis's behalf.
7   You receive a cheque from Avis for £1,000 on account of costs. You do not split the cheque.
9   You pay counsel's fee of £400 plus VAT on behalf of Avis. The invoice was addressed to you but you add the name and address of Avis.
11   You pay surveyor's fee of £200 plus VAT. The invoice was addressed to you.
13   You send Avis a bill. Your profit costs are £600 plus VAT.
15   You transfer the £530 remaining in client account in part payment of your bill. You receive a cheque from Avis for the balance of £510.

Comment on the application of the Accounts Rules and explain what steps you will take to deal with the VAT elements involved in this transaction. Make the appropriate entries on the relevant ledger accounts.

Solutions

Exercise 13A

The fee is inclusive of VAT. If the profit costs are regarded as 100% the solicitor can be said to have received 100% *plus* 17.5% (profit costs *plus* VAT). To calculate the profit costs it is, therefore, necessary to divide by 117.5 to give 1% of the receipt and to multiply by 100 to give 100% of the receipt.

$$\text{Receipt} \quad \times \quad \frac{100}{117.5}$$

$$\text{£200} \quad \times \quad \frac{100}{117.5} \quad = \text{£170.21}$$

$$\text{VAT} \qquad\qquad = \text{£ 29.79}$$

Exercise 13B

Notes

July

8   The money is client money. It will be paid into the client bank account in the usual way pursuant to Rule 15.

10   Rule 22(1)(b) permits the payment out of the client bank account. The court fees are exempt from VAT.

22   The invoice was addressed to you, so the disbursement must be paid using the principal method out of office money. Remember that the solicitor is responsible for paying the input tax.

At this stage, the solicitor only debits the fee, not the VAT, to the client. The cash account records the fee and the total paid, ie the VAT. The solicitor debits the VAT to the Customs & Excise ledger account.

[*Note:* You will see a note in the details column of Barton's ledger account that the solicitor has paid input tax. This is a reminder to the solicitor to charge the client output tax later.]

July

29   The counsel's invoice was addressed to Barton and is therefore payable using the agency method.

There is sufficient money in the client bank account and it is sensible to make the payment out of client's money as permitted by Rule 22(1)(b).

August

7   You debit Barton's ledger account, office section, with costs and VAT. What you must consider carefully is how much output tax to charge.

The solicitor must charge output tax at the standard rate on the value of his legal services, ie:

(1)   the value of the profit costs of £800; plus

(2)   the value of any general disbursements – there are none in this case; plus

(3)   the value of any taxable disbursements paid on the principal method – in this case the accountant's fee of £400.

Therefore, the solicitor must charge VAT on £800 profit costs plus £400 accountant's fee, which makes a total of £1,200. VAT @ 17.5% is £210.

The double entries for costs and VAT will be in the costs ledger account (not shown) and Customs & Excise ledger account respectively.

[*Note:* There is no entry in the cash account as no movement of money is involved.]

August

9   Rule 22(3)(b) permits the withdrawal from the client bank account for payment of expenses and costs. Rule 23(3) provides that the withdrawal shall be by way of transfer to the office bank account.

11   This money is received from Barton specifically in payment of the outstanding costs and expenses. The money must be paid straight into the office bank account under Rule 19(1)(a) (unless it is paid into client account in accordance with Rule 9(1)(c)).

The accounts will look like this:

Client: Barton							
Matter: Tax Dispute							

Date	Details	Office account			Client account		
		DR	CR	BAL	DR	CR	BAL
Jul							
8	Cash. On account					1,000	1,000CR
10	Cash. Court fee				100		900
22	Cash. Accountant's fee						
	[VAT £70 paid]	400		400DR			
29	Cash. Counsel's fee				705		195
Aug							
7	Costs.	800		1,200			
	VAT (£70 + £140)	210		1,410			
9	Cash. Transfer from client to						
	office		195	1,215	195		—
11	Cash. From Barton.						
	Balance due		1,215	—			

Date	Details	Office account			Client account		
Cash account							
		DR	CR	BAL	DR	CR	BAL
Jul	Balance			xxx			xxx
8	Barton				1,000		
10	Barton					100	
22	Barton		400				
	VAT		70				
29	Barton					705	
Aug							
9	Barton	195				195	
11	Barton	1,215					

Customs & Excise account				
Date	Details	Office account		
		DR	CR	BAL
Jul 22	Cash. Re Barton	70		70DR
Aug 7	Barton		210	140CR

The CR balance shown on Customs & Excise ledger account represents the output tax charged to Barton less the input tax paid by the solicitor. The solicitor will have to account to Customs & Excise for this amount.

Exercise 13C

(1) 5 November   You are not holding any money for Avis. Therefore Rule 22(5) applies and the money cannot be paid out of client account. The payment is made out of office account.

> *Entries:*
> DR Avis ledger account
> CR Cash account   } Office section

7 November   The money is office and client money. You pay it into client account – Rule 20(2)(b).

> *Entries:*
> CR Avis ledger account
> DR Cash account   } Client section

9 November   The invoice is addressed to Avis so the payment must be made using the agency method. You pay an inclusive sum of £470 with no separate record of VAT. There is sufficient money in client bank account, so make the payment out of client bank account – Rule 22(1)(b).

> *Entries:*
> DR Avis ledger account
> CR Cash account   } Client section

11 November   This invoice was addressed to you so you must pay it using the principal method. You record the fee and VAT separately. You DR the fee to Avis and the VAT to Customs & Excise.

Even though there is enough money in client bank account you must make a payment on the principal method out of office bank account.

> *Entries:*
> Fee   DR Avis ledger account
>   CR Cash account   } Office section
>
> VAT   DR C&E ledger account
>   CR Cash account   } Office section

13 November   You make entries for costs and VAT separately. The DR entry in the client's ledger account is in the *office* section.

You calculate VAT on the total of profit costs, general disbursements (none in this case) and taxable disbursements paid on the principal method. The surveyor's fee was paid on the principal method. VAT is therefore charged on £600 profit costs plus £200 surveyor's fee, making a total of £800. VAT will be £140.

Entries:

Costs   DR Avis ledger account
         CR Costs account   } Office section

VAT   DR Avis ledger account
         CR C&E ledger account   } Office section

15 November   You have £530 remaining in client bank account. Avis owes you £1,040. You will transfer the £530 and receive a cheque for £510 from Avis.

Rule 22(3)(b) allows the withdrawal of £530 from the client bank account in payment of your expenses and costs respectively.

The money has been received to repay the disbursements and to pay your costs where a bill has been sent. Subject to Rule 19(1)(c), the money must not be paid into the client bank account. It is paid straight away into the office bank account.

Entries:

For transfer
Withdrawal from client account

         DR Avis ledger account
         CR Cash account   } Client section

Receipt into office account

         CR Avis ledger account
         DR Cash account   } Office section

For receipt of money from Avis into office account

         CR Avis ledger account
         DR Cash account   } Office section

Client: Avis
Matter: Boundary dispute

Date	Details	Office account			Client account		
		DR	CR	BAL	DR	CR	BAL
Nov							
5	Cash. Court fee	100		100DR			
7	Cash. From Avis.						
	On account of costs					1,000	1,000CR
9	Cash. Counsel's fee				470		530
11	Cash. Surveyor's fee						
	[VAT £35 paid]	200		300			
13	Costs	600		900			
	VAT (£105 + £35)	140		1,040			
15	Cash. Transfer from						
	client to office account		530	510	530		—
	Cash. From Avis.						
	Balance due		510	—			

Cash account							
Date	Details	Office account			Client account		
		DR	CR	BAL	DR	CR	BAL
Nov	Balance			xxx			xxx
5	Avis		100				
7	Avis				1,000		
9	Avis					470	
11	Avis		200				
	C&E		35				
15	Avis	530				530	
	Avis	510					

Customs & Excise account				
Date	Details	Office account		
		DR	CR	BAL
Nov				
11	Cash. Re Avis	35		35DR
13	Avis. VAT		140	105CR

Chapter 14

SPLITTING CHEQUES AND RECEIVING CHEQUES IN PAYMENT OF A BILL

14.1   RULE 20

14.1.1   Receipts partly of office and partly of client's money (Rule 20)

A solicitor often receives a cheque which is made up partly of office money and partly of client money.

Example

You act for Carollo Ltd. You have paid £40 out of the office bank account on its behalf. In response to a request by you, it sends a cheque for £100, partly to pay back the £40 and partly to cover future disbursements. The £40 is office money and the £60 is client's money.

Under Rule 20(2)(a) you can 'split' the cheque. This means paying the different parts of the cheque into different bank accounts. Thus, you could pay the £40 into the office bank account and the £60 into the client bank account.

On splitting the cheque the entries are:

DR Office portion to Cash account	Office section
DR Client portion to Cash account	Client section
CR Office portion to Client ledger	Office section
CR Client portion to Client ledger	Client section

14.1.2   Unsplit cheque

If you do not split the cheque, you must pay it all into the client bank account under Rule 20(2)(b). You will then need to transfer the 'office' portion (ie the £40) to the office bank account within 14 days of receipt (Rule 20(3)).

You *cannot* pay the whole cheque into the office bank account and transfer the client portion to the client bank account.

If not splitting the cheque the entries are:

DR whole amount to cash account	Client section
CR whole amount to client ledger	

When later transferring office portion:

CR Cash account	Client section
DR Client ledger	
DR Cash account	Office section
CR Client ledger	

Entries (if cheque split):

Client: Carollo Ltd							
Matter:							
Date	**Details**	**Office account**			**Client account**		
		DR	**CR**	**BAL**	**DR**	**CR**	**BAL**
Feb 1	Cash	40		40DR			
10	Cash		40	—		60	60CR

Cash Account:							
Date	**Details**	**Office account**			**Client account**		
		DR	**CR**	**BAL**	**DR**	**CR**	**BAL**
							xxx
Feb 1	Carollo		40				
10	Carollo	40			60		

*Entries (if cheque **not** split and a transfer is later made of the office money element):*

Client: Carollo Ltd							
Matter:							
Date	**Details**	**Office account**			**Client account**		
		DR	**CR**	**BAL**	**DR**	**CR**	**BAL**
Feb 1	Cash	40		40DR			
10	Cash					100	100CR
	Cash Transfer		40	—	40		60

Cash Account							
Date	**Details**	**Office account**			**Client account**		
		DR	**CR**	**BAL**	**DR**	**CR**	**BAL**
				xxx			xxx
Feb 1	Carollo		40				
10	Carollo				100		
	Carollo Transfer	40				40	

Exercise 14A

You act for Brian.

March

7   Pay £30 by cheque on Brian's behalf.

15   You have an interview with Brian. You ask him to reimburse you for the £30 and to give you another £70 in respect of future items. He gives you a cheque for £100. You split the cheque.

21   Pay £50 by cheque on Brian's behalf.

31   Brian instructs you to hold the balance on behalf of Christine and you receive confirmation from Christine to hold this sum for her.

14.2 RULE 19

14.2.1 Cheques received in full or part payment of a bill

Rule 19(1) gives various options for dealing with a cheque received in full or part payment of a bill.

(a) Deal with the money in accordance with its nature. Thus, an office money cheque will be paid into the office bank account, a client money cheque will be paid into the client bank account and a mixed cheque will be dealt with under Rule 20.

(b) Where the cheque is office money plus client money in the form of unpaid professional disbursements for which the solicitor has incurred liability, the entire receipt can be paid into the office bank account. However, by the end of the second working day following receipt, the solicitor must either pay the disbursement or transfer the money for it to the client bank account.

Note: This option is not available if the cheque received contains client money of any other kind.

(c) Pay the cheque whatever its nature into the client bank account. However, any office money must be transferred out of the client bank account within 14 days of receipt. This option means that a firm can give its clients one bank account number which they can use for direct payments into the firm's account.

(d) Where the cheque is a receipt from the Legal Aid Board it can always be paid into the office bank account even if it consists entirely of client money for unpaid professional disbursements. However, the solicitor must either pay the disbursement or transfer the money for it to the client bank account within 14 days of receipt.

14.2.3 Money received for an agreed fee

An agreed fee is a fixed fee which cannot be varied upwards and which does not depend on the transaction being completed. It must be evidenced in writing. It is not necessary under the Solicitors' Accounts Rules to deliver a bill provided there is written evidence. However, a solicitor will often choose to deliver a bill even where a fee has been agreed so as to have a record for VAT purposes.

Money received for an agreed fee must under Rule 19(3) be paid into the office bank account. If no bill has been delivered the option of paying the money into the client bank account contained in Rule 19(1)(c) does not appear to be available.

14.3 REVISION OF MATERIAL IN CHAPTERS 10–14

Exercise 14B

(1) **Which one of the following receipts is entirely office money?**

    (a) Client A sends you £100 on account of costs. ☐

    (b) A deposit received as stakeholder on the sale of a house by Fred, a partner in the firm, to Joe, an assistant solicitor. ☐

    (c) Solicitor delivers a bill to Client C for profit costs of £200 + VAT of £35 and £10 for land charges for which liability is incurred but which are not yet paid. Client C sends the solicitor £245. ☐

    (d) None of the above. ☐

(2) **Which one of the following cannot be paid into the client bank account?**

    (a) Controlled trust money. ☐

(b) Office money to open the client bank account.

(c) A cheque for £235 in settlement of the solicitor's bill for costs of £200 and VAT of £35.

(d) A cheque for £500 received from Client A with a written request that the money should not be paid in until the client gives the solicitor instructions.

(3) **Client X gives solicitor a cheque for £100 on account of costs. The solicitor endorses the cheque over to an expert witness on X's behalf. Which one of the following statements is correct?**

(a) Rule 17(b) permits the solicitor not to pay the cheque into the client bank account so no entries need be made in the solicitor's accounts.

(b) Rule 32(2) requires the solicitor to record the receipt and payment on the cash account.

(c) Rule 32(2) requires the solicitor to record the receipt and payment on the cash account and client ledger account for X.

(d) Rule 17(b) provides that the solicitor must not pay the cheque into the client bank account.

(4) **Client X sends a solicitor a cheque for £235 in satisfaction of the solicitor's bill for profit costs and VAT. Which one of the following statements is correct?**

(a) The cheque is client money and must be paid into the client bank account without delay.

(b) The cheque is office money and must be paid into the client bank account.

(c) The cheque is office money and must not be paid into the client bank account.

(d) The cheque is office money and can be paid into the client bank account.

(5) **A solicitor is holding £1,000 for Client A. Client A instructs the solicitor to hold £300 of that money to the order of Client B to whom A owes money. Which one of the following statements is correct?**

(a) A client bank account cheque for £300 must be sent to B.

(b) No entries need be made.

(c) A client bank account cheque for £300 must be drawn and then the cheque must be paid into the client bank account on B's behalf.

(d) Entries must be made on the client ledger accounts of A and B and on a record of sums transferred from one ledger account to another.

(6) **Brown is a bookseller. He sells only books. He does not charge his customers VAT. Is this because:**

(a) His turnover does not exceed the limit for compulsory registration?

(b) He makes only exempt supplies?

(c) He is not carrying on a 'business' for the purposes of VATA 1994?

(d) He makes only zero-rated supplies?

(7) **A solicitor (registered for VAT) agrees to draft a will for Client X for £100. Which of the following statements is correct?**

    (a)   He must charge £17.50 VAT on top of the fee. ☐

    (b)   He must not charge VAT. ☐

    (c)   The client will pay him £100 plus VAT. ☐

    (d)   The client will pay him £100. ☐

(8) **A solicitor completes the administration of an estate on 31 March and delivers a bill on 2 April. When is the tax point?**

    (a)   31 March. ☐

    (b)   2 April. ☐

    (c)   14 April. ☐

    (d)   30 June. ☐

(9) **A solicitor receives an invoice from an expert witness for £200 + VAT in respect of litigation being conducted for Client X. The invoice is addressed to the solicitor's firm. The solicitor holds £1,000 in the client bank account for X generally on account of costs. Which one of the following statements is correct?**

    (a)   The solicitor can pay the invoice from the client bank account. ☐

    (b)   The solicitor must pay the invoice from the office bank account. ☐

    (c)   The solicitor must debit the client ledger account immediately with £235. ☐

    (d)   All of the above statements are incorrect. ☐

(10) **You receive a cheque from the client made up partly of office money and partly of client money. Which one of the following statements is correct?**

    (a)   You must split the cheque. ☐

    (b)   You may split the cheque. ☐

    (c)   You must pay the cheque into the client bank account. ☐

    (d)   You must pay the cheque into the office bank account. ☐

Solutions

Exercise 14A

Notes:

7 March	No client money, so office money must be used.
15 March	This cheque includes office and client money, so can be split under Rule 20. If split, you must record two separate receipts, one for client money and one for office money. If not split, it must be paid into the client bank account.
21 March	Client money is available and can be used.
31 March	This is an inter-client transfer. No entry is made on the cash account.

DR Brian ledger
CR Christine ledger } Client section

Client: Brian
Matter:

Date	Details	Office account			Client account		
		DR	CR	BAL	DR	CR	BAL
March							xxx
7	Cash. Payment	30		30DR			
15	Cash. From you		30	—		70	70CR
21	Cash. Payment				50		20
31	Christine. Transfer				20		—

Client: Christine
Matter:

Date	Details	Office account			Client account		
		DR	CR	BAL	DR	CR	BAL
March							
31	Brian. Transfer					20	20CR

Cash Account:

Date	Details	Office account			Client account		
		DR	CR	BAL	DR	CR	BAL
				xxx			xxx
March							
7	Brian. Payment		30				
15	Brian. Amount from Brian	30			70		
21	Brian. Payment					50	

Exercise 14B

(1) (c) The money is received in payment of 'costs' and a bill has been delivered. In (b) the money is held for a partner in the firm **and someone else**. Therefore the money is client money.

(2) (d) Note that although the receipt in (c) is office money it can be paid into the client bank account under Rule 19(1)(c). However, it must not be left longer than 14 days.

(3) (c)

(4) (d) See Rule 19(1)(c).

(5) (d) See Rule 32.

(6) (d)

(7) (d) The solicitor must apportion the fee between the VAT and the VAT exclusive element.

(8) (b)

(9) (b) It must be treated on the principal basis and, therefore, must be paid from the office bank account.

(10) (b)

Chapter 15

MISCELLANEOUS MATTERS

15.1 RECEIPT OF A CHEQUE MADE OUT TO THE CLIENT OR A THIRD PARTY

A solicitor who receives a cheque made out not to the firm but to the client (or a third party) *cannot* pay that cheque into a firm bank account. The firm is not the payee.

The solicitor's only obligation is to forward the cheque to the payee without delay. The solicitor has not dealt with client money because the cheque is not 'money' as far as the solicitor is concerned; it is a piece of paper which the solicitor cannot turn into cash. As the solicitor has not dealt with *client money*, there is no obligation under Rule 32 to record the event on the client ledger account and cash account. However, the solicitor will want to keep a written record on the correspondence file.

Many firms will have a special control account where all cheques received by the firm will be recorded irrespective of the payee. This is not required by the Rules but is a useful precaution to prevent cheques being overlooked.

15.2 ENDORSED CHEQUES

A solicitor may receive a cheque made out to the firm on behalf of a client. Instead of paying the cheque into the client bank account, the solicitor is free under Rule 17(b) (assuming the cheque is endorsable) to endorse the cheque to the client or to a third party on behalf of the client. However, as this is a *dealing* with client's money, it must be recorded under Rule 32 on the client ledger account and cash account as a receipt and payment of client money. As the cheque passes through the solicitor's hands having no effect on the balances of the accounts, it is common to make the entries for receipt and payment on the same line.

Example

A solicitor acting for Brown in a debt collection receives a cheque for £1,000 in settlement of a debt due to Brown. The solicitor endorses the cheque to Brown.

Client:	Brown							
Date	Details	Office account			Client account		
		DR	CR	BAL	DR	CR	BAL
	Cash. From debtor. Cheque endorsed				1,000	1,000	—

Cash account								
Date	Details	Office account			Client account		
		DR	CR	BAL	DR	CR	BAL xxx
	Brown. From debtor. Cheque endorsed to Brown.				1,000	1,000	

15.3 RETURNED CHEQUES

There is nothing in the rules to prevent a solicitor drawing against a cheque which has been paid into the client bank account but which has not yet been cleared. However, if that cheque is then dishonoured, there will be a breach of Rule 22 and the solicitor will have to transfer money from the office bank account to the client bank account to make up the deficiency.

Example

On 1 March you receive £500 on account of costs from your client, Smith.

On 2 March you pay a court fee of £100 out of the client bank account on behalf of Smith.

On 4 March Smith's cheque is returned by the bank marked 'Return to Drawer'.

On 7 March Smith tells you that there has been a mistake and that the cheque should have been met. He asks you to re-present it. You do so on 7 March and it is met.

Because it turns out that you have no money for Smith, you must have used £100 belonging to another client for the benefit of Smith. You must transfer £100 from the office bank account to the client bank account to remedy your breach of the rules.

When you re-present the cheque, you can either split it or you can pay the whole amount into the client bank account and transfer the £100 to the office bank account at a later stage.

Notes:

1 March   The money is client money and is paid into the client bank account (Rule 13).

 Entries
   CR Smith ledger account
   DR Cash account   } Client section

2 March   Rule 22 allows the money to be paid out of the client bank account even though the cheque from Smith has not yet been cleared.

 Entries:
   DR Smith ledger account
   CR Cash account   } Client section

4 March   You must make entries reversing those made when you received the cheque.

 Entries:
   DR Smith ledger account
   CR Cash account   } Client section

This results in a DR balance of £100 on Smith's ledger account and you are in breach of Rule 22(5). Effectively you have used client money on behalf of a client for whom you were not holding any.

4 March   You must make an *immediate* transfer of £100 from the office bank account to the client bank account to rectify the breach.

Entries:
Withdrawal from office account
  DR Smith ledger account
  CR Cash account   } Office section

Receipt into client account
  CR Smith ledger account
  DR Cash account   } Client section

7 March   When the cheque is re-presented you can, under Rule 20, either pay the whole amount into the client bank account; or, as in this example, split it so that £100 goes into the office bank account and £400 into the client bank account.

Entries if split:
£100 Office money
  CR Smith ledger account
  DR Cash account   } Office section

£400 Client money
  CR Smith ledger account
  DR Cash account   } Client section

The accounts look like this:

Client: Smith
Matter: Miscellaneous

Date	Details	Office account			Client account		
		DR	CR	BAL	DR	CR	BAL
March 1	Cash. From Smith. Advance on costs					500	500CR
2	Cash. Court fee				100		400
4	Cash. Smith's cheque – returned.				500		100DR
	Cash. Transfer from office account to rectify breach	100		100DR		100	—
7	Cash. Smith's cheque re-presented		100	—		400	400CR

Cash account

Date	Details	Office account			Client account		
		DR	CR	BAL	DR	CR	BAL
March							xxx
1	Smith				500		
2	Smith					100	
4	Smith					500	
	Smith		100		100		
7	Smith	100			400		

A well-run firm will operate a system which makes it impossible to draw against a client bank cheque before it has cleared.

15.4 ABATEMENTS

Clients frequently complain that the amount of their bill is too high. Sometimes the solicitor may decide to reduce, or abate, the costs.

In order to record the abatement, you simply reverse the entries made when the bill was delivered. You also send the client a VAT credit note.

Entries:
   DR Costs
   DR Customs & Excise   } with the reduction

   CR Client ledger (office section) with the reduction in costs and VAT.

Example

You send your client Jones a bill for £600 plus VAT on 4 May. On 6 May, after discussion with Jones, you agree to reduce the bill by £80 plus VAT.

The accounts will look like this:

Client: Jones
Matter: Miscellaneous

Date	Details	Office account			Client account		
		DR	CR	BAL	DR	CR	BAL
May 4	Costs	600		600DR			
	VAT	105		705			
6	Costs – Abatement		80	625			
	VAT – Abatement		14	611			

Costs account

Date	Details	Office account		
		DR	CR	BAL
May 4	Jones		600	600CR
6	Jones	80		520

Customs & Excise account

Date	Details	Office account		
		DR	CR	BAL
May 4	Jones		105	105CR
6	Jones	14		91

If preferred, the firm can debit abatements to a separate abatements account. At the end of the accounting period, the debit balance on the abatements account is transferred to the debit side of the costs account.

15.5 BAD DEBTS

15.5.1 The general rule

From time to time, a solicitor will realise that a client is not going to pay the amount owing to the firm. The solicitor will have to write off the amount owing for profit costs and VAT and for any disbursements paid from the office bank account. The general rule for VAT used to be that there was no VAT relief and VAT had to be accounted for to Customs & Excise even if the debt was written off. Thus, the VAT was an additional element of the bad debt and increased the amount which had to be written off.

Entries

CR Client's ledger account, office section
DR Bad debts account
} with the whole amount

15.5.2 VAT relief

However, VAT relief is now available if the debt has been outstanding for at least 6 months since the date payment was due. In this case, the solicitor will be entitled to a refund from Customs & Excise.

Entries:

When debt is written off:

CR Client's ledger account, office section, with the full amount owing
DR Bad debts account with the full amount owing

When VAT relief becomes available:

CR Bad debts account with amount of VAT
DR Customs & Excise with amount of VAT

Example

On 9 April you send Green a bill for £400 plus VAT. On 6 June you write off Green's debt.

Six months after the due date of payment of Green's bill (31 October) you become entitled to VAT bad debt relief.

The accounts will look like this:

Client: Green
Matter: Miscellaneous

Date	Details	Office account			Client account		
		DR	CR	BAL	DR	CR	BAL
Apr 9	Costs	400		400DR			
	VAT	70		470			
Jun 6	**Bad debts**		470	—			

Costs account

Date	Details	Office account		
		DR	CR	BAL
Apr 9	Green		400	400CR

Customs & Excise account				
Date	**Details**	**Office account**		
		DR	**CR**	**BAL**
Apr 9	Green		70	70CR
Oct 31	**VAT relief**	70		—

Bad debts account				
Date	**Details**	**Office account**		
		DR	**CR**	**BAL**
Jun 6	**Green**	470		470CR
Oct 31	**VAT relief**		70	400

15.6   PETTY CASH

15.6.1   Need for petty cash account

Any firm will need some petty cash on the premises to meet small cash payments. When cash is withdrawn from the bank for petty cash the entries will be:

CR Cash – office section
DR Petty cash account

When a payment is made, eg a roll of sticky tape is bought, the entries will be:

CR Petty cash account
DR appropriate ledger account, eg Sundries

15.6.2   Petty cash payments for clients

A solicitor will sometimes make a payment from petty cash on behalf of a client. The CR entry will be made on the petty cash account, not on the main cash account. The solicitor will want to DR the client ledger account to show that the client now owes the solicitor for the expense incurred. The DR entry must be made on the office section of the client ledger even if client money is held for the client. This is because petty cash is office money. Thus, by deciding to use petty cash, the solicitor has elected to use office money on behalf of the client.

Example

Solicitor holds £200 in the client bank account for Smith. Solicitor pays £20 expenses to an expert witness from petty cash.

Smith's client ledger account will look like this:

Client: Smith Matter:							
Date	Details	Office account			Client account		
		DR	CR	BAL	DR	CR	BAL
	Cash. Received on account					200	200CR
	Petty cash. Expert witness	**20**		20DR			

The corresponding credit entry will be on the petty cash account not on the cash account. Notice that the 'Details' section of Smith's ledger account refers to 'petty cash' not to cash.

15.7 INSURANCE COMMISSION

Solicitors sometimes act as agent for an insurance company and collect premiums from the company's customers. The solicitor will be entitled to a commission from the company and will normally account to the company for the premiums collected less the commission due.

The commission is charged to the company in much the same way as costs are charged to any other client.

However, because commission is an exempt item for VAT purposes, no VAT is charged. An insurance commission account similar to the profit costs account will be required. On charging commission DR insurance company ledger account, office section, and CR insurance commission ledger account.

If the commission exceeds £20 then Solicitors' Practice Rule 10 applies (solicitors must account to their clients unless they have client's agreement to retain commission).

Example

You hold £300 client's money for Black. On 1 May, Black asks you to make £100 available to ABC Insurance Company in payment of an insurance premium. On 2 May, Brown, a client for whom you arranged insurance with ABC Insurance Company sends you this year's premium of £200. You act for ABC Insurance Company which allows you 10% commission on premiums collected for them.

Both Black and Brown have authorised you to retain the commission. On 4 May you deduct your commission and send ABC the net amount due.

Notes:

1 May   You must do an inter-client transfer to show that £100 of the money previously held for Black is now held for the insurance company.

2 May   You receive £200 *for* the ABC Insurance Company. You never hold it for Brown so you will credit the money straight to the insurance company's ledger account.

4 May	You must make a DR entry on the insurance company's ledger account to show that the insurance company owes your firm commission. The CR entry will be on an insurance commission ledger account.
4 May	You will record the payment of the net premium to the insurance company.
4 May	The £30 remaining in the client bank account will be transferred to the office bank account.

Cash

Date	Details	Office account			Client account		
		DR	CR	BAL	DR	CR	BAL
May							xxx
2	ABC Insurance Co. Net premium from Brown				200		
2	ABC Insurance Co. Net premium					270	
4	ABC Insurance Co. Transfer commission	30				30	

Client: ABC Insurance Company
Matter:

Date	Details	Office account			Client account		
		DR	CR	BAL	DR	CR	BAL
May							
1	Black. Premium					100	100CR
2	Cash. Premium					200	300
4	Insurance commission due	30		30DR			
4	Cash. Net premium. To ABC Co				270		30
4	Cash. Transfer commission.		30	—	30		—

Exercise 15A

You act for Forsyth.

March

1 Forsyth sends £100 on account of costs.

2 You pay court fees £40 from client bank account.

3 Bank informs you that Forsyth's cheque has been dishonoured.

15 You re-present the cheque instructing the bank that, assuming the cheque is honoured, you want £40 to be paid into the office bank account and £60 into the client bank account.

16 You pay counsel's fee £200 plus £35 VAT. The invoice is addressed to your client.

18 You deliver a bill for £440 plus £77 VAT.

19 The client complains and you reduce the bill by £40 plus £7 VAT.

31 You write off Forsyth's debt as bad, having transferred any balance in the client bank account to the office bank account.

Make the necessary entries in Forsyth's client ledger account and the cash account. The balances on the cash account were office £1,000 (DR), client £10,000 (DR).

(See overleaf for solution.)

Solution

Exercise 15A

Notes:

March

1 This was received generally on account of costs and is client money.

2 You have client money available and so can make the payment from the client bank account.

3 Drawing against an uncleared cheque is not in itself a breach of rules. However, as the cheque has been dishonoured, there has been a breach which must be remedied by transferring £40 from office to client bank account.

15 The re-presented cheque is split between office and client bank account. The portion representing reimbursement of the expense incurred for court fees is office money, the balance is client's money.

16 As the invoice is addressed to the client, the agency basis is used.

19 This is an abatement. Simply make the opposite entries you would make if delivering a bill.

31 There is £60 in the client bank account which can be transferred to the office bank account. The whole of Forsyth's indebtedness, including VAT, must be written off as a bad debt.

No VAT relief is available at present. The debt has not been outstanding for 6 months since the due date for payment.

Client: Forsyth
Matter:

Date	Details	Office account			Client account		
		DR	CR	BAL	DR	CR	BAL
March							
1	Cash. On account					100	100CR
2	Cash. Court fees				40		60
3	Cash. Dishonoured cheque				100		40DR
3	Cash. To remedy breach	40		40DR		40	—
15	Cash. Re-presented cheque		40	—		60	60CR
16	Cash. Counsel	235		235			
18	Costs	440					
	VAT	77		752			
19	Costs – abatement		40				
	VAT – abatement		7	705			
31	Cash. Transfer		60	645	60		—
31	Bad debts		645	—			

Cash

Date	Details	Office account			Client account		
		DR	CR	BAL	DR	CR	BAL
March							
1	Balances			1,000DR			10,000DR
1	Forsyth. On account				100		10,100
2	Forsyth. Court fees					40	10,060
3	Forsyth. Dishonoured cheque					100	9,960
3	Forsyth. To remedy breach		40	960	40		10,000
15	Forsyth. Re-presented cheque	40		1,000	60		10,060
16	Forsyth. Counsel		235	765			
31	Forsyth. Transfer	60		825		60	10,000

Chapter 16

ACCOUNTING TO THE CLIENT FOR INTEREST

16.1 WHEN MUST A SOLICITOR ALLOW INTEREST?

Study Rule 24.

Under Rule 24(1), a solicitor must account to a client for all interest earned on money held in a separate designated deposit bank account.

Under Rule 24(2), a solicitor must pay a client a sum in lieu of interest where client money is not held in a separate designated deposit bank account. The amount is calculated by reference to the amount which the relevant bank or building society would have paid if a separate designated deposit bank account had been opened.

There are some exceptional cases set out in Rule 24(3) where the solicitor need not make any payment to the client. Notably:

- if the amount calculated is £20 or less;
- the amount held and the period for which it is held does not exceed the amounts and periods set out in the table in Rule 24(3).

Rule 24(7) states that Rule 24 does not apply to controlled trust money. Under the general law of trusts, trustees must account to the trust for all interest earned.

For further problems relating to trust money, see **16.3.3** below.

16.2 THE METHODS

16.2.1 Separate designated deposit bank account

Rule 14(5) defines this in relation to a client as a deposit account which includes in its title a reference to the identity of the client.

The solicitor simply opens a separate deposit account at the bank designated with the name of the client and pays the client money into it. All interest allowed by the bank belongs to the client.

The disadvantage of this method is that, if the solicitor uses it for every client, there will be an enormous number of separate deposit bank accounts. Each bank account will require its own cash account designated with the name of the client so the solicitor will have an enormous number of separate cash accounts. The solicitor also loses the opportunity to benefit from interest earned by client money.

16.2.2 Payment of the solicitor's own money in lieu of interest earned on separate designated deposit bank account

The solicitor must bear in mind the table set out in Rule 24 which shows when the obligation to account arises.

Assume that as a solicitor you hold £1,600 of client's money for 9 weeks on behalf of your client Smith. Rule 24 applies and you must account to Smith, out of office money, for an amount equal to the interest that would have been earned if the money had been put on deposit.

The disadvantage of this method is that the solicitor has to calculate how much would have been earned in respect of each individual client to whom the rules apply. Also, at first sight, it appears that the solicitor will be out of pocket. However, consider the following.

As a solicitor you are likely to hold a large sum of client money made up of relatively small amounts from each individual client. The Solicitors Act 1974 allows solicitors to put client money on deposit to earn interest for themselves. You will probably be able to earn a relatively high rate of interest. You must still comply with your obligation to the clients, but not every client will be entitled to interest and for those who are, interest is paid at a rate applicable to that which would have been earned had the money been deposited separately; this is likely to be a relatively low rate.

16.3   ACCOUNTING ENTRIES

16.3.1   Separate designated deposit bank account

The solicitor will instruct the bank to open a deposit bank account – the separate designated deposit bank account – and to transfer the appropriate amount from the (current) client bank account into it. You will record the receipt into the separate designated deposit bank account by making a DR entry on the designated deposit cash account.

When you put client money on deposit it is important that your client ledger accounts show what has happened to the money.

Rule 32(3)(b) requires that where a solicitor opens a separate designated deposit account, entries must be made in a separate client ledger account. This new ledger account can be presented as an additional 'client-deposit' section on the ordinary client ledger account.

When you pay the cash into the designated deposit bank account and make the appropriate cash entries, you will also debit the existing client ledger account and credit the new client ledger account with the appropriate amount.

Entries:
To record payment from current client bank account

    CR Cash
    DR Original client ledger account   }   Client section

To record receipt into separate designated deposit bank account

    CR New client ledger account
    DR Separate designated deposit (SDD) cash account

Interest earned will be paid by the bank into the separate designated bank account. The solicitor will record the interest as a CR in the client's new ledger account and a DR in the SDD cash account.

Before returning money to the client the solicitor must transfer the total sum including interest from the separate designated deposit bank account to the current client bank account so that a cheque can be drawn on the current account.

Example

You act for Dash Ltd which is owed £2,200 by Bingley. You write to Bingley and you receive a cheque for the money from him on 3 April. On 4 April Dash Ltd tells you to hold the money for 5 weeks until 9 May. You put the money on deposit in a separate designated deposit bank account. On 9 May you tell the bank to close the account. They tell you that they have allowed £18 interest. The £2,218 is transferred to the current bank account. You send Dash Ltd the £2,200 plus accumulated interest of £18.

Notes:

3 April   The money is received as client money and paid into the current client bank account.

    Entries:
       CR Dash Ltd (debt collection) ledger account ⎫
       DR Cash account   ⎬ Client section

4 April   The bank will transfer the cash from your ordinary current client bank account to the separate designated deposit (SDD) bank account. You will need an SDD cash account to record the transactions relating to Dash Ltd's separate designated bank account and a new client ledger account (or additional deposit section on the old client ledger).

    Entries:
       CR Cash account   ⎫
       DR Dash Ltd (debt collection) ledger account ⎬ Client section

       DR SDD Cash account
       CR Dash Ltd (money held on deposit) ledger account

Note:

Had you known on 3 April that you would want to put the money on deposit you could have paid the money straight into the separate designated deposit bank account without passing it through the ordinary current client bank account.

    Entries:
       DR SDD cash account
       CR Dash Ltd (money held on deposit) ledger account

9 May   Deal with the interest first. The interest has been earned on behalf of Dash Ltd and belongs to it. It is client money and the bank will pay it into the deposit bank account.

    Entries:
       DR SDD Cash account with interest
       CR Dash Ltd (money held on deposit) ledger account with interest

Then pay out the total from the separate designated deposit bank account.

    Entries:
       CR SDD Cash account
       DR Dash Ltd (money held on deposit) ledger account

Then receive the total into the current client bank account.

Entries:
DR Cash account
CR Dash Ltd (debt collection) ledger account $\Big\}$ Client section

You can now pay Dash Ltd the total sum you are holding on its behalf.

Entries:
CR Cash account
DR Dash Ltd (debt collection) ledger account $\Big\}$ Client section

The completed accounts look like this:

Client: Dash Ltd
Matter: Debt Collection

Date	Details	Office account			Client account		
		DR	CR	BAL	DR	CR	BAL
April 3	Cash. Bingley					2,200	2,200CR
4	Cash. On deposit				2,200		–
May 9	Cash. Off deposit					2,218	2,218
	Cash. Returned				2,218		–

Client: Dash Ltd
Matter: Money held on deposit

Date	Details	Office account			Client account		
		DR	CR	BAL	DR	CR	BAL
April 4	Deposit cash					2,200	2,200CR
May 9	Deposit cash interest					18	2,218
9	Deposit cash. A/C closed				2,218		–

Cash account

Date	Details	Office account			Client account		
		DR	CR	BAL	DR	CR	BAL
April				xxx			xxx
3	Dash Ltd. (Debt collection)				2,200		
4	Dash Ltd. (Debt collection) On deposit					2,200	
May 9	Dash Ltd. (Debt collection) Off deposit				2,218		
	Dash Ltd. (Debt collection) Return					2,218	

Separate designated deposit client cash account – Dash Ltd								
Date	**Details**	**Office account**			**Client account**			
		DR	**CR**	**BAL**	**DR**	**CR**	**BAL**	
April 4	Dash Ltd (Money on deposit)				2,200		2,200DR	
May 9	Dash Ltd (Money on deposit) Interest				18		2,218	
	Dash Ltd (Money on deposit)					2,218	—	

The solicitor may choose to have a separate deposit section on the existing client ledger account instead of a separate client ledger account. In this case the Dash Ltd example would appear as follows.

Client: Dash Ltd Matter: Debt Collection								
Date	Details	Office	Client			Client – Deposit		
			DR	CR	BAL	DR	CR	BAL
Apr 3	Cash. Bingley			2,200	2,200CR			
4	Cash. On deposit		2,200					
4	Deposit cash						2,200	2,200CR
May 9	Deposit cash. Interest						18	2,218CR
9	Deposit Cash. A/c closed					2,218		—
9	Cash. Off deposit			2,218	2,218CR			
9	Cash. Returned		2,218		—			

Cash account					
Date	**Details**	**Office**	**Client**		
			DR	**CR**	**BAL**
April 3	Dash Ltd. Debt collected		2,200		xxx
4	Dash Ltd. On deposit			2,200	
May 9	Dash Ltd. Off deposit		2,218		
9	Dash Ltd. Returned			2,218	

Separate designated deposit client cash account: Dash Ltd					
Date	**Details**	**Office**	**Client**		
			DR	**CR**	**BAL**
April 4	Dash Ltd. On deposit		2,200		2,200DR
May 9	Dash Ltd. Interest		18		2,218DR
9	Dash Ltd. Off deposit			2,218	—

16.3.2 Paying from the solicitor's own money

Using this method the payment is an expense of the business and will be recorded on an interest payable account. It is equivalent to the firm paying any other business expense, such as electricity or wages.

To comply with Rule 32(4) the office money dealing must be recorded in the office section of the client ledger account. If the money is transferred from the office bank account to the client bank account and held for the client, entries must be made on the client ledger.

Example

To enable you to make a direct comparison we will use the same basic facts as in the previous example, except that the money is not put into a separate designated deposit bank account.

Notes:

3 April   You receive the £2,200 on behalf of Dash Ltd and pay it into the current client bank account. Entries as before:

> *Entries:*
> CR Dash Ltd ledger account
> DR Cash account   } Client section

9 May   You have to allow Dash Ltd £18 interest and, therefore, have to account to Dash Ltd for £2,218. You can do this in either of two ways.

Method 1   Send two cheques: one drawn on the office bank account for the £18 in lieu of interest and the other drawn on the client bank account for the £2,200.

Entries must be made on the client ledger office section to record the dealing with office money.

> *Entries:*
> To record £18 owed to client in lieu of interest
> DR Interest payable ledger account
> CR Dash Ltd ledger account   } Office section
>
> To record £18 office cash sent to client
> CR Cash account
> CR Dash Ltd ledger account   } Office section
>
> To record £2,200 client cash sent to client
> DR Dash Ltd ledger account
> CR Cash account   } Client section

The accounts will look like this:

Client:	Dash Ltd						
Matter:	Debt Collection						
Date	**Details**	**Office account**			**Client ledger**		
		DR	CR	BAL	DR	CR	BAL
April 3	Cash. Bingley					2,200	2,200CR
May 9	Interest payable		18	18CR			
9	Cash in lieu of interest	18		—			
9	Cash. Returned				2,200		—

Cash account								
Date	**Details**	**Office account**			**Client account**			
		DR	**CR**	**BAL**	**DR**	**CR**	**BAL**	
April 3	Dash Ltd. Bingley				2,200			
May 9	Dash Ltd. In lieu of interest		18					
	Dash Ltd. Returned					2,200		

Interest payable account				
Date	**Details**	**Office account**		
		DR	**CR**	**BAL**
May 9	Dash Ltd	18		18DR

Method 2   Transfer the £18 from office bank account to client bank account and then send Dash Ltd one cheque drawn on client bank account for £2,218. In this case, additional entries must be made on the client section of the client ledger and on the client section of the cash account to show that money has been held for the client in the client bank account.

Entries:
To record £18 owed to client in lieu of interest
   DR Interest payable ledger account   ⎫
   CR Dash Ltd ledger account   ⎬   Office section
                                           ⎭

To record £18 office cash paid out
   CR Cash   ⎫
   DR Dash Ltd   ⎬   Office section
                                           ⎭

To record £18 received into client bank account
   CR Dash Ltd ledger account   ⎫
   DR Cash account   ⎬   Client section
                                           ⎭

Payment to Dash Ltd of £2,218 from client bank account
   DR Dash Ltd ledger account   ⎫
   CR Cash account   ⎬   Client section
                                           ⎭

The accounts will look like this:

Client: Dash Ltd Matter: Debt Collection								
Date	**Details**	**Office account**			**Client account**			
		DR	**CR**	**BAL**	**DR**	**CR**	**BAL**	
April 3	Cash					2,200	2,200CR	
May 9	Interest payable		18	18CR				
9	Cash. In lieu of interest	18						
9	Cash. In lieu of interest					18	2,218	
9	Cash. Returned				2,218		—	

Cash account							
Date	**Details**	**Office account**			**Client account**		
		DR	**CR**	**BAL**	**DR**	**CR**	**BAL**
April 3	Dash Ltd. Bingley				2,200		
May 9	Dash Ltd. In lieu of interest		18				
	Dash Ltd. In lieu of interest					18	
	Dash Ltd. Returned					2,218	

Interest payable account				
Date	**Details**	**Office account**		
		DR	**CR**	**BAL**
May 9	Dash Ltd	18		18DR

Looking at this example, you may object that by using this method of paying interest the solicitor is out of pocket by £18 as compared with using a separate designated deposit bank account. You are perfectly correct *if* the solicitor does nothing more. However, as we said earlier, a well-organised firm would always put a proportion of its client money on deposit in a general deposit bank account. It will then be entitled to keep the interest earned on that general deposit bank account. Provided the firm organises its bank accounts sensibly it should earn more interest on its general deposit bank account than it has to pay to individual clients. A firm can never put all of its client money on deposit since it must ensure that it has sufficient client money readily available to meet all day-to-day expenses for clients.

If a firm puts client money into a general deposit bank account the entries will be:

> CR Cash account
> DR General client deposit cash account   } Client section

Any interest earned will belong to the firm and will be office money. The bank must be instructed to pay all interest into the office cash account.

> *Entries:*
> DR Cash account – office section
> CR Interest received account

16.3.3   Trust money

Trustees must be careful not to profit from their trust directly or indirectly. If a solicitor puts controlled trust money into a separate designated account, there is no problem. If it is a deposit account, the solicitor accounts to the trust for all interest allowed by the bank. If it is not a deposit account, the solicitor calculates how much interest the bank would have allowed and pays the trust that amount in lieu of interest.

If the solicitor puts controlled trust money into the general client bank account, there are problems for the solicitor.

Any interest earned on the general client bank account is office money. To avoid profiting from the trust the solicitor must allocate the appropriate amount of interest to the controlled trust without delay.

The solicitor must avoid obtaining an indirect benefit from the controlled trust money. For example, the bank may pay a higher rate of interest because the general client bank account has a higher balance than it would without the controlled trust money.

Where a solicitor does not wish to put all controlled trust money into a separate designated bank account, it may be desirable to have a general client bank account reserved for only money of controlled trusts. All interest earned can be allocated amongst the trusts and the solicitor will not derive a benefit.

Exercise 16A

You act for the executor of Swan deceased and for Cygnet, the residuary beneficiary of Swan's estate. You complete the administration and ask Cygnet for instructions on what to do with the money due to him. Cygnet tells you to hold the money pending his instructions as he is hoping to buy a house in the near future.

March

20   You transfer Cygnet's residuary entitlement of £200,000 from the executor's ledger account to Cygnet's ledger account.

April

15   You realise that Cygnet will be entitled to interest on the money held for him. You calculate that he is entitled to £100 for the period from 20 March. You pay the sum from the office bank account into the client bank account.

16   You tell the bank to open a separate deposit bank account designated with Cygnet's name and to pay all the money held for Cygnet into that deposit bank account.

30   Cygnet tells you to send him the amount to which he is entitled. The bank credits £120 interest. You close the deposit bank account, transfer the money to the current client bank account and send Cygnet a cheque for the whole amount.

May

6   Cygnet tells you he thinks he is entitled to more interest for the period 20 March – 15 April.

You agree and send him an office bank account cheque for £30.

Show relevant cash accounts and client ledger entries for Cygnet.

(See overleaf for solution.)

Solutions

Exercise 16A

Notes:

20 March This is an inter-client transfer from the ledger account of the executor to the ledger account of Cygnet. No entries will be made on the cash account as the money remains in the client bank account. A note would be made in the transfer journal.

15 April To record the payment of interest from the office bank account:

> DR Interest payable
> CR Cygnet (conveyancing) – Office section

> CR Cash   ⎱
> DR Cygnet (conveyancing)   ⎰   Office section

Since the interest is going to be held by the solicitor for Cygnet, it must be received into the client bank account:

> DR Cash   ⎱
> CR Cygnet (conveyancing)   ⎰   Client section

16 April To record the transfer of the money into a separate designated deposit bank account:

> CR Cash   ⎱
> DR Cygnet (conveyancing)   ⎰   Client section

> DR SDD cash
> CR Cygnet (money held on deposit)

30 April To record bank's payment of £120 interest:

> DR SDD cash
> CR Cygnet (money held on deposit)

To record the transfer of £200,220 back to current client bank account:

> CR SDD cash
> DR Cygnet (money held on deposit)

> DR Cash   ⎱
> CR Cygnet (conveyancing)   ⎰   Client section

To record the payment of £200,220 to Cygnet:

> CR Cash   ⎱
> DR Cygnet (conveyancing)   ⎰   Client section

6 May To record the payment of £30 office money in lieu of interest:

> DR Interest payable
> CR Cygnet (conveyancing) – Office section

> CR Cash   ⎱
> DR Cygnet (conveyancing)   ⎰   Office section

As the £30 is paid out to Cygnet directly and is not held by the solicitor in the client bank account no entries need be made on the client section of Cygnet's ledger account or on the client section of the cash account.

Client: Cygnet
Matter: Conveyancing

Date	Details	Office account			Client account		
		DR	CR	BAL	DR	CR	BAL
March							
20	Executor of Swan. Residuary entitlement (TJ)					200,000	200,000CR
April							
15	Interest payable		100	100CR			
15	Cash. In lieu of interest	100		—			
15	Cash. In lieu of interest					100	200,100
16	Cash. On deposit				200,100		
30	Cash. Off deposit					200,220	200,220
30	Cash. Returned				200,220		
May							
6	Interest payable		30	30CR			
6	Cash. in lieu of interest	30		—			

Client: Cygnet
Matter: Money held on deposit

Date	Details	Office account			Client account		
		DR	CR	BAL	DR	CR	BAL
April							
16	Deposit Cash					200,100	200,100CR
30	Deposit Cash. Interest					120	200,220
30	Deposit Cash				200,220		—

Cash

Date	Details	Office account			Client account		
		DR	CR	BAL	DR	CR	BAL
April	Balance			xxx			xxx
15	Cygnet. In lieu of interest		100				
15	Cygnet. Conveyancing				100		
16	Cygnet Deposit. On deposit					200,100	
30	Cygnet Deposit. Off deposit				200,220		
30	Cygnet. Conveyancing. Returned					200,220	
May							
6	Cygnet. In lieu of interest		30				

Separate designated deposit client cash – Cygnet

Date	Details	Office account			Client account		
		DR	CR	BAL	DR	CR	BAL
April							
16	Cygnet Deposit				200,100		200,100DR
30	Cygnet Deposit. Interest				120		200,220
30	Cygnet Deposit					200,220	—

Interest payable				
Date	Details	Office account		
		DR	CR	BAL
Apr 15	Cygnet	100		100DR
May 6	Cygnet	30		130

Chapter 17

FINANCIAL STATEMENTS

17.1 PURPOSE

A solicitor who has handled money for a client should always prepare a written statement explaining how the client's money held has been dealt with.

The statement is particularly important in conveyancing transactions where it is likely to be sent to the client part-way through the transaction to inform the client how much he will have to provide or how much will be available to the client at the end of the transaction.

17.2 LAYOUT

There is no set layout but the statement must be clear and easy for the client to follow. It can be presented in two columns.

Example

FINANCIAL STATEMENT [date]
TO: MR AND MRS BOUNDS

PURCHASE OF 3 WICKET STREET

	Receipts £		Payments £
From you. On account of costs	400	Search	20
Mortgage advance net of legal fees	22,340	Stamp Duty	400
From you. For deposit	3,000	Land Registry Fees	100
		Deposit	3,000
		Balance Purchase Price	27,000
		Our Professional Charges	400
		VAT	70
Balance required from you to complete transaction	5,250		
	30,990		30,990

Another common layout is to show the statement in the form of a sum, starting with the purchase price, adding expenses and deducting receipts (or in the case of a sale, starting with the sale price, deducting expenses and adding receipts).

Note: Items to be deducted are frequently shown in brackets.

Example

FINANCIAL STATEMENT [date]
TO: MR AND MRS BOUNDS

PURCHASE OF 3 WICKET STREET

	£	£
Purchase price		30,000
less: Prepaid deposit	(3,000)	
Mortgage advance net of legal fees	(22,340)	
		(25,340)
add: Search	20	
Stamp duty	400	
Land Registry fees	100	
Professional charges	400	
VAT	70	
		990
less: Received on account of costs		(400)
DUE FROM YOU		5,250

Where a simultaneous sale and purchase is involved it is good practice to show separate sub-totals for the sale and for the purchase so that the client can see how much the purchase cost and how much is available from the sale. The statement will then show the total amount due to or from the client in respect of both transactions.

Exercise 17A

You act for Clara who is selling 6 High Street for £65,000 to Priscilla and buying The Cedars for £80,000 from Viola.

The Bayswater and District Building Society, for whom you act, is granting a mortgage on The Cedars of £45,000 and there is a mortgage to redeem on 6 High Street of £40,000.

June

1   Clara gives you £200 on account of costs.

3   You pay search fees £10 by cheque on The Cedars.

5   You receive a cheque from Clara for £8,000 (the deposit on The Cedars) made out to Viola's solicitors.

7   You send the cheque for £8,000 to Viola's solicitors to hold as stakeholders. You receive a cheque for £6,000 from Priscilla's solicitors which you are to hold as stakeholders.

16   You deliver a financial statement to Clara which shows the total required from her to complete both transactions. You also present your bill which includes £200 costs on sale and £300 costs on purchase plus VAT. Your charges to the building society which Clara is to pay by way of indemnity are £40 on the mortgage advance and £20 on the mortgage redemption plus VAT in each case.

18   You receive from Clara the amount requested on 16 June and you receive the mortgage advance from building society.

20 You complete sale and purchase.
21 You pay land registry fees £100 and stamp duty £50 on The Cedars and transfer amount due to you for costs, etc.

Prepare the financial statement sent to Clara on 16 June.

(See overleaf for solution.)

Solutions

Exercise 17A

FINANCIAL STATEMENT 16 JUNE
TO: CLARA

PURCHASE OF THE CEDARS

		£	£
Purchase price			80,000.00
less:			
	Prepaid deposit	(8,000.00)	
	Mortgage advance	(45,000.00)	(53,000.00)
			27,000.00
add:			
	Our costs	300.00	
	VAT	52.50	
	Building society costs and VAT	47.00	
	Land registry fees	100.00[1]	
	Stamp duty	50.00[1]	
	Search fees	10.00	
			559.50
Required for purchase			27,559.50

SALE OF 6 HIGH STREET

		£	£
Sale price			65,000.00
less:			
	Mortgage redemption	(40,000.00)	
	Our costs	(200.00)	
	VAT	(35.00)	
	Building society costs and VAT	(23.50)	
			(40,258.50)
Available on sale			24,741.50

SUMMARY

		£
	Required for purchase	27,559.50
less:	Available on sale	(24,741.50)
		2,818.00
less:	Received on account	(200.00)
DUE FROM YOU		2,618.00

[1] Although you have not paid these on 16 June you know that they will be required and will, therefore, include them on the Financial Statement.

Chapter 18

ACCOUNTING PROBLEMS FOR SOLICITORS

18.1 HOW MANY LEDGER ACCOUNTS?

18.1.1 The problem

A solicitor must show the amount of client money held for each client. This requires a separate ledger account for each client for whom money is held. (There is one exception contained in Rule 32(6) – see **18.1.6**.) A solicitor must consider carefully which client the firm is holding money for and whether money ceases to be held for one client and becomes held for someone else.

18.1.2 Funds originally held for one client being held for another

This can happen in a number of different types of transaction.

Example

You act for the executors of a deceased person. You complete the administration of the estate and inform the residuary beneficiary of the amount of his entitlement. The residuary beneficiary asks you to hold the money for him pending completion of a transaction on his behalf.

The money will stay in your client bank account so no entries are made on your cash account. However, you must mark the fact that the money is no longer held for the executors, but is now held for the residuary beneficiary. You do this by an inter-client transfer.

Entries:

DR executors' ledger
CR residuary beneficiary's ledger
⎫
⎬ Client section
⎭

Exercise 18A

You act for George and for George & Co Ltd. George is a director of George & Co. George is selling land to George & Co for £120,000. The sale is to be completed on 5 June.

On 1 June George tells you that he will be investing in a venture capital trust and asks you to hold the proceeds of sale of the land until he gives you further instructions.

On 4 June the company gives you the funds to complete the purchase. On 5 June you complete the sale. On 7 June George tells you to pay the sale proceeds to the Gallymead Venture Capital Trust.

How will you deal with the sale proceeds of the land?

18.1.3   One party paying the legal costs of another

Quite frequently, one party to a transaction will agree to pay the legal costs of another. The solicitor must consider which client received the legal services and which client the bill (and VAT invoice if the client is entitled to receive one) should be addressed to.

The bill (and VAT invoice if required) will be addressed to the client for whom the services were provided (A) even if another person (B) is paying.

(1)   VAT

If A is a registered fully taxable person, and the supply of legal services is obtained for the purpose of the client's business, A will be entitled to an input tax credit. In that case, B need only pay the amount required for the costs exclusive of VAT.

If A is not a registered taxable person and cannot obtain an input tax credit, B is liable to pay the costs and VAT as well. However, B cannot recover the VAT. This point has been considered by the High Court in *N.O. Turner (trading as Turner Agricultural) v Commissioners of Customs & Excise* [1992] STC 621.

In no circumstances may a VAT invoice be issued by the solicitor or the solicitor's client to B. B is not entitled to receive an input tax credit, as the services have not been rendered to him. B should therefore receive a note of the other party's costs in such terms that the note cannot be mistaken for a VAT invoice issued to the paying party (eg a photocopy of the invoice stamped 'copy').

(2)   Entries

Costs and VAT are debited to the ledger account of A.

When cash is received, whether from client A or from the other party, the solicitor will make the following entries.

> *Entries:*
> DR Cash
> CR Client A's ledger account
> } Office section

Alternatively, if the solicitor is acting for both parties, the amount of costs and VAT of the first party can be transferred as a debt to the ledger account of the second party.

> *Entries:*
> CR A's ledger account
> DR B's ledger account
> } Office section

Then when the cash is received, it is credited to the ledger account of the second party in the normal way.

> *Entries:*
> CR B's ledger account
> DR Cash
> } Office section

Example

Solicitor acts for Schiller. On 20 January he delivers a bill showing profit costs as £200 plus £35 VAT. Goethe has agreed to pay them. Solicitor does not act for Goethe. On 30 January Goethe pays.

Client: Schiller
Matter:

Date	Details	Office			Client		
		DR	CR	BAL	DR	CR	BAL
Jan 20	Costs	200		200DR			
	C&E: VAT	35		235			
30	Cash. From Goethe		235	—			

Cash

Date	Details	Office			Client		
		DR	CR	BAL	DR	CR	BAL
Jan 30	Schiller. From Goethe in payment of costs	235		xxx			xxx

18.1.4 Stakeholder money

A solicitor may receive a deposit to hold as stakeholder. This is clearly a receipt of client money and so must be held in the client bank account. Who is it held for?

The solicitor is holding it jointly for the buyer and the seller. It will not become the property of the seller unless and until completion takes place. Therefore, the solicitor cannot record the money as held for the seller.

The solicitor must have a separate stakeholder ledger account to which the money is credited when it is received.

Entries:
DR Cash
CR Stakeholder
⎫ Client section

As soon as the completion takes place, the solicitor starts to hold the money for the seller alone. The solicitor must record this by doing an inter-client transfer from the stakeholder ledger account to the seller's ledger account.

Entries:
On the day of completion:
DR Stakeholder ledger
CR Seller's ledger
⎫ Client section

Note: Had the money been received as agent for the seller, it would have been held for the seller from the moment of receipt.

> *Entries:*
> DR Cash
> CR Seller's ledger   } Client section

18.1.5   Bridging finance

A deposit received as stakeholder is not available to the seller until completion. A seller who is also purchasing a property may have insufficient cash available to pay the deposit on the purchase. It is fairly common to take a bridging loan from a bank to cover the period from exchange of contracts on the purchase to completion of the sale, when cash will become available.

A bridging loan is a personal loan to the borrower and once received belongs to the borrower and not the bank. Hence, when the solicitor receives the cash (whether direct from the bank or via the borrower) it will be held to the order of the borrower and must be credited to the borrower's ledger account not to a ledger account in the name of the lending bank.

On completion of the sale, the loan, together with interest, must be repaid to the bank.

18.1.6   Mortgages

(1)   Introduction

Many clients who buy property need to borrow money on mortgage. A client who sells property which is subject to a mortgage will have to redeem, ie repay, that mortgage after completion.

A solicitor who acts for a conveyancing client can also act for the lender, provided that there is no conflict of interests and that the solicitor complies with Practice Rule 6. Practice Rule 6 prohibits the solicitor from acting for lender and borrower in a private mortgage at arm's length except in very limited circumstances.

Where a solicitor is instructed to act for both the borrower and the lender the solicitor must bear in mind that there are two separate clients. The solicitor must consider carefully for which client the solicitor is holding client money.

(2)   Mortgage advances – solicitor acting for buyer and lender

When solicitors receive a mortgage advance, they hold it for the lender until the day of completion when it becomes available to the borrower. A solicitor's ledger accounts must clearly distinguish money held for one client from money held for every other client. This normally requires a separate ledger account for each client so that there would have to be a separate ledger account for the lender. However, Rule 32(6) provides a limited exception to the rule that money held for each separate client must be shown on a separate ledger account.

The exception in Rule 32(6) applies only to institutional lenders which provide mortgages on standard terms in the normal course of their activities. Banks and building societies are examples of such lenders.

Where a mortgage advance is provided by an *institutional lender* which provides mortgages in the normal course of business the solicitor need not have a separate ledger account for the lender. Instead, the advance can be credited to the ledger account of the borrower. However, it is important that the funds belonging to each client are 'clearly indentifiable'. This is done by including the name of the lender in the details column of the borrower's ledger account and describing the funds as 'mortgage advance'.

Example

The Southern Cross Building Society advances £50,000 to Brown on 6 June for his house purchase.

Client: Brown
Matter: House Purchase

Date	Details	Office			Client		
		DR	CR	BAL	DR	CR	BAL
June 6	Cash. Mortgage Advance held for Southern Cross Building Society					50,000	50,000DR

It is important to remember that Rule 32(6) applies only to loans from institutional lenders. A loan from a private lender must be dealt with in the ordinary way so a separate client ledger account is required in the name of the lender.

(3)   Costs on mortgage advance

The solicitor is entitled to charge the lender for work done in connection with the mortgage advance as well as charging the buyer for the work done in connection with the purchase. The buyer will frequently have agreed with the lender to pay the costs charged to the lender. As we have already seen, the normal rule is that costs and VAT *must* be debited to the ledger account of the person (A) to whom the legal services were supplied. If another person (B) is discharging the debt by way of indemnity, the debt can be transferred from A's ledger account to B's ledger account.

In the case of a mortgage advance from an institutional lender the normal rule has to be varied because the solicitor will probably not have a ledger account for the lender. Thus, the mortgage costs will have to be debited from the beginning to the ledger account of the buyer/borrower. The conveyancing costs and the mortgage costs with appropriate VAT will be shown separately in the ledger account kept for the buyer/borrower.

Entries:

DR Buyer's ledger account, office section, with purchase costs and VAT
CR Costs account and Customs & Excise account, with costs and VAT

DR Buyer's ledger account, office section, with mortgage costs and VAT
CR Costs account and Customs & Excise account, with mortgage costs and VAT

(4)   Mortgage redemption – solicitor acting for both lender and seller

Rule 32(6) applies only to mortgage advances, not to mortgage redemptions. This means that the solicitor will need one ledger account to show dealings with the seller's money and a separate ledger account to show dealings with the lender's money.

When the solicitor receives the balance of the price from the buyer, it is client's money and must be paid into the client bank account. The receipt is normally shown with an initial CR entry in the seller's ledger account to give a full picture of amounts handled for the seller.

Entries:
  CR Seller's ledger account
  DR Cash account   } Client section

However, part of the receipt is required to redeem the mortgage. That money belongs to the lender and it must be shown as such in the lender's ledger account. It must be immediately transferred from the seller's ledger account to the lender's ledger account.

Entries:
  DR Seller's ledger account
  CR Lender's ledger account   } Client section

The solicitor will then send the lender a cheque for the mortgage redemption money out of the client bank account.

Entries:
  DR Lender's ledger account
  CR Cash account   } Client section

Note 1: It is permissible to argue that the solicitor receives part of the proceeds for the seller and part for the lender so that it is correct to split the credit entries at the time of receipt. If this is done, the solicitor will credit part of the proceeds to the seller's ledger account and part to the lender's ledger account. The whole amount is debited to the cash account client section.

Note 2: Frequently, the money due for the mortgage redemption will be paid direct to the lender. In such a case, as the solicitor does not handle that money, there will be no entries relating to the money in the solicitor's accounts.

(5) Costs on mortgage redemption

The seller may have agreed to pay the profit costs of the lender. The solicitor will address a bill to the lender. As there is a separate ledger account for the lender, the mortgage redemption costs must initially be debited to the lender's ledger account. The debt will then be transferred to the seller's ledger account to show that the seller will discharge it, not the lender.

Entries:
  DR Seller's ledger account, office section, with sale costs and VAT
  CR Costs account and Customs & Excise account with sale costs and VAT

  DR Lender's ledger account, office section, with mortgage costs and VAT
  CR Costs account and Customs & Excise account with mortgage costs and VAT

Transfer debt from Lender's ledger account to Seller's ledger account as follows:
  CR Lender's ledger account with mortgage costs and VAT added together
  DR Seller's ledger account with mortgage costs and VAT added together

(6) Private lenders

Rule 32(6) states that the solicitor must open a separate ledger account for each client.

(a) **Costs.** The mortgage costs will be charged to the lender; the purchase/sale costs will be charged to the buyer/seller. The buyer/seller is likely to be responsible for the lender's costs which may be transferred as a debt from the lender's ledger account to the buyer/seller's.

(b) **Receipt of mortgage advance for purchase.** The solicitor receives this on behalf of the lender. It is shown in the lender's ledger account. It is transferred to the buyer's ledger account immediately before completion of the purchase to show that it is now available to the buyer.

(c) **Redemption of mortgage on sale.** The solicitor receives the proceeds of sale on behalf of the seller and then deals with the redemption in the same way as for the institutional lender.

Below are examples of transactions involving two clients.

Example 1

Purchase – with mortgage advance

Your firm is instructed by Eliot who is purchasing The Wilderness for £127,000 with the aid of an £85,000 mortgage from Garden Building Society for whom you also act. The following events occur:

August

4   Eliot tells you that he has paid £500 preliminary deposit to the estate agents, Crumble & Co.
5   Pay local search fee of £25.
12 Receive £12,200 from Eliot being balance of deposit.
15 Receive and pay surveyor's invoice in Eliot's name of £161 including VAT.
20 Exchange contracts. Pay net deposit.
27 Send financial statement and bill of costs to Eliot (Costs on purchase amount to £400 plus VAT and on mortgage £80 plus VAT.)

September

2   Pay bankruptcy search fee of £10.
4   Receive mortgage advance from Garden Building Society.
5   Receive sum due for completion from Eliot.
7   Complete purchase of The Wilderness.
8   Pay Land Registry fees of £200 and stamp duty of £1,270. Transfer all sums due to the firm to close the account.

Show the entries necessary to record the above transaction in the client ledger and cash account together with the financial statement sent on 27 August.

Notes:

4 August   You do not need to make any entries – but remember that, when contracts are exchanged and the 10% deposit is payable, £500 of the deposit has already been paid.

5 August   There is no money held in client bank account for Eliot. The payment cannot be made from client bank account. The money is paid from office bank account.

> *Entries:*
> DR Eliot ledger account
> CR Cash account   } Office section

12 August The money is client money and is paid into client bank account.

> *Entries:*
> CR Eliot ledger account
> DR Cash account   } Client section

Remember that £500 has already been paid. This money makes up the balance of £12,700.

You cannot reimburse yourself for the search fee out of this money. You have received it for a particular purpose and you can only use it for that purpose.

15 August The invoice is addressed to Eliot and so you must pay it using the agency method. The money in the client bank account is specifically for payment of the deposit. It cannot therefore be used for payment of this bill. The bill must be paid out of office money as you have no client money available.

Entries:
DR Eliot ledger account
CR Cash account   } Office section

20 August   The payment can be made out of the client bank account as you have client money available.

Entries:
DR Eliot ledger account
CR Cash account   } Client section

27 August   The delivery of the financial statement does not require any entries in the accounts. The purpose is to show the client how much is required from the client, bearing in mind this time that part of the money is being borrowed on mortgage. A suitable financial statement is shown at the end of this example.

Costs and VAT: A bill is delivered so the usual entries are made. Remember to charge the costs on the mortgage advance as well as those on the purchase to Eliot. They should, however, be shown on separate lines.

Entries:
Costs   DR Eliot ledger account
        CR Costs account   } Office section

VAT   DR Eliot ledger account
        CR Customs & Excise ledger account   } Office section

(Costs and Customs & Excise accounts are not client ledger accounts and are not shown.)

2 September   There is no money in client bank account. The money is paid out of office bank account.

4 September   The money is client money. It is paid into client bank account. You are receiving the money on behalf of your client Garden Building Society. However, Rule 32(6) allows you to show the money in Eliot's ledger account provided it is labelled as held for the Garden Building Society and described as a mortgage advance.

Entries:
CR Eliot ledger account
DR Cash account   } Client section

5 September   This is the amount shown in the Financial Statement. The money is a mixture of office and client money. We have not split the cheque but have paid it all into the client bank account (Rule 20).

Entries:
CR Eliot ledger account
DR Cash account   } Client section

7 September   On completion the balance of the purchase price owing is paid out of the client bank account.

Entries:
DR Eliot ledger account
CR Cash account   } Client section

8 September   The financial statement took into account the amount which would be payable for Land Registry fees. There is therefore enough money in the client bank account to cover them so the payment can be made from the client bank account.

> *Entries:*
> DR Eliot ledger account ⎫
> CR Cash account   ⎬ Client section
>   ⎭

The transfer from the client to office bank account is recorded in the usual way.

> *Entries:*
> Withdrawal from client bank account
> DR Eliot ledger account ⎫
> CR Cash account   ⎬ Client section
>   ⎭
>
> Receipt into office bank account
> CR Eliot ledger account ⎫
> DR Cash account   ⎬ Office section
>   ⎭

The *completed* accounts look like this:

Client:	Mr Eliot						
Matter:	Purchase of The Wilderness						
Date	Details	Office account			Client account		
		DR	CR	BAL	DR	CR	BAL
Aug 5	Cash. Local search fee	25		25DR			
12	Cash. From Eliot. Balance of deposit					12,200	12,200CR
15	Cash. Surveyor's fee	161		186			
20	Cash. Vendor's solicitor. Balance of deposit				12,200		—
27	Costs on purchase	400		586			
	VAT	70		656			
	Costs on mortgage	80		736			
	VAT	14		750			
Sep 2	Cash. Bankruptcy search fee	10		760			
4	Cash. From Garden Building Society. For mortgage advance					85,000	85,000
5	Cash. From Eliot					31,530	116,530
7	Cash. Vendor's solicitor. Completion				114,300		2,230
8	Cash. Land Registry fee				200		2,030
	Cash. Stamp Duty				1,270		760
	Cash. Transfer costs and disbursements		760	—	760		—

Cash account							
Date	Details	Office account			Client account		
		DR	CR	BAL	DR	CR	BAL
	Balances			xxx			xxx
Aug							
5	Eliot		25				
12	Eliot				12,200		
15	Eliot		161				
20	Eliot					12,200	
Sep							
2	Eliot		10				
4	Eliot				85,000		
5	Eliot				31,530		
7	Eliot					114,300	
8	Eliot					200	
	Eliot					1,270	
	Eliot	760				760	

FINANCIAL STATEMENT 27 AUGUST

TO: ELIOT
PURCHASE OF THE WILDERNESS

	£	£
Purchase price		127,000
less: Prepaid deposit		(12,700)
		114,300
less: Mortgage advance		(85,000)
		29,300
add: Costs on purchase (inc VAT)	470	
Costs on mortgage (inc VAT)	94	
Local search fee	25	
Bankruptcy search fee	10	
Surveyor's fee (inc VAT)	161	
Land Registry fee	200	
Stamp duty	1,270	
		2,230
DUE FROM YOU		31,530

Example 2

Sale and purchase – mortgage redemption and advance

You are acting for Laura who is selling Obrion for £40,000 and buying The Tower for £100,000. There is an existing mortgage of £20,000 on Obrion in favour of Bonnet Building Society. This is to be redeemed following completion of the sale. Bonnet Building Society has also agreed to a new mortgage to Laura of £50,000 for the purchase of The Tower. You have been instructed to act for the Bonnet Building Society in connection with the redemption and the new advance. Laura has agreed to pay Bonnet's legal costs in connection with the advance and redemption.

The following events occur:

May

17 Obtain office copy entries relating to Obrion (pay £12 by cheque). Pay £25 by cheque for local land charges search in respect of The Tower.

24 Receive £10,000 from Laura to use as the deposit on The Tower.

28 Exchange contracts on sale and purchase. Receive £4,000 deposit on Obrion as stakeholder. Pay deposit on The Tower.

31 Send completion statement in respect of Obrion showing the balance due (£36,000).

June

1 Receive completion statement in respect of The Tower showing the balance due (£90,000).

3 Send bills of costs and financial statement to Laura. Costs on sale are £400 plus VAT; on purchase £600 plus VAT; on mortgage redemption £40 plus VAT; and on the new mortgage advance £80 plus VAT.

5 Pay bankruptcy search fee (£5) by cheque.

8 Receive £23,548 from Laura being the amount shown due in the financial statement.

9 Receive the mortgage advance of £50,000 from the building society.

10 Complete the sale and purchase.

11 Send the building society a cheque to redeem the mortgage. Pay stamp duty (£1,000) and Land Registry fee (£250) in respect of The Tower.

12 Pay the estate agent's commission of £800 plus VAT. The invoice was addressed to Laura. Transfer all costs and disbursements owing to you.

Show the entries necessary to record the above transaction in the client ledger and the cash account together with the financial statement sent on 3 June.

Notes:

17 May   These payments must be made from the office bank account as we have no client money.

> *Entries:*
> DR Laura ledger account ⎫
> CR Cash account   ⎬ Office section
>   ⎭

24 May   Client money must be paid into client bank account.

> *Entries:*
> CR Laura ledger account ⎫
> DR Cash account   ⎬ Client section
>   ⎭

28 May   £4,000 deposit received is client money, so is paid into client bank account, but CR stakeholder ledger account, not Laura ledger account.

Entries:

> CR Stakeholder account
> DR Cash account
> } Client section

The £10,000 deposit will be paid out of client money.

> *Entries:*
> DR Laura ledger account
> CR Cash account
> } Client section

31 May No entries are required. There are no apportionments referred to, so at completion only the balance of the sale price (£36,000) will be received.

1 June This confirms that only the balance of the purchase price (£90,000) will be payable at completion.

3 June The usual entries for costs and VAT are made.
Remember that Laura is responsible for your charges to her and for your charges to the Bonnet Building Society. You must debit the mortgage redemption costs and VAT to Bonnet's ledger account and then transfer the debt to Laura's ledger account. The mortgage advance costs and VAT will be debited directly to Laura's ledger account. A financial statement is given at the end of this example.

5 June There is no client money available, so payment must be from the office bank account.

8 June The cheque is a combination of office and client's money. We have not split it but have paid it into the client bank account (Rule 20).

> *Entries:*
> CR Laura ledger account
> DR Cash account
> } Client section

9 June The money is received on behalf of your client Bonnet Building Society but Rule 32(6) applies and the mortgage advance can be shown immediately as a CR in Laura's ledger account.

10 June **Completion of sale:**
£36,000 is received from the purchaser's solicitor. It is client money and paid into the client bank account.

> *Entries:*
> CR Laura ledger account
> DR Cash account
> } Client section

Then transfer the deposit, which now belongs to Laura, from stakeholder account.

> *Entries:*
> DR Stakeholder ledger account
> CR Laura ledger account
> } Client section

There will be a record of the transfer made in the transfer journal (Rule 32(2)).

Redemption of mortgage:
Part of the sale proceeds (the portion required to redeem the mortgage) is held for the building society. Transfer the redemption money from Laura to Bonnet Building Society. Keep a record in the transfer journal.

Entries:
DR Laura ledger account
CR Bonnet Building Society ledger account } Client section

Completion of purchase:
Send the vendor's solicitor the balance required of £90,000 from the client bank account.

Entries:
DR Laura ledger account
DR Cash account } Client section

11 June   Send the Bonnet Building Society a cheque for £20,000 from the client bank account.

Entries:
DR Bonnet Building Society ledger account
CR Cash account } Client section

The Land Registry fees and stamp duty can be paid from the client bank account.

Entries:
DR Laura ledger account
CR Cash account } Client section

12 June   The estate agent's bill is paid from the client bank account using the agency method.

Entries:
DR Laura ledger account
CR Cash account } Client section

Transfer money from the client to office bank account in the usual way.

Entries:
Withdrawal from client bank account
DR Laura ledger account
CR Cash account } Client section

Payment into office bank account
CR Laura ledger account
DR Cash account } Office section

The *completed* accounts look like this:

Client: Laura
Matter: Sale of Obrion; Purchase of The Tower

Date	Details	Office account			Client account		
		DR	CR	BAL	DR	CR	BAL
May							
17	Cash. Office copies. Obrion	12		12DR			
	Cash. Local search. The Tower	25		37			
24	Cash. From Laura. For deposit on The Tower					10,000	10,000CR
28	Cash. To Vendor's solicitor. Deposit on The Tower				10,000		—
June							
3	Costs: Sale	400		437			
	Purchase	600		1,037			
	VAT	175		1,212			
	Costs: mortgage advance	80		1,292			
	VAT	14		1,306			
	Bonnet BS. Transfer mortgage redemption costs and VAT	47		1,353			
5	Cash. Bankruptcy search	5		1,358			
8	Cash. From Laura					23,548	23,548CR
9	Cash. From Bonnet Building Society. For mortgage advance					50,000	73,548
10	Cash. Purchaser's solicitor. Complete sale					36,000	109,548
	Stakeholder. Transfer deposit (TJ)					4,000	113,548
	Cash. Vendor's solicitor. Complete purchase				90,000		23,548
	Bonnet Building Society. Transfer mortgage redemption (TJ)				20,000		3,548
11	Cash. Stamp duty. The Tower				1,000		2,548
	Cash. Land Registry fee. The Tower				250		2,298
12	Cash. Estate agent. Obrion				940		1,358
	Cash. Transfer costs and disbursements from client to office account		1,358	—	1,358		—

Client:	Bonnet Building Society						
Matter:	Mortgage redemption re Laura						

Date	Details	Office account			Client account		
June		DR	CR	BAL	DR	CR	BAL
3	Costs	40					
	VAT	7		47DR			
	Laura. Transfer mortgage redemption costs and VAT		47	—			
10	Laura. Transfer mortgage redemption (TJ)					20,000	20,000CR
11	Cash. To Bonnet Building Society				20,000		—

Cash account:							

Date	Details	Office account			Client account		
		DR	CR	BAL	DR	CR	BAL
May				xxx			xxx
17	Laura		12				
	Laura		25				
24	Laura				10,000		
28	Stakeholder				4,000		
	Laura					10,000	
June							
5	Laura		5				
8	Laura				23,548		
9	Laura				50,000		
10	Laura				36,000		
	Laura					90,000	
11	Bonnet Building Society					20,000	
	Laura					1,000	
	Laura					250	
12	Laura					940	
	Laura	1,358				1,358	

Stakeholder account							

Date	Details	Office account			Client account		
		DR	CR	BAL	DR	CR	BAL
May							xxx
28	Cash. Deposit on Obrion re Laura					4,000	
June							
10	Laura. Transfer deposit (TJ)				4,000		

FINANCIAL STATEMENT 3 JUNE

TO: LAURA

SALE OF OBRION

		£	£
	Sale price		40,000
less:	Mortgage redemption		(20,000)
			20,000
	Costs on sale (inc VAT)	470	
	Costs on mortgage redemption (inc VAT)	47	
	Estate agent's commission (inc VAT)	940	
	Office copy entries	12	(1,469)
	Available on sale		18,531

PURCHASE OF THE TOWER

		£	£
	Purchase price		100,000
less:	Prepaid deposit		(10,000)
			90,000
	Mortgage advance		(50,000)
			40,000
add:	Costs on purchase (inc VAT)	705	
	Costs on mortgage advance (inc VAT)	94	
	Stamp duty	1,000	
	Land Registry fees	250	
	Local land charge search	25	
	Bankruptcy search	5	2,079
	Required for purchase		42,079
	SUMMARY		
	Required for purchase		42,079
less:	Available from sale		(18,531)
	DUE FROM YOU		23,548

18.2   AGENCY TRANSACTIONS

A firm of solicitors may decide to use another firm as its agent. This can occur in any type of transaction but probably happens most often in the context of a litigation matter.

18.2.1   The agent solicitor

The agent solicitor treats the instructing solicitor like any other client. There will be a client ledger account in the name of the instructing solicitor and the normal entries will be made to deal with any client money and the delivery of the bill.

18.2.2   The instructing solicitor

The fees of the agent solicitor are not a disbursement paid by the solicitor on behalf of the client. The instructing solicitor is providing legal services to the client using an agent. The cost of the agent is, therefore, an expense of the instructing solicitor's firm. The firm will charge more for its legal services in order to cover the expense of using an agent. Any true disbursements will be charged to the client as usual and it is irrelevant whether the agent or the instructing solicitor pays them.

When the instructing solicitor pays the agent solicitor's bill he sends one office bank account cheque for the total amount. There can be three different elements of that total, the agent's profit costs, VAT on those costs and any disbursements paid by the agent. The different elements will be recorded separately in the instructing solicitor's accounts.

Entries:

Agent's profit costs	CR Cash account DR Agency expenses account	} Office section
Agent's VAT	CR Cash account DR Customs & Excise account	} Office section
Agent's disbursements	CR Cash account DR Client's ledger account	} Office section

When the instructing solicitor sends his own client a bill, he adds the agent's profit costs to his own solicitor's profit costs and passes on the agent's disbursements to the client.

Example

You act for Williams. You instruct Gibson, Weldon & Co, Solicitors, as your agents. On 17 May you receive their bill showing their profit costs of £200 plus VAT and a court fee of £70. You pay their bill on the same day. On 18 May you send Williams a bill. Your own profit costs are £400 plus VAT.

Notes:

17 May   When you pay the agent's bill you will pay a total of costs £200 plus VAT £35 and court fee of £70, ie a total of £305. However, you will make three separate pairs of DR and CR entries to record the three separate elements of the bill.

The accounts will look like this:

Cash account

Date	Details	Office account			Client account		
		DR	CR	BAL	DR	CR	BAL
				xxx			xxx
May 17	Agency Expenses VAT Williams		200 35 70				

Client: Williams
Matter: Miscellaneous

Date	Details	Office account			Client account		
May		DR	CR	BAL	DR	CR	BAL
17	Cash. Gibson, Weldon & Co. Court fee	70		70DR			

Agency Expenses account

Date	Details	Office account		
		DR	CR	BAL
May 17	Cash. Williams	200		200DR

Customs & Excise account

Date	Details	Office account		
		DR	CR	BAL
May 17	Cash	35		35DR

18 May   When you deliver your bill, you add the agent's profit costs to your own and make the usual entries for costs and VAT.

The accounts will look like this:

Cash account

Date	Details	Office account			Client account		
		DR	CR	BAL	DR	CR	BAL
				xxx			xxx
May 17	Agency Expenses		200				
	Customs & Excise		35				
	Williams		70				

Client: Williams
Matter: Miscellaneous

Date	Details	Office account			Client account		
May		DR	CR	BAL	DR	CR	BAL
17	Cash. Gibson, Weldon & Co.						
	Court fee	70		70DR			
18	Costs (400 + 200)	600		670			
	VAT (70 + 35)	105		775			

Costs account

Date	Details	Office account		
		DR	CR	BAL
May 18	Williams		600	600CR

Agency Expenses account

Date	Details	Office account		
		DR	CR	BAL
May 17	Cash. Williams	200		200DR

Customs & Excise account				
Date	Details	Office account		
		DR	CR	BAL
May				
17	Cash	35		35DR
18	Williams		105	70CR

18.3 MUST CLIENT MONEY ALWAYS BE PAID INTO THE CLIENT BANK ACCOUNT AND MUST A RECEIPT ALWAYS BE RECORDED?

18.3.1 Rule 16 and Rule 17 exceptions from need to pay money into client bank account

As we saw in Chapter 10, there are situations where client money does not have to be paid into a client bank account.

Under Rule 16, client money can be held outside the client bank account, for example in the solicitor's safe or in a different bank account.

However, the client must have instructed the solicitor to this effect and the instructions must either have been given in writing or confirmed by the solicitor in writing.

Under Rule 17, the solicitor can withhold money from the client bank account without written instructions or written confirmation of instructions in six situations. For example, where cash is received and is without delay paid in the ordinary course of business to the client or on the client's behalf.

18.3.2 Rule 32(2) – the need to record dealings

Whenever the solicitor is dealing with client money, the dealing must be recorded on the cash account and on the client ledger account.

18.3.3 Non-recording

The only receipts which will not be recorded are those which are not regarded as 'money' in the solicitor's hands, eg a postdated cheque (until the post date arrives) and a cheque which is made out not to the firm but to someone else. Such cheques could not be paid into the firm's bank account and are not regarded as 'money' for this purpose.

Exercise 18B

Which of the following receipts must be paid into the client bank account? Which must be recorded as a receipt of client's money?

(1)   You act for the executor of Alan. The executor gives you £250 cash which he found in Alan's house. You authorise the executor to take back the cash in partial payment of a debt due from Alan to the executor.

(2)   You act for Brian in a debt collection. You receive a cheque for £5,000 from the debtor. The debt is in part payment of the debt due to Brian and the cheque is made out to Brian.

(3)   You act for Clay. Clay gives you a cheque for £500 on account of costs. He is unsure whether or not he has sufficient funds to cover the cheque and, in his accompanying letter, asks you not to pay the cheque in until he instructs you to do so.

(4)   You act for the executors for Diana. You have negotiated a loan from Diana's bank of £3,841 to cover the inheritance tax due on application for a grant of probate. The bank sends you a cheque made out to the Inland Revenue.

Solutions

Exercise 18A

When the company gives you funds on 4 June you must record a receipt of the company's money.

Entries:
DR Cash
CR George & Co Ltd   } Client section

When the sale is completed on 5 June you must show that the money is now held for George. You show this by doing an inter-client transfer.

Entries:
DR George & Co Ltd
CR George   } Client section

When you complete the investment for George on 7 June you must record a payment of George's money.

Entries:
DR George
CR Cash   } Client section

Exercise 18B

(1) This is a receipt of client money. It need not be paid into the client bank account under Rule 17(a). However, you are dealing with client money and must **record** the receipt (and payment) on your client ledger for the executor and on your cash account.

(2) This is not a receipt of money so the question of 'office or client?' does not arise. No entries need be made to record the receipt. The cheque could not be paid into the firm's client bank account.

(3) This is a receipt of client money. You will not pay this cheque in as the client has given you written instructions not to (Rule 16). However, as in (1) above, you must record the receipt on your client ledger for Clay and on your cash account.

(4) As in (2) above, this is not a receipt of money so no entries need be made. The cheque could not be paid into the firm's client bank account.

Chapter 19

COMPLIANCE

19.1   INVESTIGATIVE POWERS

*Chapter 19
contents*
**Investigative
powers**
**Delivery of
accountants'
reports**

The Law Society, through the Monitoring and Investigation Unit of the Office for Supervision of Solicitors, has extensive investigative powers. Any solicitor must, at a time and place fixed by the Society, produce any papers, files, records, documents and other information requested in writing by the Society. The Society's powers override any solicitor/client confidentiality or privilege.

A solicitor must be prepared to explain and justify any departures from the guidelines for accounting procedures and systems published as Appendix 3 to the 1998 Rules.

Any report produced by the Society may be sent to the Crown Prosecution Service or Serious Fraud Office and/or used in proceedings before the Solicitor's Disciplinary Tribunal.

19.2   DELIVERY OF ACCOUNTANTS' REPORTS

Every firm which has handled client money must deliver an Accountants' Report to the Society within 6 months of the end of the accounting period (Rule 35). The rules relating to Accountants' Reports were amended in 1995 and are now incorporated into the Solicitors' Accounts Rules.

The amendments stem from The Law Society's attempts to reduce the costs of default. It became apparent from the reports of the Monitoring Unit and from its inspections that some reporting accountants were not carrying out their duties effectively and that serious breaches of the Rules (and in some cases fraud) had not been identified.

The 1998 Rules require that reporting accountants must have registered auditor status, together with membership of one of the major accountancy bodies. So that The Law Society can maintain accurate records, solicitors must inform the Society of any change in the reporting accountant.

Solicitors have to produce a letter of engagement for accountants, incorporating the terms set out in the Rules. These cannot be amended. The letter (and a copy) have to be signed by the solicitor (or a partner or director) and by the accountant. The letter has to be kept for three years and produced to The Law Society on request (Rule 39).

Reporting accountants have to complete and sign a Law Society checklist which the solicitor must keep for three years and produce to The Law Society on request (Rule 46 and Appendix 4). The checklist is intended to be an assurance to the solicitor and to The Law Society that the work required to be done has indeed been done.

The reporting accountant has to check that records, statements and passbooks are being kept as required by liquidators, Court of Protection receivers, etc. Accountants are also required to report on any substantial departure from the guidelines for procedures and systems.

INDEX